Our first child was anxious to be born. My wife's labor increased in frequency and intensity; obviously it was time to go to the hospital.

I warmed up the car but had not turned off the TV. Detroit and Montreal were playing hockey. Joyce was at the door, beckoning. I turned for one last look. It was late in the third period. The score was tied and Detroit had a power play.

"Just one more rush, honey," I said. "Just one more rush . . ."

She gaped at me unbelieving. I don't believe it either . . . now.

Sports have become almost a national addiction; competition, not religion, could be called the opiate of the people. Yet the competitive urge is a two-sided coin—with both benefits and dangers, uses and abuses. . . .

ALSO BY GARY WARNER:
  Out to Win
  The Home Team Wears White
  A Special Kind of Man

COMPETITION

GARY WARNER

David C. Cook Publishing Co.
ELGIN, ILLINOIS—WESTON, ONTARIO

COMPETITION
© 1979 David C. Cook Publishing Co.

First printing, July 1979
Second printing, January 1980

Scripture quotations, unless otherwise noted, are from the Revised Standard Version.

Published by the David C. Cook Publishing Co.
850 N. Grove, Elgin, IL 60120
Cover photo by Jim Whitmer
Cover design by Kurt Dietsch
Printed in the United States of America
LC: 79-51747
ISBN: 0-89191-074-3

To Katherine,
who had to compete too hard

ACKNOWLEDGMENTS

The result might well have been stronger were there more people to embrace as co-laborers in this effort. In actuality, it was primarily a solitary pursuit.

My appreciation to the writers before me whose wisdom and insights add immeasurably. If any have been quoted and not properly acknowledged, my apologies.

My gratitude to several members of the Fellowship of Christian Athletes national staff who encouraged me, brainstormed with me, and assured me such a "white paper" on faith and competition was needed. Especially to Skip Stogsdill, who was there at the beginning.

My thanks to Mrs. Wanda Wiley, for years my secretary with the Fellowship, who typed the manuscript with her usual diligence and excellence.

A hug for Jeff, Wendi, and Gregg, who waited while dad worked.

My love to Katherine, who was always there when the uncertainty and the pain took hold.

And my special thanks to those aware and concerned athletes and coaches at all levels of competition who burn to compete and also desire, beyond all else, to live out a Christian life-style in the labyrinth of competitive sport. Their questing and questioning formed a significant part of the motivation behind this book.

Some have dropped out. Given up athletics. A few, given up the faith. Too many, given up bringing the healing of their passion for sport to the entrenched system of competitive sport in America.

There are hope and time. Come back. Come compete with me.

CONTENTS

PREFACE

Broadly speaking, outside of a national character and an edu-cated society, there are few things more important to a country's growth and well-being than competitive athletics. . . . It has been said, too, that we are losing our competitive spirit in this country, the thing that has made us great. I don't agree with that; the competitive urge is deep-rooted in the American character.

Gerald R. Ford
Former president of the United States
Sports Illustrated

Former President Ford captained the Michigan football team in 1934 and, according to his former congressional adversary Lyndon Johnson, "played football too long without a helmet." President Ford got humorous mileage out of that remark but did speak seriously of the "competitive urge." He also thought and strategized in terms of competitive athletics.

So did Ford's predecessor, who sent plays to coaches and telephoned winners of major sporting events. And before that, there was the touch footballer from the lawns of Hyannis Port, before him the man who gave golf a strong impetus, and even before that a man who talked in salty terms about "staying out of the kitchen if you can't stand the heat," which certainly involves competition.

Why do we compete? What are our attitudes about competition? What *can* we gain from competition and what *do* we too often end up receiving instead? Could—and should—the climate of organized sport be altered or affected by a different outlook on competition? What is the thrust of both human nature and God's Spirit toward competition? Are the two identical? Or incompatible? Should the Christian have a similar or different view of competition than a person without a faith perspective?

Questions. Through the years I've had a ton of them and a handful of answers. As a lover of sports, a competitor, a coach, a spectator, a sportswriter, the father of three athletes, a Fellowship of Christian Athletes staff member, I have encountered a distinctive ambivalence in my competitiveness.

My concern is: can Christians establish a value system, a barometer, perhaps even a theology, that would enable us to evaluate the who, what, where, when, why, and how of the Christian competitors?

I not only believe we can establish a higher competitive value system, I believe we must. The model is desperately needed.

This book grew from a series published in *The Christian Athlete* while I was editing that magazine for the Fellowship of Christian Athletes, FCA. It was a three-month series, running in January, February, and March, 1975. After studying reactions over the next several years, I was left with one overriding impression—most athletes, coaches, parents, and fans struggle with their competitiveness. But no one talks about it. It's like suffering from a yet-to-be-determined disease. There are no handles. No one to understand; no apparent helps. We're overwhelmed by the competitive system. You get in the "rat race" or perish. What can one person do? So the issue lies dormant, muted.

The genesis of the series was an athletic seminar at the University of Missouri—Kansas City. The protagonists were Dave Meggysey, well known in the athletic counter-culture as a pro footballer turned kiss-and-tell author; former Kansas City Chiefs defensive end Jerry Mays; former UMKC basketball coach Bill Ross; and *Kansas City Star* sports editor Joe McGuff.

The deck was obviously stacked against Meggyesy, but

the results were embarrassing. Three to one was unfair. It should have been fifty to one.

"We live in a society based on antagonistic relationships. . . .We should help each other push beyond our limits. . . .We should love our opponents even more than our teammates; without them there is no game. . . .To be totally exhausted and to have competed and helped each other push beyond limits is the highest level of brotherhood. . . .Football is theater, not sport. . . .People are disenfranchised. . . .I love athletics, but the horror is what we do to each other in the name of the system."

And on Meggysey went. A jumble of truth, and common sense, coated with a thin veneer of philosophical jargon and sloganized humanism. But he had done his homework and had his lines down pat.

There was no debate. The rejoinders were platitudes and cliches and, at times, so childishly sophomoric that the audience broke into laughter. I wanted to cry. Upon leaving I determined that the ramifications of competition for the Christian had to be spoken to.

The athletic profile is often unfortunately stereotyped. An example is the fine play, *That Championship Season*. Through a long night of conflict and self-realization when a coach and the members of his championship basketball team gather for a 20-year reunion, the coach issues such supposed virilities as "Exploiting a man's weakness is the name of the game. . . .Don't grow old on me, boys; I carved your names in silver and nothing changes but the date. . . .That trophy is the truth, the only truth."

The Christian in sports—athlete, coach, parent, fan—must move beyond that level of competitive superficiality. Perusing the athletic scene today, one can be encouraged and discouraged in almost the same breath.

"I don't see any conflict between hard, clean competition and my religious values," said former University of Oklahoma All-America quarterback Steve Davis. "God gave me a durable body and the ability to compete in the most interesting sport in his world, and competition is the big drive in my life. . . .I play hard and pray hard."

On the other hand, *Sports Illustrated* reported that on the same team, "Tinker (Owens, Oklahoma receiver) had to share playing time with another gifted end, the bigger, faster Billy Brooks. Competition between them was so intense they hardly spoke—even though they were roommates on the road."

The televised "Superstars" competition, while hokey in some aspects, has afforded glimpses of fun and camaraderie between the performers. In an obstacle race between baseballers Reggie Jackson and Pete Rose, both dove at the finish line, rolled up from the ground, shook hands, and embraced in obvious affection. It was a lofty example of tough head-to-head competition concluded in an atmosphere of warm respect.

On the other hand, a well-known coach of a professional football team, known for his pre- and post-game prayers and "chaplain" on the sidelines, invited an FCA staff member to lunch. It was the week before an important game, and the coach asked about the weaknesses of a player on the opposing squad. The FCA man said the player had none. The coach retorted that every man has weaknesses. The FCA staffer's reply was that the player was a close friend (they had played together in college . . . a fact the coach knew), and he would not share weaknesses even if he knew some. End of lunch. Next day the FCA man went to the team's practice and discovered that his press pass, issued by the coach, had been mysteriously canceled. He has not heard from the coach since.

Eventually, as with all such matters, it boils down to a personalized decision. Regardless of circumstances, societal pressure, environment, the expectations of others—one must determine his own course. Before a Christian theology of competition can become corporate it must be the overt choice of many individuals.

Let this be our prayer for this book: that it can help develop for all those in athletics—performer or onlooker—a Christian perspective on competition affording peace and fulfillment for ourselves and harmony in the games.

A number of Baltimore Colt players and wives were in a Bible study prior to a recent season. Ken Mendenhall and Fred Hoaglin were vying for offensive center. With both wives present, Jan Hoaglin prayed, "Lord, I don't know all about this competition, but help Myrlane and me stay close in Christ."

And this author does not know all about "this competition," but as we learn together through these pages about the relatedness of faith and athletic competition, may we draw closer to Christ and radiate a competitive theology that will attract others to his Kingdom.

PART

1

A PERSONAL ODYSSEY

1

THE BOY

We were, in some ways, the odd couple, but it was inevitable that we would become friends.

Each of us was the only "next door" the other had.

My family moved to the country when I was in the fourth grade. "Gentleman farmer" is what the real farmers labeled us: twenty acres, some chickens, a couple of hogs, a milk cow and calf, and enough land for berries and a monstrous (it seemed to us who worked it!) garden.

Dad worked five miles away in Adrian, an industrial oasis in the southern Michigan farmland. We rented out the land. A team of plow horses was pastured there. The fields were planted in corn and oats, and the barn was stuffed with hay, great for jumping into from the pinnacle of the imposing red structure. We marked the seasons by how high the jump was. When it took your breath away and you wondered if you'd ever touch, you knew school would soon be out.

The hay loft was being filled when we moved in that fall. I ran down the lane toward the distant woods, past the murky swale with its mysterious sounds and movements. I circled back through harvested corn stacked in little teepees. If ever a boy had been ushered into heaven, surely I was that boy.

I walked a mile to a one-room country school. Riverside, District 15. One teacher, about forty students, a grumbling coal furnace, and outside two-holers. There were three in my class. Larry Francouer became a baseball teammate in later years. I was an even better influence on his sister Marilyn: she became a nun.

I saw my closest friend-to-be while walking home from school shortly after moving in. His farm was next to ours, and there was no one across, beside, or behind. He was doing chores, and I wondered where he went to school. We stared at each other a minute, then hesitantly went our ways.

A few days later we nodded. A week later we each said, "Hi."

It was a colorless November afternoon when we consummated our nods and "hi's." Deliberately meandering past his farm and trying to appear inconspicuous as I searched for him, I encountered a peculiar sight. He was sliding on his sizable rump down a man-made barnyard mountain. In polite company one would refer to it as a haystack; however, it had already played its initial role in the life cycle of the farm. The weather being enough chilled, there appeared to be no danger to my riding britches (my mother's continuing concern), there was no wind to stir the tempest, and it looked to be good fun.

He glanced up. "Wanna slide?"

"Sure."

His name was Elwood Stock. He was the first and last Elwood I ever knew, my companion for the next nine years.

Had there been any choice, we may have picked other friends. I was slender, with elbows, knees, and toes pointing in different directions; he was pear-shaped, like those man-size balloons with sand in the feet that pop back up when you knock them over. I was quick in talk and movement; he was so slow we joked that the grass wilted where his shadow fell when we ran together.

He was easy-going and late, and I was punctual and responsible (a mantle the oldest child was expected to wear). And he was German and his mother had a funny accent and they were Roman Catholics. I was American and Protestant.

All that mattered little. We were there and no one else was.

I'm not sure how many hours we spent together. Number them in the thousands. We would grudgingly help each other clean chicken coops and weed vegetables and shell corn and slop hogs so we could play sooner.

And play we did. We built tree forts in the woods with secret messages hidden in them. We skinny-dipped in the muddy, weed-infested ponds and skated in the winter on the glazed surface they offered, using a couple of sticks and a tin can to play hockey. We hunted and rode sleds and skied and caddied together.

It was the first spring and summer of our friendship that I encountered my first man-against-man competitive trauma.

The only competition I had known before had been impersonal, me versus machine (learning to ride a bike), or me versus nature (learning to ski). Trying and not quitting. Overcoming fear to do something I was not sure I could do, although I was assured that millions of others before me had done it.

With spring came baseball, the game that was to burn a fever course through my life the next thirteen years. Michigan is Detroit Tiger country, and I idolized the Tigers. Remember your most emotional, thrilling moment, and you know how I felt the first time I entered (then) Briggs Stadium. The cavernous expanse, the green of the fifty-five thousand seats a dark contrast to the manicured lighter green of the outfield. The delicately cut design of the infield, the dugouts from which sauntered professional athletes who were actually paid to do what I wanted to do all day long for free, the sounds of the vendors, the massive scoreboard, the pennants of the teams stretched in the breeze, the crack of wood in the batting cage. I was awestruck as dad smiled and winked at mother.

I was barely breathing and found it hard to move my legs toward our seats. I did not eat or talk that day. I just looked, enchanted. Had I died before reaching ten, it would have been all right. I had seen all this world had to offer.

Mother and I would talk about school when I'd come home—unless there was a game on the radio, even when Harry Heilmann would make up the action while reading from the teletype reports. In 1945 we interrupted moving procedures for only one thing—to listen to Detroit play the Chicago Cubs in the World Series. Birdie Tebbetts, Hal Newhouser, Jimmy Outlaw, Skeeter Webb, and Doc Cramer against Phil Caverreta and his band of scoundrels. Mother would be at the ironing board, doing a little dance when fortunes were good and offering profound managerial asides ("I knew they left him in too long") when fortunes waned.

Mother became my batterymate. Dad would be long in the city, so mother would catch for me until he got home. Then it was dad's turn. I could never understand how they could tire first when there were two arms to my one. I never recall saying "that's enough for right now."

When they stopped, I turned to a stoic, reliable receiver: our barn. I drew a bull's-eye on its side to serve as my plate and catcher. At Woolworth's for a matter of pennies you could buy hard, red rubber balls. I kept them stocking hard, red rubber balls. I would pitch entire games, inside the bull's-eye, a strike, outside a ball— Detroit versus New York or Boston or Cleveland or Chicago. Detroit usually won. Always won. A ten-year-old's strike zone tends to expand or contract depending on which team is at the plate.

Elwood and I played ball. We'd toss up rocks and drive them whining across the road into the woods, the results disastrously evident on a bat that should have won the Medal of Honor.

And that first spring we played "the game."

I'm not sure how it started. A challenge, perhaps. "Can you do this?" "Bet I can!" "Bet you can't!"

There was a sunken spot in our yard we used as home plate. The idea was to toss the ball up and slam it across the yard, past the lean-to chicken coop that slanted off the barn, and over the fence into Stock's corn field.

For some days the goal was possibility thinking only. Elwood was a year younger but heavier and stronger. Each day his drive edged precariously closer to the promised land. And I was still circling in the wilderness.

"Pretty soon," he'd assure me. "Before you."

"Maybe," I'd grimly reply. "But you ain't done it yet."

Each day I'd practice. I'd swing the bat hundreds of times to build my wrists and arms. I analyzed my swing. How to get more power? I'd daydream while hoeing and would swing the hoe, checking my stance, my hip rotation (Doc Cramer said hip rotation was important), and my bat speed until mother's command from the house got me pursuing weeds again.

I'd lie awake in bed thinking, planning, worrying. I had to be first. I had to hit it farther.

At that time World War II had just ended. The world was in chaotic condition. Millions had died. Whole nations were devastated. The problems of postwar reconstruction were overwhelming. But to a ten year old whose life was school, work, play, eat, and sleep, hitting a ball into that field first and farthest was the most crucial matter confronting the universe.

Then Elwood did it. Hit it over. He jumped and hol-

21

lered and ran in little circles. I looked at the ball planted in that field as a testimonial to my inferiority. Tears filled my eyes and my stomach fell away. I told him he didn't have to make such a big deal out of it. That made him whoop all the more. I began to cry and told him to go home. He did, laughing and taunting me. I threw a rock after him.

Kids are like that. At each other's throats one minute, dealing out the usual childish cruelties, and then playing in harmony five minutes later as if nothing had happened. We played the game many more times that spring and summer.

Elwood would occasionally clear the fence. I learned to control myself and wait . . . wait . . . wait. I knew I would not quit until I had matched him. It ate at me, and I could not let go.

One typical Michigan summer afternoon, with cotton balls drifting overhead, we played. Five swings. Confidently, Elwood went first. We both missed through the first four swings. For me it was expected, although two did bounce on a couple hops to the fence. Elwood grumbled about his bad luck—a line drive, a pop-up off an errant toss, and a couple of grounders.

His fifth hit was near the fence but not over. I had escaped embarrassment for that day.

I am not sure how or why things happen as they do. What makes a first? What makes the mind and body coordinate into one smooth, perfectly timed swing? But there it was, against the clouds in a lazy arch, down past the barn to bury itself with a triumphant thud about three rows deep in the corn field—over the fence. Into Canaan.

I was stunned. My heart was pounding. My legs wobbled. Neither of us said anything until I raced to the house, screaming, "Ma, guess what!"

"About time," Elwood groused.

I'm not sure if I was a decent sport about it, probably not, as I retrieved the ball. A part of me wanted to hit again right then, and a part of me wanted to retire immediately, preferably to Cooperstown.

Elwood had had enough for the day. He walked slowly home. I put the ball back in the field where it had landed, sat on home plate, and relived my triumph.

I could not sleep that night. In later years I would know what it was to be "pumped up." Then I would get up and take a walk or a shower or get something to drink and forget about sleep, because when the adrenalin is flowing and your mind is racing, sleep is a lost cause.

But at ten years old it was fun just to lie there. Why do people close their eyes to remember even when it is cavern dark? But I did; closed them and saw the event again. Over and over I picked up the bat, took my stance, choked slightly on the handle, tossed the ball into the air, stepped with the swing, turned into the ball, and felt the contact.

And then the ball climbing, hanging at its apex, descending lazily and then with swift determination . . . and then the prettiest sight of all.

I recalled previous nights when I had thought about "the game" and would rehearse it inside me, little Gary and little Elwood hitting fly balls in my stomach, and every now and then putting their arms around each other in a fantasy fresco and shouting up the tunnel of my throat to my brain, "You can't do it."

But they were wrong.

For there it was: toss, thunk, thud.

Toss, thunk, thud.

I have never counted sheep when needing a formula to clear my head for sleep. I simply go to sleep the way I did that night, curled on my side, smiling and watching in my mind's instant replay—toss, thunk, thud.

I had competed. It was to be the first of many such nights.

THE PLAYER

Someone misled me. They said it would get better. It never did.

"They" would include parents, friends, coaches, sportswriters, broadcasters . . . all those communicating the blessedness of sports competition.

They did not intend to lie. They intended only for my best interests, my completion. I was having fun and desiring more. So they gave me Uncle Sam style everybody-does-it and don't-you-miss-out competition. It turned out to be a sometimes spirit-numbing compulsion that made a sport junkie of me and sentenced me to a lifetime addiction. Once I had made contact with this intriguing, alluring new world, I could not retreat without regret to the purity of play.

One summer afternoon I went to my favorite park in Kansas City to sort out my thoughts on this process. While at a picnic table jotting notes, the contrast was lived out before me.

To my right, grade-school children played. They had chosen up sides, whiffle ball served dutifully to plastic bat by a harried, bored teacher. There were more accusations, arguments, and herding of wandering players than actual game playing.

One boy stood out; a boy who is "all boy" if he's yours and "that little monster" if he belongs to someone else. The oak tree near my table was first base. And first baseman John kept me informed of the proceedings:

"I'm the best hitter. . . . She can't hit, she's a creep. . . . C'mon, hit the ball, you dummy. . . . Whadayamean, didn't know we were calling strikes; you're out. . . . I'm gonna be with the Royals when I grow up. . . . Hey, four eyes, you run like a girl. . . . Boy, do I like to play ball!"

To my left was a group of elderly men and women bused to the park from a home for the aged. Their play was what John's should have been, only late in their day. Youth, once again, wasted on the young.

One couple was center stage. They were playing catch with a balloon-light beach ball, perhaps remembering when movements were quicker and the laughter giddy. Now there was only a firm, quiet intensity as they faced each other no more than ten feet apart, legs spread for balance, hunched forward. Little smiles crinkled lips and the eyes sent appreciative messages when one made a good catch. The dropping was painful . . . the walk . . . the bending. He retrieved and she thanked him.

After a short time they sat down, tired, rewarded. They'd had fun. More fun, I suspect, than John and his friends. They had survived the competitive fires of our culture and could still have fun with a ball. I selfishly wished the same for myself.

Tim Davenport, a bright and articulate quarterback at Harvard, wrote me, "Why, as a junior in college, am I just learning to enjoy the sport that has been such a big part of my life? The Game is such a small portion of the total time, effort, and commitment involved in most any sport that it is a shame it receives so much emphasis. I wish someone had helped me learn to enjoy the preparation and expect less of the outcome. The championship season or the game won seldom results in expectation fulfilled."

In those years as a farm boy when I was hero-worshiping the Detroit Tigers and already dreaming of a pro career before I had ever played an organized game, I received almost everything one can realize out of play . . . and I never realized it until much later.

One hears it especially from runners, the breaking through "the wall" away from the pain and entering a spiritual experience in which body and spirit intermingle in a joyous dance.

But athletes in every sport have sensed it, reached it: that coming together, that intimate ecstasy when one senses he has arrived at the quintessential harmony of life.

Former New York Knick great Bill Bradley wrote, "What I'm addicted to are nights when something special happens on the court. . . . It is far more than a passing emotion. It is as if a lightning bolt strikes, bringing insight into an uncharted area of human experience. It makes perfect sense at the same time it seems new and undiscovered. . . . It goes beyond the competition that brings goose pimples or the ecstasy of victory. . . . It's my private world. No one else can sense the rightness of the moment. A back-door play that comes with perfect execution at a critical time charges the crowd, but I sense an immediate transporting enthusiasm and a feeling that everything is in perfect balance."[1]

Runner Tom Derderian wrote of the Boston Marathon: "I don't actively motivate myself to make this almost religious pilgrimage to Boston any more than the robins who return every spring need to decide to migrate. They are just drawn, not as a foolish moth to a flame but by a sixth sense that is absolutely necessary for their survival. Did you ever run Boston? Did you notice the children? They stand with their hands outstretched wanting to touch the runners as if they are carrying some magic from the gods."

The truest beauty of sport comes when one isolates and

enters this private, enchanted world.

Competition, as America defines it, is play intensified; play related to another's play with more than mere fun the essence. It is a long maturing process before one can consistently find the magic of play within these parameters of competition. When one arrives at that point, he has truly arrived. Within organized sports few get that far, either being hurt out, cut out, burned out, or bored out along the way.

For me, the earliest magic I found came during the years of playing and dreaming about the athlete I would one day be:

With a buddy on the diamond . . . blue jeans and T-shirt . . . old bat and beat-up browned ball . . . out at shortstop trying to smooth a place in the impossibly rutted, stone-strewn infield . . . the feeling of readiness, no tension, loose, sweated . . . a last pat of the glove and a look to the plate . . . hands on knees and, as the ball is tossed and the bat arched back, crouching, two little pitty-pat steps forward, glove low and open.

The ball, coming as if shot from a gun down a long tunnel . . . the world is only a ball, coming. Deflecting here, then there . . . picking up speed . . . gathering dust like an avalanche, swelling, faster, faster . . . but not too fast to me . . . looking like a basketball . . . so easy. Is it confidence? Am I smiling? The eyes locked on like a targeting system . . . the ball tries to elude, escape. The move left, glove low. One last frantic effort by the ball to slide under. The eyes riveted, the glove pancaking the dirt . . . the ball hitting with a shiver felt in the hand and telegraphed through the arm . . . the top hand closing the trap. The straightening . . . the phantom throw to first. Looking into the sun, hands raised, eyes closed. It is beautiful.

I never understood when once full force into the competitive milieu that the preparation is certainly as important, and maybe more important, than the game. Grantland Rice to the contrary, our culture barely acknowledges the concept of play without some sort of payoff. That payoff is winning and losing. It is the bottom line. There is no respite from it in any area of our lives. We're all involved in "competition shock."

As a farm boy who worked the fields and caddied and then worked until early morning in the kitchen of the country club washing dishes, I was quite satisfied with play. I didn't need a team or anyone else, for that matter. I just wanted to do something besides work!

My earliest organized competition was loosely structured kid baseball. Maybe a handful of games in one season. But there was no thought of "being better" or destroying someone else. The scores were 24-22 and, win or lose, it sure beat sweating in the fields.

Then I left country school and entered the ninth grade. Junior high football was my first "big team" competition. I'd never read a squad cut list before. I made it. I adapted. I competed, at first for the right reasons. I enjoyed it. Later I went on to senior high sports and college and semi-pro baseball and fencing and racquetball in my "middle young" years.

Along this course I often competed for the right reason—it was fun and fulfilling. But at times I competed for the wrong reasons—dreams of stardom, peer pressure, parental approval, the macho image, fear of failure, fear of losing respect and prestige should I quit or not go out.

All the questions, the struggles, the misgivings, the mixed emotions I experienced about the whole competitive process between the ages of fourteen and forty were leading me toward what Dr. Howard Mickel in *The Complete Runner* has called "the humanistic athlete": "What distinguishes the humanistic athlete is that he feels the major purpose of athletics is to produce the playful enjoyment and sense of achievement that comes from self-actualizing activity. The values he receives from sport do not depend ultimately on the competitive system. He may, for example, run all of his life without entering a race. . . . I found myself getting a kick out of bettering my own earlier performances, transcending my own potential rather than beating opponents. . . .

"At the psychological level, the competitive athlete may be fulfilling what Abraham Maslow calls 'basic needs'— the need for respect, self-esteem, worth—while the humanistic athlete may be making headway toward the higher needs of self-actualization, the fulfillment of potential."[2]

Do not think the transformation complete. For one conditioned by 'most every circumstance and relationship of life, and motivated by personal competitive attributes, to a daily pattern of "competing," change is painful, long, and marked by backsliding. There is still the force, the voice within that urges me to beat, to win, to hurt, to humiliate, to conquer, to destroy, to waste, to put in his place, to be on top, to dominate, to whip, to blitz, to smear, to teach a lesson and on and on and on.

But I am more quickly aware now. And able more often and more rapidly to smother the potential violence of the competitive urge.

Every life needs moments of exultation. This is why competition is so valuable. Too many of us—even those of faith—are culturally and socially packaged in mundane containers. We need the simple joy of a long putt that drops, a tennis shot that hits the line, a diving catch, a basket that swishes, a happy, sweating run.

In a world often at the precipice of some cataclysmic event, these may not seem the most significant achievements. But for the moment—and we must have moments—there may be no greater, more meaningful thrill than that of athletic achievement. For the moment nothing is more important.

But can we allow it to happen within the spirit of controlled, low-key competition and play rather than striving for what society assures us is "more"?

I pray we can. I believe we must.

One summer night in Michigan while at an FCA conference, I was arrested by a glow of light and a cacophony of sound on the far side of the athletic complex. I homed in on the glow.

Sound preceded the movement . . . clapping . . . little bursts of delight that tickled the ears, then grew decipherable like a tape slowing to the right speed. "C'mon, girls . . . get together now . . . we need a rally . . . nice play! . . . looking like a team now."

It was a women's softball tournament. Twelve teams on six fields. I looked for pretty faces and nice shapes, settling on Ace Hardware and Sports versus The Store. Kids played in the sandpile behind the home-plate screen. Coors cans and cigarette packs mocked the exercise from the bench. A few fans watched from lawn chairs.

The players seemed either too skinny or packing too much backside into jeans and shorts. Perhaps the lights distort. The pitcher was cute and very serious about her work. The first baseman disgustedly inspected a broken nail. The blond at second was pretty. The third baseman had her hair in a scarf and throwing hand in her pocket. The shortstop played a grounder safely to the side, hoping it would come and go and not inflict pain. She escaped unscathed.

On the bench the girls sat quietly, cheered their hitters, talked about kids and dates and the miseries of work. The managers half-heartedly tried to get them fired up. They paid momentary attention, promised to do better.

"This is class D, the lowest flight," a coach explained. "As you can see, the play is kinda poor. No relays or cutoffs; bad throws. Nobody thinks. I don't believe these gals know what it is to be competitive. They don't care if they win or lose; they're just out to have a good time. But that will change. Women's softball is the fastest growing sport in Michigan."

The second baseman blew me a bubble as I left.

From a distance I studied the scene again. Little specks under tall candles. Cheers and specks jumping. Looking around I noticed the university's darkened physical education plant and football stadium. The candle lights were a world unto themselves. But the night air grew cool and heavy on my shoulders as I realized it would not stay that way. The competitive world will suck it in. Next-day office stories about how cute someone's little girl looked or what they did after the game will change to who won and who lost and why.

With men it went from competitive baseball to fun slow-pitch softball. With women the process will reverse. Players will be chewing nails, not manicuring them. The gum chewing will be to calm nerves. The shortstop will charge the grounder properly and make the play or else some other player will be in there to make it. Insecure players who secretly hope the ball is not hit to them will be replaced by confident athletes who want to control the game and compete . . . and be the best . . . and win.

The little island of light seemed sad. I turned and did not look back.

THE SPORTSWRITER

The problem with being an overachiever in a competitive society is that one has an excruciating time determining his level of contentment. Outside forces exalt upward mobility. Inner drives keep one questing for "the top," wherever that may be. It was while I was a sportswriter that I realized these ideas might be important.

For six years, I beat out copy for a small daily newspaper in my home town—the *Adrian Daily Telegram*–, and I began to seriously grapple with my competitiveness and all the ramifications of the competitive process. I underwent an experience that brought the Holy Spirit into play. As I hammered out words on that ancient, manual typewriter, I no longer sought merely to make an impression on a piece of paper but, prayerfully, to make an indelible impression on the heart.

I never intended to be a writer. I never intended to be anything, really, except a major league baseball player. I wasn't sure what one did for "a job." Others could worry about that.

I considered coaching. Enrolling at Michigan State University, I uncovered such winners in the physical education curriculum as fly casting, canoeing, and group games. I had a small scholarship and was paying my way through school, working as a dishwasher. Group games did not seem the best conceivable use of my time and dollars.

I'd entered a high school writing contest—one

thousand words on "What the Constitution Means to Me." I took the fifty I could think of, puffed it to the required thousand, and to my amazement, won fourth place and fifty dollars. My English teacher told me I had "some small flair for writing."

I checked the MSU journalism courses. Of the 192 credits needed to graduate, only 36 were in journalism, the rest in liberal arts. A balanced education. And no group games. It seemed plausible.

Writing became a mild—then a growing—addiction. One of the reasons was a professor of mine, one of only two people who has ever identified me by my real name, Kenneth. He loved objective journalism. He believed reporting to be an honorable calling.

He started us with D's and challenged us to work our way up. A portion of my advanced reporting class was a mock murder trial. We'd write a daily story as he played all the roles in the unfolding case. He introduced us to pressure. Fifteen minutes before the period ended he would suddenly interject some startling development in the case. The students would moan and typewriters were activated as stories already written had to be rewritten before the class ended. Newspaper deadlines were never so frightening after his class.

I graduated with the grades (a 3.7 average and Magna Cum Laude) and the accolades (named "outstanding journalism graduate" of my class) but not the experience. Because of baseball, studies, and work, I had no actual newspaper time. My wife, Joyce, was expecting our first child, so we returned to the familiar environment of home at the modest salary of seventy-two dollars a week.

(Several years later when our second child was born I was given a $2 a week raise and made farm editor. So, as reward for parenting, I was allowed to tromp around the county's barnyards as well as its playing fields. Miserly management could be the strongest incentive for family planning!)

One would not consider the *Telegram* utopia. Being a "college boy" brought initial ostracism from old timers who felt J-school to be the ruination of the newspaper, just as ROTC has ruined the army. The building was so decrepit that snow drifted under the windows. The summers were so hot that big fans blew constantly, meaning we typed with one hand and held everything on our desk with the other.

But there was no better place to learn. I covered the school board, city hall, circuit court, and the police station. When a siren blew, anyone available grabbed a camera and followed the trucks to the fire or the police to an accident or the ambulance to the hospital. It was a crash course toward seasoned newspapering.

The best part was writing sports. We were surrounded by the big events. Detroit with its professional Tigers, Lions, and Red Wings was only seventy miles away. The University of Michigan, its massive football bowl holding over a hundred thousand only forty miles north, and Michigan State another forty beyond that.

However, these were largely the territory of the metro papers. My select domain was Lenawee County, its college and high schools. I knew every coach, every player, every statistic, every aspiration. I went to any game I wanted and had free access to every event. My byline was better known than the names of local senators and congressmen. In a limited sense, I was "somebody." It was the happy environment some sports editors spend fifty years in.

Football and basketball were the main sports of the late 1950s and early 1960s. And all male. Girls played intramural field hockey after school. We featured all the teams with each new season. "Lenawee Louie" made predictions. "Love Letters" poured in. The remembrance of football Friday in a small town with leaves burning and the fog and the smoke creating a smoky aura over the dimly lighted field is still vivid.

During basketball season I would select the particular game to cover each Tuesday and Friday. Before watching the varsity I would officiate the JV game. Returning to the paper, I'd write my feature and help with telephone stories. Three of us worked this schedule every football and basketball night, finishing about 2:00 A.M. and returning at 7:00 A.M. to get the wire news. In another few hours it was all there to read and have read.

And through those years of addiction I learned numerous lessons that shaped my competitive philosophy.

First, there are no such things as "major" and "minor" sports, as sometimes labeled. Our pages covered every imaginable athletic and recreational pursuit. While criticized by those who think football, basketball, and baseball to be the only sports in the universe, I enjoyed meeting fishermen, soaring enthusiasts, dog trainers, trap shooters, and ice-boat racers.

I drove the sulky around the track to better understand the harness race driver. I hovered over a small hole in the ice in below zero temperatures to empathize with the ice fisherman. I suffered through tight upward spirals in the thermal and thrilled at the wondrous glide out to better know the glider pilot. I was a small-scale George Plimpton. But it gave me a lasting appreciation and respect for the feelings people develop about those athletic pursuits special to them.

Also, I had my first reservations about the organization of youth league sports. At first I was more PR agent than objective newspaperman. Then one afternoon I saw a mother run on the field, shake and slap her startled son and send him crying to the dugout after he had struck out. It opened my eyes to further atrocities. It caused me to reevaluate the press's responsibility in covering youth league activities. While it brought considerable criticism from angry parents, we eventually cut our coverage back to a list of scores. My feeling was that the publicity at that age was more harmful than helpful. The kids would struggle with their egos enough in senior high when they read their names and saw their pictures. Let them wait until then.

There were also numerous incidents that confirmed within me that competition can produce incredible highs for both player and fan. Clean and decent and understood for what it is, concentrated competition can leave branded impressions.

One season Adrian high school had a basketball team with no player over six feet two inches. Yet, somehow, they managed to go to the state finals. I had covered these kids for three years. They were like family. They lost the championship game before twelve thousand fans in a game so exciting that twice I nearly fell from the press box. That event, and others, made me realize how arresting competition can be and allowed me the faculty to empathize with men and women who try to explain the personal meaning of athletic events in which they have performed.

It also helped me realize that for every winner there is a loser, and forever buried the cliche, "I look at the sports page because I want to read about winners." I discussed this with Bill Smith, sports editor of the *Charleston* (West Virginia) *Mail,* and he had an interesting comment: "Remember the TV show 'Something for Joey' about John Cappelletti of Penn State and his brother Joey who was dying of cancer? Well, I was at that Penn State-West Virginia game in which John told Joey he would score four touchdowns and did. That's fine, but all the TV show played up was the winner. Across the stadium in the West Virginia dressing room the losing coach, a Christian named Bobby Bowden, was hurting, too. His team was blitzed and his job was in jeopardy. Competition has losers as well as winners. That's always part of the story."

I also learned about the false impressions, the influence, the prestige that the media can build way out of proportion. Perhaps the all-star team, in all its forms, is one of the most dishonest, unfair, and most uncalled-for part of athletics. And the media, as well as the athletic profession, is responsible.

I served on Michigan panels to select the All-State high school football and basketball teams. They were largely a farce. Average players often made it. And some excellent players never had a chance because they had no advocate.

For example, Adrian High School had a halfback who was truly outstanding. But I knew he would not be heard of in Detroit, Grand Rapids, or Flint. So I eliminated other good players from my select list. I informed the other five sportswriters on the panel that I had one player for whom I wanted their support, and I would vote for any of theirs they felt likewise about in return. We all horse-traded this way. Doug Nelson was All-State. So were a number of other players I knew nothing about.

Through the years with the Fellowship of Christian Athletes, I have been involved with Christian newspapermen and college sports information directors. With a few qualifications they agree, almost to a man, that the whole high school and college all-star process is unrealistic.

The most revealing story comes from Ohio University SID Frank Morgan: "Former great coach Adolph Rupp of Kentucky once told a press conference he could make an All-American out of anyone. A newsman challenged this and they made a wager. From that moment on Rupp began calling his blue-eyed, golden-haired center Cotton Nash "My All-American center." Nash, an average player by any standard, did make All-America—three years in a row!"

I found sportswriting can be intoxicating. It is easy to shill, to become little more than a PR agent for the home team. The reason so many men remain in sports all their lives without expanding their horizons, or broadening their perspective, or taking on new challenges with a keener edge is because sportswriting is so predictable, easy, and comfortable. Too much sportswriting has a numbness, a dull mediocrity. Sportswriters become fans and cheerleaders rather than reporters. And the buying price is cheap—a pat on the back from a coach, a free ticket, a dinner, a team trip.

And it didn't take long to learn that the most overwritten and overbroadcasted part of American life is sports. Sport interviews on radio and television are among the most banal contrivances of the English language. Most writers have nothing new to ask and most athletes and coaches have nothing new to say. But it is asked and said anyway; over and over like the dripping of the Chinese water torture. And it will be asked and written in ever expanded fashion because the public demands its mediocrity in large doses.

On the plus side, however, I learned what a tremendous forum the press can be for the Christian . . . and how it can be overdone if one is not prayerfully careful.

I became a Christian while sports editor. It was Dicken's *Christmas Carol* revisited. Biting and sarcastic before that (called "poison pen" by some), it was as if Scrooge had awakened and found employment covering Tiny Tim's cricket team.

A PERSONAL ODYSSEY

My column regularly featured profiles of Christian athletes—Bobby Richardson of the Yankees, Dave Wickersham of the Tigers, the "skating parson" Dave Burnham. A member of a legalistic congregation, I became sanctimonious, narrow, overzealous, and, certainly, unloving (garbage in, garbage out). To me, however, in my immaturity and eagerness to witness, I was doing just what a Christian with such an obvious platform should do.

My editor indulged me. My readers, who, at first, must have thought I'd gone mad, stayed with me. Eventually maturity and wisdom under the Spirit's teaching began to creep in. I learned that one can make a point and express love and establish a higher standard without spraying spiritual napalm.

At age twenty-nine my sportswriting career ended. I moved on to the Billy Graham Evangelistic Association, and then the Fellowship of Christian Athletes.

But the lessons learned have remained.

THE CHRISTIAN

I did not come into the Kingdom kicking, screaming, and dragging my feet. I was more like a wary child, peering around corners, a cautious half-smile on my face as if someone would, at any moment, jump out and scream "April Fool!" and the joke would be on me.

While I came from a home of loving, hard-working, morally and ethically upright parents, there was no religious vista. Through junior high and high school, my spring, summer, and fall Sunday mornings were spent caddying. We were "Christian people" all right, and pledged allegiance to it on the essential occasions—births, deaths, holidays, severe weather that devastated crops, and other acts of benevolence or judgment.

By the time I graduated from college, my theological background consisted of several consecutive weeks in Sunday school when I was twelve years old. All I remember is that we called the teacher "Uncle Dick," and one Saturday we took a hike. I have since heard several preachers who, I'm certain, had the same depth of instruction.

My withdrawal from agnosticism was caused by several key factors. The first was a Christian athlete, the only such breed of man that I knew in high school, college, and subsequent semi-pro years.

Larry Foster had the potential to be a great pitcher. He was also a kind and humble young man and a Christian.

The first characteristic appealed to me. We played together at Michigan State, and, if he helped the team, he helped me. I was willing to overlook his religious fervor on one condition: that he never mention religion to me. He didn't, and we became friends.

Larry could throw BBs. The problem was no one, most of all Larry, knew where they were going. Teammates would not hit against him in batting practice. It was rumored that catchers caught him with a mitt and a motorcycle. The classic joke among his teammates went:

"Hey, did you hear Larry lost his cool today?"

"No! Larry?"

"Yeah. He got so mad he threw the ball at the ground."

"So?"

"He missed!"

We traveled to Iowa and Minnesota the last weekend of our senior year, needing to win two of three games to cop the Big Ten title. We beat Iowa, 6-5, and stayed on the Hawkeye campus that night. I was tight and couldn't sleep. Larry took a walk with me. He tried to share in his unobtrusive way. He told me to relax. I was incredulous. Relax? As much as these games meant? How could he say that?

"A game is never everything in life," he smiled. "I'd tell you what's more important, but I don't think you'd let me."

"You're right." We walked on in silence.

The next day at Minnesota we lost the first game, 3-2. One game for the title. But we were low on pitching. The coach had a hunch—how about Larry? We gasped as he led Larry to the mound (it had been some time since he'd been there), and we hoped and prayed (yes, in our way), for a Frank Merriwell/Horatio Alger finish.

You only get that in storybooks. Larry lasted less than two innings. He could not get the ball over the plate. We

42

lost the title 2-1 in the final league game of my college career.

In the dressing room players wept, cursed, sat stunned; the crushing end of high expectations. Yet in this bleak setting I experienced one of my profoundest athletic moments. It was a crucial point in time which, eventually, helped lead me to a sport/faith ministry and convinced me of the powerful witness available in the community of athletes.

Larry, his eyes red from the tears but the ever-present smile on his face, came around to each of his teammates to apologize for letting them down and to thank them for playing so hard that day and for being his friend. A pitcher given the biggest chance of his career and failing, yet with the courage and (what?) faith to overcome even this. When he gripped my hand and looked into my eyes I knew he had finally found a way to tell me about Jesus Christ.

The second factor was my wife, Joyce. Her church, a severe sort of experience that left me repulsed, was important to her. At night in bed she would ask me about death, heaven, and hell, and what I believed. I had never thought about it, and I was afraid—afraid of the dark, afraid of the unknown, afraid of a God who would laugh gleefully while condemning me to an eternity of suffering. At least she focused my thinking on the subject for the first sustained period of time.

My spiritual vacuum became apparent to me. At night when she was asleep or on Sunday morning when she was in church, I'd sneak out an old Bible and read it. From the standpoints of common sense, the intellectual approach, and the feelings rampant inside me, Jesus made sense. So one night in the living room of our home, with a local Baptist minister present, I knelt by our sofa and stammered a prayer something like, "God, if there is a

God, I've tried it my way for twenty-five years. I want to give you a chance. Prove you are real, Lord. I need to know."

The next night I stood shivering in a half-lighted hole in the ground that was to be a new church, a shovel in my hand, surrounded by my new brothers eager to have an extra worker, and wondering what in the world I had gotten into.

The ensuing years were a time of stumbling, change, and growth. I grimace at the mistakes I made and the activities I condoned, but I am grateful that the Lord understood and was patient with me. My church was built on rules, and I adopted all of them, assured this was what love and faith entailed. The preacher, a red-haired pulpit thumper, told jokes in dialect about "old Rastus, the colored boy" in his sermons, and I, shamefully, grinned along with the rest of the congregation when I should have been denouncing his blatant racism. Five years later he would no longer speak to me because I was going to join Billy Graham who, as anyone could see, had "sold out to the world."

Slowly, the Spirit began to nudge me to open my eyes to what Jesus-style love, concern, and caring were all about. I especially recall Wednesday night prayer meetings and "testimony time." One after another the old standbys, who could always be counted on for a word, stood and related, sober, stone-faced, how all their problems had gone away and they were happy all the time since they met Jesus. Yet there was no laughter, no warmth; only gossip, jealousy, and fierce judgment. Screwtape was right—Christians will do most of the work to keep the number of believers in check.

The words didn't square with the lives. One was a lie. Once I honestly tried to apply Jesus to the events of my daily life, my newly sensitized awareness gave me more struggles than before. I cared about right and wrong; I hurt for people in need; I wrestled with the contradictory forces inside me. Didn't anyone else? And if they did, why didn't they say so?

I wanted to stand up in prayer meeting and scream, "No, it's not that way!" "Poor Brother Warner" would have been counseled, prayed for; but not heard, and most of all, not understood.

And it struck me what the charade most reminded me of—losing. Losing! We were singing "victory in Jesus" . . . and I was losing.

I am equally as chagrined and appalled when I recall how my faith first intersected with my athletic career. If I mirrored what being Christian is all about, I would not want to be one now. I played and officiated in church leagues. The attitudes and sportsmanship were as crude and vicious as any industrial league, and worse than some. Teams used any tactics, brought in ringers, anything to win. Is there nothing new, not even under the Son?

My faith had no practical application to my competitiveness. I was the same old person between the base lines. I cursed, I lost control, I was obsessed with winning. I would manipulate and do whatever it took to win. I slid into bases with my spikes high, and if a baserunner did not get down on the double play, I had no qualms about putting the ball between his eyes. From the bench I heaped abuse on opponents and referees. After all, this was competition. This was being an athlete. And no one modeled a Christian difference for me to see.

Off the field I would again put on my cloak of righteousness. My sport columns testified to my faith. I was called on to give my testimony—turn on the recorder and out it comes. I was a Sunday school teacher, then superintendent; I won prizes for bringing the most people to revival meetings. I drove the church bus to youth rallies. I was "Mr. Christian."

In the church I made friends. But the friendship was surface level. There was no community, no commitment, no bond of love—only a form of religion built around church attendance and meetings.

My real community had been in sports with guys I had sweated with and won and lost with. They were my brothers, and, in my immature zeal, I did my utmost to nearly lose the only community I had. In my efforts to evangelize this lost and wandering tribe, I forgot to love and respect them first.

While I'd never had more than an occasional beer on the farm, I'd always found it very comfortable after baseball games on the road to sit in a bar and have a hamburger and soft drink with my teammates. Just a few months A.J. (after Jesus) I would piously remain in the car alone rather than sully my soul in those dark and degrading watering holes. My buddies got along quite nicely without me. Soon I was having a tough time finding someone to ride with.

I was taught to consider martyrdom essential to witnessing. One night before a game, George Burk, a six-foot-five, zany figure of confidence who threw left and, some of us figured, also thought that way, ran to the bench from where he'd been warming up, threw himself at my feet, and began to implore, "Oh, save me, Gary. Save me right now, brother. Here's a quarter. I can't go out there tonight unless you save me now." Everyone else got a laugh out of it, but I played it stiff upper lip all the way, feeling most righteous, thanking God I was not the likes of them.

The Spirit is gracious. He regenerates us, seals us, convicts us, pardons us, strengthens us, loves us. But he does not coerce us or denigrate our personhood in the process of teaching us. Slowly, gently, the Spirit helped me see myself. It was especially after I joined the Fellowship of Christian Athletes that the scales fell rapidly away. I saw miniature "me's" all around, and it was not a pleasant sight.

There were the extremes. When I joined the FCA staff, I worked editorially with Dr. LeRoy King, six foot nine, who had played college and professional basketball. While LeRoy did not know a deadline from next year, he was one of the kindest, most affable men I knew. He had his competitiveness in perspective. He knew who he was and had nothing to prove.

In three-on-three basketball, he'd have fun, not caring who won or who lost. I always wondered if he was "competitive," if he ever got upset. One day I challenged him, ridiculous at my height, on the boards. After taking enough of my shoving and holding, he threw an elbow as I went for a rebound and sent me sprawling. He helped me up with a knowing glance as if to say, "I understand. And now you know." He never showed me again. He didn't have to.

At the negative pole, or nudging near it, is where a large cluster of Christian athletes and coaches stand. James Jeffrey, a good old boy from the South, was FCA executive director from 1964 to 1972.

His oldest son, Neal, played at Baylor, tried out with several pro teams, and then entered seminary. A fine young man, he accomplished all this though plagued by an acute case of stuttering (an especially difficult obstacle for a quarterback) and a father who could not let him fail. One afternoon we were playing football in the backyard, Jeff and his kids, me and mine. Neal was getting tired, discouraged, letting down a little. The next play his dad lined up close to him at the line of scrimmage and, as Neal came off the ball, Jeff hit him across the nose with a forearm. His son sprawled on his back, blood gushing from his nose. "Got to teach him to be meaner," Jeff explained to me, "or he won't make it."

Neal did not get meaner. And he did make it.

This unenlightened mindset about competition prevails among Christian athletes and coaches. I learned that faith applies to everything but playing or coaching.

Where it should apply most, it is least actualized.

When our competitive house is cleaned out by the Spirit, unless he is filled with a godly approach to competitiveness, the sin that initially bedeviled him will be joined by seven fellow demons (as in the example in Luke 11:24-26) to make it even more difficult for that person to be God's man or woman on the playing field. This wraps us in a costume of false righteousness, which Jesus denounced: "You Pharisees clean the outside of the cup and dish, but inside you are full of greed and wickedness. You foolish people! Did not the one who made the outside make the inside also? But give what is inside to the poor, and everything will be clean for you" (Luke 11:39-41).

A significant number of Christian athletes are much like the Pharisee—clean on the outside but dead on the inside.

As long as athletes and coaches verbalize their faith but give it no application to the world of sports or their competitiveness, it is not only suspect but deceptive.

Tom Landry, coach of the Dallas Cowboys and a pillar in the FCA, having served as its chairman, once made this classic statement to an FCA leadership gathering, "The sports world is changing and the opportunity for hero-worship may not exist a few years from now as it does today, so we need to *use* sports as long as we can to get our message across."

USE sports? Exactly.

Frank Deford riled the sport/faith waters several years ago with his three-part "Religion in Sports" series in *Sports Illustrated*. It was, in part, shallow, inaccurate, and biased. But he did include some noteworthy assessments, including, "The feeling seems to be within the organizations that rather than attacking the abuses in sports, the attempt is to save souls to make sports better. After dozens of interviews no one in 'Sportianity' remotely suggested any direct effort made to improve the morality of athletics. . . . Instead all the talk was about the celebrity, the 'market figures.' Striving to foster better athletic morality just did not occur to anyone. . . . They take the big name out of sports, use him, and put back nothing. That's the extreme, but the danger exists."

It should be obvious that Jesus presents an alternative to life. But this alternative must be substantiated in its fullness, regardless of the cost, if the message of the sport/faith organizations and individual Christian athletes and coaches is to have merit. At present, it does only in rare cases. Taking Jesus with us into all of our lives is a faith venture: the essence of costly grace whereas now cheap grace is largely practiced. If the sport/faith organizations, the chapel speakers, the sharing athletes and coaches do not apply faith to the playing of games and the actions and attitudes this involves, it will never take place in sports. There is no other inside force or vehicle for the Spirit to function through to make it happen.

When Jesus addressed the people in Luke 20:46-47, he was indicating the kind of surface coat too often brushed on in the sport/faith ministries to cover "business as usual" underneath.

"Beware of the teachers of the law. They like to walk around in flowing robes and love to be greeted in the marketplaces and have the most important seats in the synagogues and the places of honor at banquets. They devour widows' houses and for a show make lengthy prayers. Such men will be punished most severely."

I can recognize the flowing robe. I too often wear one. I saw them years ago in those Wednesday night prayer meetings. I see them now in the athletic community. We must strip them off and bare ourselves to apply Jesus to all of our lives, including our competitiveness.

PART

2

THE BENEFITS OF COMPETITION

5

TWO SIDES
OF COMPETITION

The competitive coin has two sides: heads and tails, plus and minus, assets and liabilities. While the game itself is neuter, our approach to the game—our attitudes, the pressures on us from outsiders, the tactics adopted by coaches, the atmosphere and environment in which the contest is staged—determines what we carry away from the game. And the vibes—good or bad—will reverberate for a long time.

Ever flip a coin and, after it somersaults to the floor, see it land on its edge . . . and roll . . . and circle . . . and finally fall? In this section there may appear to be some edged landings. The pluses and minuses of competition are not absolute. Competition can help one person become more responsible. It can also nourish irresponsibility. It may help us understand winning or losing, or it can precipitate a "must win, cannot lose" mentality. It can teach teamwork or breed a ruinous selfishness. It can be a healer or a destroyer.

"You have to be careful not to generalize too simply about sports being related to life," said teacher/author Jack Scott. "After a game, you can pretty easily determine who has won and who has lost. There is more ambiguity to life."[1]

According to "A Christian View of Sports" by the Canadian Catholic Conference and the Canadian Council of Churches, "Sports do not automatically and infallibly produce the benefits attributed to them . . . they possess no magical powers; they possess neither the pristine purity nor the recreative power nor the basic integrity which their ideologists too easily attribute to them."

Agreed. Through the ages the sporting theorists have rolled out their cannons and fired volley after volley about the corollary of sport to life. The "playing fields of Eton" mentality has impaired too many competitors. I've seen the carnage and am sensitive to the danger.

But this is no reason to ignore the fact that competition—given the proper environment, emphasis, and perspective—can help build beneficial character traits. As Royal Robbins wrote of rock climbing in *Sports Illustrated,* "If we are keenly alert and aware of the rock and what we are doing on it, if we are honest with ourselves and our capabilities and weaknesses, if we avoid committing ourselves beyond what we know is safe, then we will climb safely. For climbing is an exercise in reality. He who sees it clearly is on safe ground, regardless of his experience or skill. But he who sees reality as he would like it to be, may have his illusions rudely stripped from his eyes when the ground comes up fast."[2]

Insert *compete* for the word *climb* and you have an excellent description of what healthy competing can do for the competitor.

RESPONSIBILITY

As the oldest of five children, I was expected to grow up quickly, not in the areas of social adjustment or competitive play, but as a worker, as a contributor to the family. And I did.

That earned me a title. When introduced to friends, I was the son colored "responsible." I winced at the term. At least once I would like to have been "handsome" or "clever" or "talented." I wanted to be the T-bone on someone's plate and not lukewarm vegetable soup. "Responsible" sounded so bland, so lackluster.

Now I'm grateful I learned early about responsibility. And despite its pitfalls, I believe sports can help implant responsibility, a major plus factor in competition.

For my working definition, the responsible competitor is "a competitor with a commitment to a set of worthwhile priorities that help produce maturity." Being a responsible person, to me, is understanding commitment, having high-minded priorities, and evidencing growth.

Commitment involves such attributes as obedience, single-mindedness, and discipline. Psalm 37:5 says, "Commit your way unto the Lord and he will act." Commitment is the starter button on the engine of responsibility; the "Here I stand; I can do no other." Commitment is the hand to the plow and not looking back of Luke 9:62. Commitment is the exact opposite of the "aimless running" Paul refers to in 1 Corinthians 9:24-26.

The discipline implied in a commitment to healthy

competition, which helps produce a responsible life-style, is the discipline described in *Desiderata,* "Beyond a *wholesome* discipline, be gentle with yourself."

The "wholesome discipline" of Christian competition is a far cry from the discipline exerted by authoritarian coaches who still live in the dark ages of sport. An exchange in the debate between Jerry Mays, former Kansas City Chiefs defensive end, and former St. Louis Cardinal linebacker Dave Meggyesy, evidences the contrast.

Commenting that self-discipline was unrealistic, Mays said, "I happen to feel that hitting him (a player) on the head with a clipboard and shaming him in front of his teammates is fine if a player has it coming. I happen to believe in strong discipline."

Meggyesy countered, "What you're talking about is the essential fascist mind." He then deplored the rationale behind athletic training, which "is not to develop the body, not to develop skills, but to teach respect for authority."

While granting the need for discipline and the value of respect for authority in its rightful place and time, it is not this mindset that will lead to responsibility. The responsible athlete is not one who salivates on the coach's command just as a computer springs into action when a button is pushed. Responsibility bred from competition is cultivated from an inner self-discipline issuing from a "commitment to a set of worthwhile priorities."

One can read about authoritarian discipline, with trumpet fanfare as background, and pray this idiocy continues to disappear in sporting competition: "On the first day of the Battle of the Somme, July 1, 1916, some 60,000 British troops were killed. They went walking across no-man's land in neat rows, led by an officer kicking a soccer ball. And they died and are buried in the same neat rows."[1]

56

Even coaches from the old Lombardi era are realizing that, other than to keep incorrigibles in line, self-discipline is the only accurate barometer of genuine commitment. Dallas Cowboys coach Tom Landry said, "I've had a few bad characters come to me, and I've never reformed one of them. Athletes in the pro ranks either have character or they don't. I can't give it to them."[2] Said University of South Carolina football coach Jim Carlen, "I want a boy with inner strength, self-discipline. I'm not gullible enough to take a Sunday school teacher who can't play football, but I want young men with character."[3]

The philosophy of self-discipline must become gospel, must be expanded, encouraged, fostered in the early stages of our play when children begin competing. Athletes need to learn early that a self-disciplined commitment to competitive excellence is the valid and healthy approach.

"I coached six-foot-eight-inch Paul O'Gorek," said former University of Pittsburgh basketball coach Buzz Ridl. "He was the committed competitor coaches love. Our boys had to run a preseason mile in 5:50 or less. Paul could have jogged home in that but he ran a 4:36 at his size! After that season, he had a tonsillectomy. I visited him at the hospital late one night. He was asleep. Only two items were on his bed stand—a hand gripper and his Bible. The evidence of his commitment."[4]

Ed Defenbaugh fell from a moving car when he was five years old. His right arm was almost completely paralyzed. He became a standout track performer at Graceland College in Lamoni, Iowa, but he also excelled in high school football, basketball, and baseball. He gained 1,269 career yards, taking handoffs "with his good arm." He was a starter in basketball, although only five foot nine and 145 pounds. "He was really something to watch in the outfield," said his baseball coach. "He'd whip off his glove and put it under his paralyzed arm, and throw left-handed."[5]

The Bible is full of stories of committed people. Perhaps the least lauded but most humanly empathetic is Joseph, the husband of Mary. The first two chapters of Matthew fashion a primer on commitment.

We know Joseph's story: engaged to a young girl who becomes pregnant, the disbelief, the social stigma, the right to cancel the engagement, his decision to marry. The baby is born. Standing aside as Mary and the baby share the spotlight. Fleeing to Egypt, coming back, settling as instructed in Galilee.

Joseph responded to and acted upon an inner conviction—not mindless obedience, but a commitment, despite misgivings, to what he considered to be right and worthy. A self-discipline, which is part of commitment, which is part of being responsible, which is part of being mature.

Another indispensable part of becoming a responsible human being in a competitive context is that we have the right priorities. If our competitive priorities are of a low nature (to keep from losing, pride, ego, to "get ahead," to "be somebody," greed, etc.), it leads to irresponsibility. If our priorities are of a high nature—if sport is seen as but one part of life and kept in its proper place—then the chance for building a responsible life-style is increased immeasurably.

Gus Ganakas, former Michigan State basketball coach, was an assistant under John Benington when John was head coach of the Spartans: "We made a lot of trips between Detroit and East Lansing when we were recruiting the great Ralph Simpson. One afternoon we got a call that Ralph was ready to sign his letter-of-intent. John and I took off.

"It was tense. Rocketing along the highway, we passed

four elderly people standing beside their beat-up car, looking helplessly at a flat tire. John stopped. I pleaded that we didn't have time, that Simpson might change his mind. John said, 'Gus, you always have time to help people.' I never forgot that. We landed Simpson, so I guess we got to Detroit on time."[6]

Life is forks in the road, alternatives, choices. What is worth committing one's self to? George Hill said, "More and more I see that the Christian life is simply a matter of choosing which side to be on, living as consistently as possible with that choice, and trusting God to make something good come of it."[7]

From the "choose you this day" of Joshua 24:15 to the "seek first his kingdom and righteousness" of Matthew 6:33, the seeker of faith is faced with choices he must make—God or mammon, right or wrong, justice or injustice, the broad way or the narrow way, the committed life or the uncommitted life, the responsible life or the irresponsible life.

When the athlete brings his life to spiritual completeness through trust in Jesus Christ, a responsible life-style can be the result. This commitment to responsible competing and responsible living probably won't make the headlines, as irresponsibility too often does, but the result means changed lives and a saner society.

Kent State University. What do you immediately think of? Probably protests, National Guard, four students dead, and a legacy of investigations and bitterness.

There's another picture painted by the Christian athletes at Kent State. Through the years of tragedy the Kent State Fellowship of Christian Athletes group witnessed throughout Ohio, gave blood to buy Christmas gifts for disturbed and abandoned children, and spearheaded the "Kent Stay United" campaign on subsequent anniversaries of the shooting to head off further disruption and bloodshed on the campus.

A matter of priorities. A matter of athletes combining their competitiveness and their faith to live out their lives responsibly.

When we become self-disciplined and committed through sports, when our priorities are of a high nature and in order, when we have learned what it is to be responsible, then we have followed one of the most important scriptural imperatives—to grow.

When doctor Luke repeated in Luke 1:80, 2:40, and 2:52 that "Jesus grew," he meant not simply physical growth, but that the child was maturing into manhood. Throughout the Gospels and the Epistles the command is to grow, to mature.

Self-discipline, commitment, right priorities, and growth—these are the marks of responsibility, and these are the signs of a mature competitor.

7

SELF-CONTROL

Sport competition both requires and teaches self-control. Plato wrote, "You can discover more about a person in an hour of play than in a year of conversation." Napoleon said that most any person can evidence courage and self-control in the warmth of the sunshine amid the plaudits of the crowd. But, he contended, few evidence the "2 A.M. variety," to be awakened in the deep of night and be in instantaneous control.

Satchel Paige made only one mistake when he threw his fastball: the fingers that released the white horsehide were black. The ball didn't care. But certain people minded. They kept him out of the major leagues for years.

Satch was indomitable. He persevered. He became a legend. And along that way the venerable Paige set down his "rules for longevity" for those planning to travel the road of competitive sport:

1. Avoid fried meats, which angry up the blood.
2. If your stomach disputes you, lie down and pacify it with cool thoughts.
3. Keep the juices flowing by jangling around gently as you move.
4. Go very light on the vices, such as carrying on in society. The social ramble ain't restful.
5. Avoid running at all times.
6. Don't look back. Something might be gaining on you.

BENEFITS OF COMPETITION

Ol' Satch appears to have had tongue-in-cheek, but there's a lot of depth in this folksy wisdom.

Jesus also set down some guidelines for those setting out along the competitive road of turning people to the new message of hope. When he commissioned his disciples, his paraphrased instructions included:

"Go where people need you . . . preach . . . heal . . . cleanse. . . give freely . . . don't worry about material needs . . . give your peace to deserving people . . . be aware . . . be gentle . . . don't be afraid . . . don't worry . . . don't be jumping about from place to place . . . go easy."

The advice of both Paige and the Lord could be summarized concisely as "stay cool." Staying cool means having yourself in check, having your emotions in control.

Self-control is such an important prerequisite to the growing process of the believer that the apostle Paul lists it in Galatians 5: 22-23 among the fruit of the Spirit. And in sports, self-control is often the difference between being an average or an above-average competitor.

Outstanding athletes have emotional control. The Athletic Motivational Inventory, created by the Institute for the Study of Athletic Motivation, lists emotional control as one of eleven traits in the "description of a high scorer." Emotional control being defined as: "Tends to be emotionally stable and realistic about athletics; is not easily upset; will rarely allow his feelings to show and his performance is not affected by them; not easily depressed or frustrated by bad breaks, calls, or mistakes."[1]

Baseball's legendary Connie Mack said, "I guess more players lick themselves than are ever licked by an opposing team. The first thing any man has to know is how to handle himself."

In a 1978 update of this, Pittsburgh Pirate manager Chuck Tanner told shortstop Frank Taveras, "Frank, you've got to stop getting angry at yourself, throwing your helmet, and getting tossed out of games. In order for you to use the talent that could make you the best shortstop in the National League, you first have to be in emotional command of yourself."

The controlled athlete is the cream who rises to the surface, as a tableau of ancient sport cliches testify: "We knew they'd find a way to lose"; "He's his own worst enemy"; "If you wait long enough, he'll beat himself."

The irony of sports competition, however, is that much of what we salute and applaud is totally contradictory to what it is to be a controlled competitor. I squirm almost every time I hear the expression "He's a real competitor." It's usually used to define a particular breed of athlete—one who throws his glove against the dugout wall, kicks over a bench, or attacks his locker. One who brutalizes an opponent, and then stands over him glowering. One who is also sometimes referred to (more accurately) as "an animal." One given to continual rages, who skirts the rules or makes his own rules, who cannot temper the emotional fires burning inside him.

And the saddest part is that in the competitive community his lack of control is not only tolerated but winked at or even artfully encouraged, which not only destroys the merits of sporting competition, but erodes and sabotages the person's maturity. Sport competition can be a strong force to foster one's control of his will and emotions. But this must, first, become a modeled and valued characteristic of competition.

Self-control is perhaps best ingrained through individual sports. And there may be no better game to teach it than golf. Club throwers are legion. But seldom does loss of control intimidate a golf course. There is no evidence of a water hazard drying up, a hole shortening, or a cup expanding because of the rage of a practitioner.

I recall with anguish playing in the finals of a district

caddy championship at age fifteen. The opponent was my brother, Ron, three years younger. I was four up with four to play—and lost five holes in a row, missing a short putt on the first sudden-death hole. I threw my putter into the nearby power lines—where it lodged for several days as the pennant flag of my outburst—and ran home, weeping uncontrollably. As I bolted away I heard the caddymaster say, "He's a real competitor. Sure hates to lose."

No, not a real competitor. Just a kid who had to grow up.

About that same age I played on my first organized school baseball team. In one game I'd had a routine day at the plate. In the late innings the opposing coach brought in a squinty-eyed lefthander who looked as if he were throwing his fastball into a hurricane. In the on-deck circle I nearly squeezed sawdust out of the bat, I was so eager to hit.

Overanxious, I swung at his first offering, lifting a lazy pop foul off first base. Perhaps no out in baseball is as maddening as a foul pop-up. You just stand, watch, and walk back to the bench.

Because it was near fair territory, I started to first, throwing my bat aside in a rage. The ball drifted right over the first base line. To this day I don't know what made me do it, but instead of avoiding the first baseman, who had his arms extended—shading the sun and waiting for the ball—I lowered my shoulder into the unsuspecting and unprotected figure and leveled him.

I was, of course, thrown out of the game. Chagrined, tearful, my pulse thundering, I slinked to the bench. The reaction amazed me. My teammates had nothing but respect in their eyes—"Wow, don't mess with him!" While my coach verbally spanked me, I saw him wink at his assistant. Publicly rebuked and privately applauded.

My act was condoned, even appreciated. Little wonder I had minimal self-control.

It was only after becoming a Christian at age twenty-five that I began to get control of my competitive emotions. And it was a matter of simply opting for a higher level of life. I did not like being uncontrolled; I had no respect for who and what I was. I gave it to Jesus, telling him I was too weak to overcome these outbursts on my own. It did not happen overnight—and I still fight the battle—but my emotions are tempered and the necessity of gentlemanly conduct is uppermost in my mind during competition.

Joseph Roux wrote in *Meditations of a Parish Priest,* "To know one's self is the true; to strive with one's self is the good; to conquer one's self is the beautiful."[2] Through Jesus we can find "the beautiful," and this involves mastery over self, a control over what escapes the hidden, volatile inner us.

Not only is self-control a fruit of the Spirit, it is an expected quality of those in leadership positions within the Christian community. In Paul's letter to Titus, he urges self-control four times in the first two chapters. In 1 Timothy 3:2, Paul instructs Timothy that self-control is a prerequisite for becoming a bishop. It seems clear that one cannot become a model of faith unless he has self-mastery and is on his way toward "the beautiful." It is likewise true in competitive sport that self-mastery leads to all "the beautiful" that competition can bring.

Early in my adult fencing career I came up against the former under-nineteen national champion. I was hopelessly outclassed by a young man about half my age. He was a talented, veteran fencer while I was still little more than a fumbling novice.

It was late on a long tournament day. He was bored, cavalier, and abusive. Fencing is a gentleman's game and, according to the dictates of the sport, you dispatch an inferior fencer and do not cat-and-mouse him.

My young opponent had other ideas. A tall lefthander (a considerable problem in itself for a righthanded fencer) with inordinate reach, he toyed with me, baiting me into attacks and scoring on stop thrusts, the one fencing move that evidences the inferiority of the opponent.

The score, in his good time, was 5-0. When we stripped our masks to shake hands, all the old compulsions within me implored my fist to tattoo his surly mouth. But I was able to look him in the eyes and say, "Nice bout." And taking off my equipment, I felt at peace about winning a bigger victory than anyone around me could imagine.

Several years later I played in the Missouri state racquetball tournament in St. Louis. After a solid victory the night before, I had one of those matches in which I was flat and my opponent was rolling everything out. Even his mistakes were winners. He beat me in the second game, 15-0.

It was the only time I have ever been skunked. He would look at me, shaking his head in disbelief. I could only shrug. It seemed inevitable. I was seething more from frustration and embarrassment. I just prayed that the Lord would let me keep control and learn what this competitive lesson had to offer.

Afterwards, Eddie was apologetic. "I'm sorry," he said. "It was one of those days. I hope we play again so you have your chance. I'm sure, if you were hot and I was off my game, it could be just the reverse."

But there was a greater victory for me. Years before I would have set up a match on the spot and returned the 250 miles just to get even, just to salve my pride, just to "show him." But I didn't have to. It was a game, and I was in control despite the seemingly humiliating situation. If we never play again, it's all right. What does it matter?

Joseph Roux, I understand.

The Scripture has much to say about anger and our control of it. In Colossians 3:8, the apostle Paul lumps anger with malice, slander, and filthy language and tells us in no uncertain terms to get rid of it. Why? In Ephesians 4:27, he says anger that is not dealt with is a foothold for the devil.

One gets closer to the elegant experience that competitive sport can be when he sees Christian athletes replacing their anger with self-control. Curt Tong, basketball coach at Williams College (Massachusetts), faced anger and the need for self-control early in life. His parents were missionaries in the Philippines when World War II erupted. When the Japanese invaded, his father was in another part of the islands. Curt, his two sisters, and their mother were interned. He did not see his father for nearly three years. Few children experience this kind of life. The self-control Curt learned in that trying circumstance influenced his competitiveness.

"What would I tell my children about competitiveness?" he said, responding to my question. "I'd tell them it can be a beautiful or an ugly thing. It is ugly when we motivate and psyche and work on the brute nature of people. I don't like to see emotional stimuli as the basis for competition. Nothing is as beautiful as seeing a competitor use his intelligence in a game, thinking and adjusting and experimenting and growing. The more cerebral a contest is, the closer it comes to a beautiful experience."

Mike Durbin is a professional bowler. He describes his early competitiveness: "I grew to be a perfectionist and hothead. I had a temper that could explode faster than a strike in the 1-3 pocket. I'd kick ball racks, swear at foul lines, and pound on telescores."

Then the former PBA Rookie of the Year encountered Jesus Christ. At the Firestone Tournament of Champions, a grueling four-day, sixteen-game grind, he was in first place with four games to go.

"Then I bowled a 147, a score that would embarrass a league bowler. I was so despondent I could have cried. I nearly kicked the ball rack before I caught myself. I took the 147 score home. I didn't say anything to my wife, Debbie, until later that night. We had tried all week to seek the Kingdom of God, but now we sought a reason and an answer for the bad game. We wanted to win so badly, but we finally saw that we had to trust the Lord and let his will, not ours, be done.

"The next day was unreal. I was like a different person, knowing the Lord was with me, win or lose. The thought of getting angry over a bad ball never entered my mind. I bowled one of the best three-game series of my life, good enough to win the $25,000 championship."[3]

There is another expression frequently used in competitive sport that is unfortunately categorized with "real competitor" and, thus, misunderstood. The choice of terminology is unfortunate because the term has applicability to the competitor and the Christian and can have merit, depending on how exercised, in both spheres.

The term is *killer instinct*. It is applied to one who, sensing an opening, moves in for "the kill." But there are right and wrong ways to go for the jugular.

"Competition brings out the best in any person," says premier base stealer Lou Brock of the St. Louis Cardinals. "That's the ace in the hole. When the pennant race is close, the killer instinct comes out."

The concern for the Christian and the competitor is not that the "killer instinct" exists in a competitive environment but, rather, how it is to be expressed. With invective? With brute force? Or in a concentrated, controlled expenditure of physical, mental, and emotional energy?

We will become angry. We will encounter legitimate stress and emotions, both as competitor and as Christian, which are difficult to control. Self-control does not mean self-delusion—locking our emotions away and swallowing the key. It means finding the safety vaalve of sane, caring release.

Indian tennis ace Vijay Amritraj smiles a lot. He acknowledges winners by his opponents and may even applaud them. He never berates officials. He never throws a racket in anger.

"Pancho Gonzales keeps telling me I am too polite, too social," Vijay says. "He says I don't have the killer instinct. I do have it. When I take the court I feel it is imperative to win. But I also want to win in the proper way. When I am ahead my game goes down 8 to 10 percent. But when I am behind it goes up 15 percent. I don't know why they say I lack competitive instinct."

Maybe, Vijay, because people only recognize the "killer instinct" when it is issued as hurting. What about when it is expended as healing? There was no better practitioner of this form of "killer instinct" than Jesus.

Perhaps the most telling illustration is in Mark 3:1-5. Jesus meets a man with a shriveled hand in the synagogue. The religious leaders watch to see if Jesus will heal on the Sabbath.

Scripture recounts that Jesus "looked around at them in anger" and was "deeply distressed at their stubborn hearts." Imagine the emotion stirring inside the Lord. And yet he did not lash out to hurt. He reached out to heal. "Stretch out your hand" was his command. And Mark relates that the man "stretched it out, and his hand was completely restored."

BENEFITS OF COMPETITION

The Pharisees dogged Jesus' steps through the gospel narratives. In this situation, to quote another sport cliche often accompanying "killer instinct," he "put them away" again. But not with angry hurting. Instead, with self-controlled healing. In competitive sport and in the competition of our faith, against forces and opponents who would delude us and defeat us, the "killer instinct," the "putting away" to assure victory when it is necessary, is a vital factor. How it is done determines if we experience "the beautiful" gift of self-conquest.

There is a seldom quoted verse in Proverbs that provides us with a clue connecting sport competition to faith. Proverbs 21:14 says, "If someone is angry with you, a gift given secretly will calm him down."

Self-control—the gift given secretly. The way to inner healing and relational healing in sport. We can extend this gift first to ourselves and then to others.

One needs no other account of self-control than to follow the last days of Jesus from the betrayal in the Garden of Gethsemane to Calvary's cross. No one could have displayed better self-control than did the Lord. To the angry around him, Jesus was giving a gift secretly, the gift of life he has continued giving to this day.

ENDURANCE

The card read, "To the Hearts and Flowers Kid. Don't be cynical about Valentine's Day. Love." It was accompanied by a candy heart and a paper flower, and it was from a female friend in the Fellowship of Christian Athletes' office, reminding me of a column I had written the previous year, which began:

"Valentine's Day . . . hearts and flowers . . . a sentimental interlude in the year's dreariest month . . . (But) save the box of dime store candy. I'd prefer remaining oblivious to the fact.

"Cold-hearted pessimist? Negative thinker? Maybe. But, sadly, my life is filled with angry farmers shooting their cattle and destroying their wheat, people dying in border disputes and religious wars, bewildered mothers clutching dead children to their breasts in Africa and India, profiteering industrialists, deceitful politicians, and . . . and . . . and . . . God, what do I do with the ache in my gut? Guess I'll buy some Valentine candy and forget about it.

"Trouble is, one cannot really forget, only rationalize or disregard. Suffering is not only a part of life but essential to life, and until we understand that, face up to it, and learn from it, we are sorry specimens for the Kingdom."

I enjoyed the piece of candy and good-naturedly displayed the flower. And I stood by the statement. Were one to press the issue and ask me for one word that summed up my Christian experience, I would probably opt for *endurance*.

What about joy, happiness, peace, assurance, and the other marketable commodities? I want them, believe them, appreciate them, sense them, but I am still persuaded that to "keep on keeping on" is at the core of faith.

I do not recognize this as cynicism. I prefer realism. The Scripture says we are pilgrims passing through a foreign land, and one cannot take off the blinders most Christians prefer to wear and look at the world as it is and remain oblivious to the groanings of creation.

That's where the endurance comes in. That's when the apostle Paul could write, "More than that, we rejoice in our sufferings, knowing that suffering produces endurance, and endurance produces character, and character produces hope, and hope does not disappoint us" (Rom. 5: 3-5a). No, hope does not disappoint us . . . once we make room in our comfortable faith for pain and the determination to endure.

It is at the point of endurance where sport competition and faith perhaps most closely parallel. And endurance may be the key factor that separates "sport play" from "sport competition."

When it begins to hurt, when one must elect to sacrifice and make deeper commitments, when defeats mount, when pressure and stress crest, those who choose "playing" over "competing" can sit this dance out. And whereas I advocate recreational play over brutalizing, self-destroying competition with all its harmful attitudes and perspectives, one must acknowledge that at certain points—endurance being one of them—competition can instruct us and complete us in ways play cannot. Hopefully, what one can acquire is the capacity to play while enduring and competing.

So there is nothing right or wrong about selecting

either play or competition in the sport context if one is aware of what he is choosing and why. In our faith life, however, the choices are not equally valid. Churches are filled with those who want to play at the feet of Jesus rather than getting their hands dirty in personal growth and service to others. It is at the point of endurance that one goes from player to competitor. And the qualities that can be derived from athletic competition have, I believe, strong carry-over value to what it means to be a full-fledged follower of the Lord.

Leo Tolstoy said, "It is by those who have suffered that the world has been advanced." Athletic performance does not reach the highest level of excellence, and records are not shattered, by those who want to play, only by those who want to compete. And this means suffering. It is said that you can measure a thoroughbred's speed by a stop watch but only a race can measure its heart. It is the same of play and competition. And the same of playful faith and enduring, steadfast, always-abounding-in-the-work-of-the-Lord faith. There's a lot of 40-yard speed in the church, but not an overabundance of long-distance heart.

An avid reader as a boy, the stories of athletic endurance thrilled me. Who would not break into goose flesh reading about Pheidippides, the famous Athenian runner, carrying the news of victory over the Persians the twenty-four miles from the plain of Marathon back to an anxious Athens? Running doggedly, feet bleeding, the Acropolis looming in the distance to call him on. His last words were "Rejoice; we conquer," and he fell dead. They named the marathon after his feat and many have endured in his name since then.

Novice Tibetan monks trained by running nonstop for six days and nights without food, and taking wet sheets to 10,000-foot elevations in snow and ice and drying them with the body temperature of their naked frames.

Miller Anderson bailed out of his flaming P-51 on his one hundred thirteenth, World War II mission, and the tail section snapped his leg in two. Doctors put in a six-inch silver plate rather than amputate. With one leg several inches shorter than the other, he not only competed as a springboard diver in 1948 and 1952 Olympics, but won silver medals in both games.

In 1978 Arnold Palmer was on the way to one of his worst competitive rounds, an excruciating 85. Yet on the final tee his playing partners heard him whisper grimly as he prepared to drive, "Got to get a birdie."

What made heavyweight Jim Corbett a champion? "Simple," said the titlist. "I fought one more round." Stories to thrill a kid. And as the child has grown to discover what competition involves, the thrill has been augmented by experience and knowledge as to what enduring ultimately means. To hear black golfer Lee Elder say, "If I just keep knocking on the door, one of these days it's going to open." Then to see him win. And play in the Masters under extraordinary pressure. One understands about the endurance of a black man in a white man's game.

As a boy I was thrilled by the myriad of sport cliches. The mental image of a football team making a "goal line stand" or the hitter or pitcher being "in the hole." And, of course, the ubiquitous "when the going gets tough, the tough get going." I'd prefer it to read "the tough keep going"—staying power, holding on, hanging tough.

The boy was anxious to prove himself worthy. He would be, as boxer Archie Moore stated, "a finisher." He would emulate miler Gil Dodds who said it was "too soon to quit." And while the experience and knowledge of sport, life, and faith have smoothed the childhood goose bumps, there's still an assurance that "paying the price" is still relevant and that "Rocky" might just happen to those who endure.

One cannot refute history. While the "pull yourself up by your bootstraps" philosophy is cruelly exploited by the positive thinking cult on the struggling masses who will grasp the flimsiest life preserver, the reward truly is, in some form, to those who endure. Walt Disney was dismissed from the *Kansas City Star* when told he had no talent. Explorer Richard Byrd crash-landed the first two times he soloed and the third time flew head-on into another plane. Writer Rod Serling of *Twilight Zone* wrote forty stories before he sold one. Fabled Western writer Zane Grey was fired by five papers because he couldn't do the job as a reporter.

When the apostle Paul says "I press on," he doesn't need to explain. It is the process of faith, life, and competitive sport.

Anyone who has ever played football at any level will not soon forget two-a-days in August. The heat, the weight and rub of the equipment, the screams of distended muscle and fiber, legs like anvils, lungs burning like the inside of a dry kiln, the taste of sweat, home for a lunch of iced tea—and throwing that up.

Fun? No. Anyone in the affirmative is a masochist. Why does one endure? There are reasons, but fun is not one of them.

One explanation is the relationships born of endurance. "Pain is the deepest thing we have in our nature, and union through pain and suffering has always seemed more real and holy than any other," said Arthur Henry Hallam. The enduring together of pain has brought me into a communion with my competitive teammates and opponents faster than any other factor. A look is enough. One understands.

Endurance has also brought me into a union with the

inner me. It has given me a glimpse into the deepest reservoirs of my soul that mere play would not have revealed. Many endure in sport competition because the rewards and satisfactions are consummate and closed off to those who prefer not to hurt. Said Cardinal Mercier, "Suffering accepted and vanquished . . . will give you a serenity which may well prove the most exquisite fruit of your life."

Another reason the athlete endures competitively is to move from a mundane plateau to the adventurous potential of highs and lows. As Nobel prize winner George Wald said, "When you have no experience of pain, it is rather hard to experience joy."

William Bengston, a Reformed minister in the Bronx and a former high school cross-country runner, wrote in the *New York Times* about the favorite hill he runs, "This old hill and I have battled before . . . I'm bending forward now, leaning into him, and pitting my strength against his. My step is shorter, thighs are tense, and calves are tight. I'm reaching for more air—mouth open, nostrils flaring, lungs complaining . . . I've had to take up the sword of determination to do battle with thoughts of giving up. These are the moments we both seem to relish. And then it's over. Suddenly, almost as if he has given up, my hill crests and I stand straight again. His aspect is benign, and we settle into the camaraderie felt by those who have proved themselves and 'gone through it together.' The course is easy now, and we can cross the top as friends until we meet again below."[1]

The payoff from enduring is found at the top. And you have to get there to perceive it.

Wrote L. Pearce Williams, history professor at Cornell, "I like pain. This is an acquired taste and can be overdone, but pain is important to me. Pain raises sport from the level of entertainment to that of human achievement, and I consider it central to a humane education . . . (it is) the difference between play and sport. I had a healthy fear of pain, but I realized that (through competitive sport) this fear could be overcome and that the man who could overcome it had a distinct advantage over those who lived in its thrall. Pain, of one sort or another, is everywhere . . . and I am convinced that learning to live with and transcend physical pain can give one the strength to conquer the mental variety. . . . To know of what one is capable, both mentally and physically, is to know the scope of one's freedom."[2]

Another exponent of the "pleasure/pain principle" is author Philip Yancey who wrote in his book *Where Is God When It Hurts?*—"When I am old, I hope I do not die between sterile sheets, hooked up to a respirator in a germ-free environment. I hope I am on a tennis court, straining my heart with one last septuagenarian over-head smash, or perhaps huffing and puffing along a trail to Lower Yosèmite Falls for one last feel of the spray against my wrinkled cheek.

"If I spend my life searching for happiness through drugs, comfort, and luxury, it will elude me. 'Happiness recedes from those that pursue her.' Happiness will come upon me unexpectedly, as a by-product, a surprising bonus from something I have invested myself in. And, most likely, that investment will include pain. It is hard to imagine pleasure without it."[3]

I have found a peculiar and cherishable truth about competitive enduring. It is much like the labor of a woman in childbirth. If a woman could exactly recall the pain, one might never accept the trauma of reproduction again. But while one recalls a vague nuance of it, the precise details are clouded by an apparent blanket of grace. The same is true of sport. The pain in remembrance is obscure, not copiously available for heightened extrapolation. I might not run again if I could explicitly recall the searing pain of my agonized uphill labors. I would not want to make another fencing lunge could I feel in my nerve endings beforehand the stretching, tearing rivets of searing needles up and down my leg.

There is a grace allowed the competitor. The joys of past competition come readily to mind. They leap back to us from springboards and mini-tramps. Pain does not return that way. I can indulge myself if I so wish, but it is work, grinding the turn screws and dredging up the hurt. Satisfaction is sudden, leaping back to me. Pain—the "I'll never do this again"—takes more effort to re-examine in the mind.

So the athlete has a choice. He can avoid pain. Or he can endure it and benefit from it. Through my suffering as a competitor a beautiful thing happened. After being refined in the fire of pain, there were tangible results: my body toughened; my mind and body did new things together; I formed special relationships; I gained new skills; I had new appreciation for the gifts of others; I found a new identity.

A word of caution is needed. One can overstate the case. A quote from Robert C. McQuilkin—"It is suffering and then glory. Not to have the suffering means not to have the glory"—reminds me of a T-shirt my oldest son, Jeff, wore during high school gymnastics. It read "No Guts, No Glory."

All of which is appropriate when not extended to absurdity. Some enduring can be physically and psychologically damaging when belabored. A 300-pound jockey will not win the Kentucky Derby no matter how much he endures and loves horses. Sydney J. Harris said, "Perseverance is the most overrated of traits . . . beating your head against a wall is more likely to produce a concussion in the head than a hole in the wall." Our endurance in sport and faith must be tempered with common sense, but one does not refute the benefits of endurance on the basis that some may be guilty of overindulging to the point of fanaticism.

There are times when a person is left with little else than his capacity to finish. A former Green Beret wrote Teddy Kennedy, Jr., when the twelve-year-old son of Senator Edward Kennedy had a leg amputated to arrest bone cancer, "It's a man's journey. Get on with it. I'm sending you my old green beret, not to cheer you initially, but to give you heart. I simply want to remind you that the battle must be yours alone. You will find, through a season of fear and worry, if you stand next to God alone, you will be filled with the knowledge of what you must do, and, with a steady, calm, and manly courage, do it."

Through the accounts of the Old and New Testaments there have been men who have stood next to God and endured. Endurance is a cornerstone in the character of faith. "They who wait for the Lord shall renew their strength, they shall mount up with wings like eagles, they shall run and not be weary, they shall walk and not faint" (Isa. 40:31).

James could write, "Blessed is the man who endures trial, for when he has stood the test he will receive the crown of life which God has promised to those who love him" (James 1:12). Paul could write "love . . . endures all things" (1 Cor. 13:7). But then Christ promised, "Come to me, all who labor and are heavy laden, and I will give you rest. . . . For my yoke is easy, and my burden is light" (Matt. 11:28-30).

A yoke of endurance, of pain, of suffering? Yes. And a yoke that is light? Hard to comprehend. Dietrich Bonhoeffer, in *The Cost of Discipleship*, explained it this way: "For God is a God who bears. The Son of God bore our flesh, he bore the cross, he bore our sins, thus making atonement for us. In the same way his followers are also called upon to bear, and that is precisely what it means to be Christian. Just as Christ maintained his communion with the Father by his endurance, so his followers are to maintain their communion with Christ by their endurance.

"We can, of course, shake off the burden which is laid upon us, but only find that we have a still heavier burden to carry—a yoke of our own choosing, the yoke of our self. But Jesus invites all who travail and are heavy laden to throw off their own yoke and take his yoke upon them—and his yoke is easy and his burden is light. The yoke and the burden of Christ are his cross. To go one's way under the sign of the cross is not misery and separation, but peace and refreshment for the soul, it is the highest joy. Then we do not walk under our self-made laws and burdens, but under the yoke of him who knows us and who walks under the yoke with us. Under his yoke we are certain of his nearness and communion. It is he whom the disciple finds as he lifts up his cross."[4]

It is with this assurance of the presence and the caring of One who had already been the way of endurance that the apostle Paul could write a key passage on endurance (2 Tim. 2:1-13) in which he encouraged Timothy, "An athlete is not crowned unless he competes according to the rules" (v. 5).

In my faith experience I have found that "the rules" include the virtue of "keeping on." Keeping on through a divorce; keeping on while burying a son who lived a few seconds; keeping on and on and on in the midst of pain. Thank you, Lord, for being the Keeper in the keeping on.

The seeming paradox of competition is that the more pain one endures, the deeper becomes the satisfaction of achievement. Jesus said in one breath to "count the cost" of following him and, in the next moment, he assured us that he had come to give us a life of abundance. Only those enduring the cost of discipleship may expect an abundance of love and communion.

Columnist Shana Alexander quoted *Jonathan Livingston Seagull* author Richard Bach as saying: "For me there always has to be that tension between belief and action. Why bother to believe in something unless it works in the face of a thunderstorm?"

Any insurance policy is adequate when things are good. What we need is one that works when we are suffering.

Any friend is adequate in good times. What we need is a friend who is there when we are suffering.

Any faith is adequate in good times. What we need is a faith that works when we are suffering.

Julian Dyke, an executive with the Boy Scouts of America, and I were staff members with the Fellowship of Christian Athletes. Julian was an infielder at Western Maryland University. The process of "keeping on" he underwent in athletics and faith is my exact experience and a story for other Christian athletes and coaches:

"I went through four stages as a player. First, I wanted our pitcher to strikeout every hitter. If he'd only do that, I'd have no chance to mess things up. Knowing the absurdity of this hope, I then wanted the ball to be hit to someone else. Anyone else. Anyone but me. Thirdly, I came to a growing maturity and confidence in my ability, and I was willing for the ball to come to me. But I wanted it simple: a nice, easy pop-up I didn't have to move for; a routine grounder with a 'candy hop.'

"By my senior year, however, I dared every batter to hit the ball to me. As a freshman, I never thought in this brash, self-confident, competitive manner. But I'd come to believe I could handle anything hit my way and was anxious to prove that I could.

"My Christian faith has advanced through the same procedure. At first, I just wanted Jesus to strike everybody out. If he couldn't and there had to be some struggles, I wanted anyone else but me to face them. Thirdly, if I did have to go through some struggles or face some problems or make some decisions, I wanted them simple—like a lazy pop fly right to me out of a nice cloud cover.

"And then, through the means of time and prayer and fellowship, I could actually pray for and accept the hardest play a Christian has to make—the tough, twisting grasscutter problems hit straight at you. I knew in whom I believed; I believed all things do work for good for Christ's people; I knew who lived in me and stood by me; I knew that the Lord and I could handle anything hit our way. I was ready—and even anticipated facing the challenge."

There is an apparent insanity both in competitive sport and in following Jesus. It would seem one of those cosmic jokes in which "you had to be there." Only the competitor who has endured the tortures of practice and competitive play can comprehend the joy. Only the Christian who can join Paul in being "content in all circumstances" and "giving thanks in all things" can comprehend the joy.

It's insanity to the outsider. To the insider—the sports competitor and the Christian—you just have to be there.

WINNING
AND LOSING

"What I was going to say," said the Dodo in an offended tone, "was that the best thing to get us dry would be a Caucus race."

"What is a Caucus race?" said Alice.

"Why," said the Dodo, "the best way to explain it is to do it."

First, it marked out a race course, in a sort of a circle. ("The exact shape doesn't matter," it said.) And then all the party were placed along the course, here and there. There was no "One, two, three, and away!" but they began running when they liked and left off when they liked, so that it was not easy to know when the race was over. However, when they had been running half an hour or so and were quite dry again, the Dodo suddenly called out, "The race is over!" and they all crowded around it, panting and asking, "But who has won?"

This question the Dodo could not answer without a great deal of thought, and it stood for a long time with one finger pressed upon its forehead . . . while the rest waited in silence. At last the Dodo said, "Everybody has won, and all must have prizes."

Lewis Carroll
Alice in Wonderland

Wouldn't it be nice for all to have won and all to have prizes? But life is not that way. And there are few, if any, Wonderlands to escape to where it can be that way. I asked a high school athlete in a sports seminar, "What if someone were to put you in a society or culture where there was no competition and no one cared who was first or best?"

BENEFITS OF COMPETITION

"Then I'd be the first best in that society," he replied without hesitation. And he was applauded.

"I've been rich and I've been poor . . . and rich is better" goes the old saying. The competitor alters it to read, "I've won and I've lost . . . and winning is better."

Marquette's former zany and quotable basketball coach Al McGuire garnered more press with his, "Winning is only important in war and surgery." Sure, Al. The Al McGuires of the world make news with this sort of balderdash for only one reason: they've won on the scoreboard. The very point they seem to be rebutting is what sets them apart and enhances this philosophizing.

How important is winning? "In athletics and in most other worthwhile pursuits first place is the manifestation of the desire to excel, and how else can you achieve anything? . . . It is not enough to just compete. Winning is very important,"[1] said former President Gerald Ford.

We've always lauded, praised, worshiped our heroes, our winners. Until they lose. Then we delight in their demise. But that's another chapter.

As to the heads and tails of the competitive coin, this chapter could also fit into the tail's section. But there is much to learn about and learn from winning and losing. And not many arenas in which to do it. Competitive sport is one. Competitive faith is another. That's why it goes in the plus column.

Let's deal with four certainties I feel about winning and losing:

1. Winning and losing, the high value of success, is simply not subject to drastic change. The challenge, therefore, for the Christian sport competitor is to bring a higher quality of competitiveness to the system.

"To contrive is nothing. To construct is something. To produce is everything!" said flying ace Eddie Rickenbacker, reflecting the American expectation. Every mother's son a war hero, sports champion, or business entrepreneur. Every father's daughter a beauty queen or, at least, the producer of beauty queens. Results are everything, and winning is the only result that counts.

The carry-over effect to sport is obvious. Leonard Shecter in his book *The Jocks* says, "We play our games, or watch them contested, with the same tenacious ferocity with which we fight a war in Vietnam and with as little reason or sense. We are taught from the cradle that we have never lost a war and that winning is everything."[2]

Dan Wooldridge is one of the nation's most competent football and basketball officials and has officiated basketball in the Olympic Games. He has some interesting things to say about the typical American competitor:

"Remember the controversial final game in the 1972 Olympics in which we lost in the last three seconds to the Russians? Well, from that game came a firmly held conviction among foreign competitors at the 1976 Games in Montreal: 'Americans never lose; Americans always get beat.'

"All America believes we were robbed in that game. Truth is, we weren't. We lost it through playing and coaching lapses. . .

"Our teams, athletes, and coaches, generally speaking, always have some sort of excuse. European athletes, in my experience, accept defeat much better than we do. They have a more mature grasp of the relevance and consequence of sport and competition."

Bill McClure, LSU track coach, agreed. "There are exceptions among the Europeans—East Germany and what it is attempting nationally through sport—but, basically, Europeans have been more concerned about just plain surviving through the years than anything else," he said. "Sport is an outlet. Competition is not a life and death thing. Our comfortable society has made it life and death, perhaps, in part, as a substitute for the lack of any other sort of adventure or danger. And, believe me, our international amateurs are just as professional as any other country. We must win. That is the imperative.

"That's why I want a recruit who has winning and losing in some balance. He must realize he can lose and go on. He must realize sport is not the ultimate but only a part of a full and complete life. These kids are not easy to find."

There are voices of temperance crying in the wilderness against our passion for being *"numero uno"* regardless of the price to our pocketbook or our national spirit. Wrote Clemson University gymnastics coach Jerome V. Poynton in the *New York Times,* "Why are American businessmen so concerned over the role United States athletes play in the Olympic Games? It seems peculiar that people are so eager to compete against the Russians with a win-at-any-cost attitude in such a nonconsequential activity as 'sports.'

"When it comes to the problems that create and promote human degradation, such as poverty, high health costs, and other ills of a technologically advanced society, both countries are more than willing to lose these battles over the Olympic ones."

There are other calming voices urging a return to a sensible view of winning and losing. "There is nothing wrong with winning if it is done honestly and humanely. There would be something wrong with our grasp on reality if we asked an athlete to work out two or three hours a day, preparing himself or herself for a competition, and then told the athlete that winning is not important.

"Anything a person works hard for is important. Achieving excellence is important. Accomplishing something one has not accomplished before is important. And playing well is important. However, the fine line between ethical play and unethical play is that winning should not be considered to be so important that anything should be done to obtain victory."[4]

There are few Christian athletes who do not struggle with their competitive nature. Yet Christians are called on to permeate the competitive sport process and not run from it.

The summons, as always, is to the Christian athlete and coach. If the insanity of the win-at-all-cost ethic is to be challenged, it must be Christian competitors who help create an atmosphere in which healthy renovation is encouraged and possible.

2. *There are positive qualities to be gained and lessons to be learned from both winning and losing. And both can be detrimental experiences if our attitudes and perspectives are not in order.*

"If you can meet with Triumph and Disaster,
And treat those two imposters just the same."

Kipling was correct: imposters. Not the alpha and omega of our existence—just conditions that can be faced, dealt with, and learned from.

The problem is that winning has been PR'ed out of all proportion. Again, come with me to the locker room wall: "Winning is everything," "Show me a good loser and I'll show you a loser," and so on. The shame is not that this ballyhoo takes place among the overachievers and underenlightened, but that parents and others have not laughed it away instead of pushing it on their children like some path to the Holy Grail.

Most sport addicts, however, do not like to hear a resounding "baloney!" Several years ago I was asked to address the season-culminating banquet of the Johnson County, Kansas, YMCA football league—hundreds of players, coaches, and parents from one of America's typically overorganized youth programs. Not wanting to unfairly appropriate this platform, I informed the officials of what I would be saying. They "took it to the board," calling several days later to say they were getting another speaker, a pro football player, someone safe who had little to say and would take a long time to say it.

But the outcries keep surfacing. Stewart L. Udall, former basketball star at the University of Arizona and later secretary of the interior under Presidents Kennedy and Johnson, addressed an honors luncheon at the NCAA Football Coaches Convention. Before an uneasy audience, Udall condemned "the win-or-perish approach to coaching," deplored a "greedy, weighted system that obviously promotes dynasties," took a swipe at "the extent to which anything-to-win attitudes have corrupted some schools," and then uttered the heretical "I am quite certain the most vital gift I took away from experiences in college athletics was the lesson of learning how to lose with a semblance of grace."

He went on to say, "Winning, being number one, dominating other teams, persons or countries has become, in recent years, a sort of new national disease. And in our shallow worship of the winning-is-everything cult I fear we have lost sight of the fact that at one time or another in our lives all of us are losers. Winners are often insufferable and need no creed to sustain them. However, it takes real character and courage to cope with failure and frustration, and the personal loss is immeasurable when an individual cannot conquer defeat, despair, or humiliation."[5]

As Hugh Prather commented, "There is no harm *wanting* to accomplish; the harm is in *having* to accomplish." And this attitude has been entrenched in sport to such a degree that, for reasons unknown if you put them to the test, many competitors would affirm that they *have* to win. Often the attitude is one of not needing victory as much as fearing defeat and all its dreaded consequences. And this attitude has been so firmly embedded in organized, competitive sport down through the decades that the effect is spiritual wreckage among those who have competed and lost.

The Heisman Trophy is the highest emblem of individual collegiate football achievement. Yet John Heisman was a most unhealthy model. He would not let his Georgia Tech football players use soap or water because he considered them debilitating. Nor could they eat pastry, pork, veal, hot bread, nuts, apples, or drink coffee. Why? "They don't agree with me so they'd better not agree with you."

In 1916 Heisman's team established a football record that still stands. It defeated tiny Cumberland College, 222-0. Cumberland was lured to the slaughter by a $500 guarantee. Cumberland had sixteen players (losing three at a rest stop in Nashville on the way to the game!) and a team manager as coach. So we name a prestigious trophy after this sportsman.

The Christian competitor has the edge while wandering in the win/lose wilderness—a compass to lead him from the maze and confusion. Lewis B. Smedes, writing in *The Reformed Journal,* said, "There seems to be an unbroken line between wanting to win, believing you deserve to win, and cheating to make it all come true. . . . When winning gets in your blood, you are in trouble. Winning can infect a person with George Allen's quaint heresy—'Every time you win, you're reborn.' (Do you recall reading something once about having to die to be reborn?) . . . I do not want to get so bizarre as to advocate . . . that 'losing is the only thing.' That would have its own moral and theological problems. But losing does have something to be said for it. It strikes me that personal growth is much of what life is about. And experience suggests that moral ·and spiritual growth develop as much in losing as they do in winning, in failure as much as in success. If we are sensitive enough to absorb their meaning, losing experiences are God's catalyst for the most significant personal victories. It's more fun to win. But it's terribly growth stunting to want that fun too badly."[6]

Both the concept and substance of winning and losing tie sport into faith. There is marvelous proximity. Regardless of what the athletic scoreboard registers, we may have won or lost. The scoreboard at Calvary pronounced defeat; yet victory arose from the grave.

3. Both play and competition are valuable, but there is a compulsion to be better inside some people, the competitive people, that requires a personal opponent or standard against which to test his skills.

Edward S. Beck, an instructor at Penn State University, said, "America is just beginning to realize that . . . participation in recreation is important. . . . My two activities (riding a bicycle and swimming) are less stressful psychologically and just as vigorous as any other sport. And when I'm finished with a workout, there are no losers. What a wonderful feeling."

It is a wonderful feeling. Thank you, Lord, for play. And if play is our goal and meets all our physical, mental, and emotional needs, then play is just what we should do. But we do not need to avoid competition just because of the evils of the win/loss transaction and the virtues of play for play's sake. Both are perfectly normal endeavors for the Christian sportsperson.

One must not run from himself. Jesus made this an imperative. He claimed that knowing ourselves and feeling good about what God created is the starting point for really knowing God and fully loving those around us. If we harbor competitive urges that we are afraid to express and deal with, we are living out and playing out a debilitating falsehood. Better to confess to the struggle with our competitiveness and get our house in order.

This may involve giving up competition completely and opting for some sort of recreational and exercising play. If this produces peace, it is right for the Christian. If there is still that hunger for something more, we need to continue searching within Christian guidelines to discover the peace that can only come when our competitive desires are explored and healed.

True play does not come easy in America. We have a capacity, almost a need, for organizing everything. Kids' sports attest to this. Where have all the corner lot choose-up and flies and grounders games gone? Play may not offer enough wins. And people need to win at something in some way at sometime.

It is hardly fair to fault others, however, when I sense within me that same need to win at something, anything. One part of me says that I would rather compete against someone who is superior and improve my game and have a workout, even if I lose, than to play someone who is not as good and win. And yet—and such a big yet!—another part of me, after a number of drubbings (no matter how good the workout or the learning process) still wants to win. Likes to win. Needs a win. It is a dichotomy, a weakness, to be sure, but it won't go away by pretending it is not there. And I don't believe we really get this in order unless, through Jesus, we can negotiate peace with our need to compete.

When that happens one can say with relief pitcher Mike Marshall, "All that's important is that the individual does the best he can. Victory does not elate me, nor does defeat depress me. The only victory for me is in the quality of the competition, not in the final score."

BENEFITS OF COMPETITION

In his book *The Inner Game of Tennis,* author Timothy Gallwey talks about winning/losing and competition in these terms, "What is seldom recognized is that the need to prove that you are better than someone else is based on insecurity and self-doubt. . . . If I am secretly afraid that playing badly or losing the match may be taken to mean that I am less of a man, naturally I am going to be upset with myself for missing shots. . . . Does the will to win always have to mean 'See, I'm better than you'? . . . (To me) winning is overcoming obstacles to reach a goal. . . . The obstacles are a very necessary ingredient to this process of self-discovery. . . . Reaching the goal itself may not be as valuable as the experience that can come in making a supreme effort to overcome the obstacles involved."[7]

If one can hold that, believe it, apply it, he is on his way to an attitude of being able to compete against a personal opponent, a standard, or his inner self, and benefit from it regardless of the outcome.

Ray Smith is football coach at small Hope College in Michigan. Here's what it looks like when a Christian realizes he wants to compete and teach competing according to a higher standard of excellence: "We stress teamwork, loyalty, relationships, and fun. That's all we have to offer—no scholarships. If a boy came here and made All-Conference four years and that's all he got out of his competitive experience, I would be disappointed. He'd be like a tire out of round."

4. Jesus Christ calls his followers to be successful by his standards. And winning and losing are wrapped up in that.

While Jesus calls us to walk above the world's standards, this does not mean rejecting that which may result from following and serving. If we are truly following Christ, there is nothing wrong with accepting victory. Jesus did not, for example, outright condemn wealth and glorify poverty. He did indicate it was difficult for a rich man to comprehend humility, but he did not say it was impossible. He said, "with God all things are possible." For the competitor, it is possible to both win or lose and, with Jesus as our guide, to be enriched by both experiences.

Jesus challenged those who followed him to be competitive in important areas, from his initial "come with me and I'll make you fishers of men" to his final "you shall be my witnesses to all the world." To be successful was to commit and love and follow.

In his temptation struggle (Luke 4: 1-13), Jesus refuted all the potential wins offered that would have been recognized as such on the world's scale, opting for greater wins. And yet there is a balance. Jesus indicated through the life-style he spoke and modeled that one does not become salt (Matt. 5: 13) or a light for all men to see (Matt. 5: 14-16) without being competitive and going full force for higher victories than others of lower standards would comprehend.

One can make a parallel statement for the Christian competitor. To be successful as a Christian athlete or coach is not to deny or ignore our competitive desires but to care and love and follow in the process of competing. This may involve winning or losing.

H. G. Wells said, "Success is to be measured not by wealth, power, or fame, but by the ratio between what a man is and what he might be."

My former FCA colleague Skip Stogsdill and I once engaged in a fiercely contested racquetball match. We split the first two games. In the third game he went ahead but I came slowly back. We were tied at 20, and I had the serve. The momentum had shifted; competitors can feel it. I felt assured of the win, so I tossed the ball to Skip and said, "That's it. This is too good a match to have a winner and a loser. Let's call it a draw."

I have done this in several situations. It has drawn surprised looks. I shared this with sport psychologist Dr. William Beausay, expecting a pat on the back. His response was, "You have a problem with winning and losing, don't you?" We argued it through. I believed my motivation and actions were both superior to playing out the game. He felt I was making too much of who won or lost.

He may be right. If we had both played to the best of our skills, if we had enjoyed the fellowship, if we had surfaced a good sweat, if we had tested and helped each other, then the outcome was actually unimportant. But, equally, something we needn't be afraid of.

It seems the attitude of Jesus in this situation would have been to play out the game. "You both have won all the important things from this sharing." I can see him smile. "The score is a part of the contest or else you shouldn't keep it. There's no need to shy away from it."

Tennis celebrity and noted hustler Bobby Riggs said the two greatest things in the world are playing and winning and playing and losing. That says a lot. Jesus calls us to be competitive and bids us to let the winning and losing take care of itself.

In a fit of hyperbole, a Missouri college football coach, discussing an upcoming important small college game in the state, said, "I guarantee it's the biggest game of the year. The one who wins will have a greater future than he can imagine."

One can only surmise of what such greatness consists from one game between two small Missouri schools, but in the Christian context Jesus is there to apply the stamp of eternal greatness to our faithfulness regardless of how the scoreboard reads.

During the 1965 season, Green Bay quarterback Bart

Starr had a little incentive scheme going with his oldest son. For every perfect paper Bart, Jr., brought home from school, his dad gave him ten cents. After a particularly rough game against St. Louis, in which Starr felt he performed poorly, he returned home weary and battered after a long plane ride. But he couldn't help feeling better when he returned to his bedroom.

There, attached to his pillow, was a note:

"Dear Dad, I thought you played a great game. Love, Bart."

Taped to the note were two dimes.[8]

The Christian competitor follows a Lord who takes the sting out of defeat and keeps us humble in victory by judging according to a higher win/lose standard.

10
RELATIONSHIPS

We lived in Minnesota for several years, making warm friendships among the Johnsons, Andersons, and Jorgesons. Policeman Jim Erickson gave Joyce her state driving test and introduced us to the Evangelical Covenant Church. It was a church league softball game, however, that cemented our friendship.

Men in jeans and sweat shirts on one of America's thousands of nondescript playground diamonds. To the practiced competitor, just another game, a time to break from the routine of work and have fun. To Jim, an emotive Swede who had not played at a high level of competition, this was the World Series.

We trailed by a run going into the last inning. Two were out when I hit a triple. Edging off third, I noticed the catcher sauntering to the mound with the ball. He was paying no attention to me. As he lobbed the ball to the pitcher, I broke for home.

It was a foolish play; really, a selfish play. If I'm out, the game is over and I'm saying, in effect, I don't believe the next hitter can drive me in. But the batterymates were surprised by the move. The catcher ran for the plate, the hurler's throw was high, and, as I slid in hard, the young catcher dropped the ball.

Safe!

Two bear arms were hugging me, lifting me off the ground. It was Jim. All he could say was, "Oh, wow! Oh, wow!" He was crying, so caught up in the exuberance of the unexpected dash from third and the new game when defeat had seemed imminent. Were we to meet a thousand years from now, we would always remember the sharing of that moment. It is something unique only teammates understand.

Mickey Mantle described the difference between a team and a gang: "A team is where a boy can prove his courage, on his own, on what he can do himself, and on what he can contribute to the team's good. A gang is where a coward goes to hide."

For years I harbored an almost mystical illusion about the community perpetuated and sustained by the team. As a youngster I saw a film of the University of Michigan football team annihilating Southern California 49-0 in the Rose Bowl. The next several falls I would hitchhike forty miles to Ann Arbor and climb the fence into the awesome 105,000-seat stadium to watch those Wolverines. The intricate patterns, the flow, the movement, what they gave to and did for each other—they were larger than life and so was the unity they showed. They had to be closer than brothers.

But there is no magic, no dust sprinkled by the gods. Just people relating to and working with people in pursuit of a common goal. Competitive relationships, while incomplete in and of themselves, can be an escalator carrying us to the highest level of lasting relationship, the brotherhood of faith.

The apparent togetherness of sport is part of the charisma that attracts millions of spectators to television and the arena. For the noncombatant there is envy when he is shown the victorious team in the locker room, or the NCAA basketball champions cutting down the nets. We all long for some form of community, and sport seems to offer a unique chance to overcome our unrelatedness.

Asked if he had ever worked with Marlon Brando,

actor Alan Arkin replied, "No, no one has. You work near him." People spend lifetimes working, living, feeling, being *near* others. They want to work *with* them. And sport seems the one operable channel.

The absence of community is an accepted fact of American life. Charles Reich wrote in *The Greening of America*, "America is one vast, terrifying anticommunity. The great organizations to which most people give their working day, and the apartments and suburbs to which they return at night, are equally places of loneliness and alienation. . . . Protocol, competition, hostility and fear have replaced the warmth of the circle of affection which might sustain man against a hostile universe."

But what kind of relationships does sport foster? Alvin Toffler identified a pseudo-community in *Future Shock:* "We form limited involvement relationships with most of the people around us. Consciously or not, we define our relationships with most people in functional terms. As long as we do not become involved with the shoe saleman's problems at home, or his more general hopes, dreams, and frustrations, he is, for us, fully interchangeable with any other salesman of equal competence. In effect, we have applied the modular principle to human relationships. We have created the disposable person: Modular Man. Rather than entangling ourselves with the whole man, we plug into a module of his personality."[1]

Reality Therapy's William Glasser told a Faith at Work conference of his "modular sport relationship." Mr. Glasser has a friend who has a tennis court in his backyard. The friend provides the court and takes care of it. Glasser gets to use the available court and have his exercise. The friend is a better player. The friend gets to win. Glasser gets to lose in exchange for the court. Such is a modular relationship that apparently meets the needs of both men.

Thinking back over my competitive relationships, I wonder if I am in any way superior. Baseball in college, semi-pro ball, years of touch football on Sunday afternoon with the same guys, Saturday morning basketball in Minnesota with a hardy band, up at 6 A.M. and battling thirty-below temperatures and monstrous snow drifts to get the open court. Despite the friendship and the jocularity and the fulfillment of team play, sporting competition gave me, at most, a one-dimensional relationship.

I plugged into the module of the competitive personality. But I seldom saw—or cared to see—beyond the mask of the sport relationship.

Bill Maskrey and I were inseparable in high school. He was the center on the football team; I was the quarterback. We worked by the hour on the center snap. In the split-T offense, the coordination between center and quarterback had to be precise. How many snaps did he give me? Thousands. But I never knew Bill. Never knew what he dreamed about or hurt about or cared about.

Maybe that was too much for high school pals. Our paths crossed by letter twenty years later. We may meet again. What will we say? Remember? That is what teammates say. Remember? The nostalgia of sport. But it is not *who* we were. It is *what* we were. And people crave relationships that convey us beyond the what to the who.

This deep purity of being two yet one is most readily attainable in Christian community. Faith in Christ adds further dimensions to our relationships and binds us as completed people, giving us a rallying point worth dying for and not merely worth sweating for. Sport competition provides us with instant acquaintanceship. Good and bad guys. Teammates and opponents. Friends and enemies. Immediate but disposable. One season a guy is on your team. Friend. The next season he's on another team. Enemy. It can be deeper, but it can also very often be as shallow a relationship as this is.

Sport, like war, produces instantaneous brotherhood. We hear a lot of "I really love you guys" in sport today. What it usually means is "I'm infatuated with you guys," an infatuation welded by the highs and lows of competitive emotion. It's not the "I want your body" of sexual infatuation, but the "I want your point production" of competition.

Another consequence of competitive relationships is that they are too often based on an antagonistic relationship: we band together to be against a foe rather than to be for each other. A man wrote of his friend who had gone AWOL to avoid being sent to Vietnam, "When I first met John I thought his reasons for not wanting to kill were valid, but I have learned since that while there is a time at which one must say, 'I will not do this *to* other people,' maturity and responsibility arrive only when one goes beyond that to say, "I will do this *for* other people." I knew and agreed with what John was fighting against, but I waited in vain to hear what he was fighting for."[2]

When teammates find something worth putting themselves on the line *for,* rather than merely *against,* then they have established the deeper relationships of the sport/faith context. Competitive sport is a worthy starting point, a common denominator. Join that to the call of Christ and one finds the opportunity to plug into the soul of another person, and not simply into a module of sports relationships.

Let's follow the process. The athlete, more than most other people, understands teamwork and loyalty in a relationship.

Jack Scott—"Athletics is the one area of our educational environment where people get to work cooperatively. You are willing to sacrifice the good of yourself for the good of the whole team. In the classroom, if you cooperate with the guy next to you, it's called cheating. In sports, it's teamwork."

Donn Moomaw, former UCLA football All-American and pastor of Bel-Air Presbyterian Church in California—"I was taught coordination with a team. I'm on a team now. We have twenty-seven people on our staff. I learned a lot about what it means to work within the team structure through athletics."

Bill Curry, former pro center with Baltimore and Green Bay—"The main thing that makes me come back up to the ball is the fact that I know the guys next to me are going to come off the ball a little harder than they did the time before, with this reserve of strength or courage or moral fiber or commitment to each other or love or whatever you want to call it, which means I've got to do it if I want to be a part of this. It's not for the bucks. It's not for a fancy ring, either. It's so that I can go back in the locker room with my arm around Bob Vogel or Danny Sullivan or Tom Matte and know that we did that together, and that we all gave it a little more than we really had. Now, that may sound real phony. But I promise you, it's the reason we play."

Phony? No. Sport competition can bring that to the participant. And beyond teamwork and loyalty, the athlete may experience stronger relational prospects:

Kent Kramer, former pro tight end—"In 1969 with Minnesota we were losing to Los Angeles in the playoffs. At the half we held a team meeting. Clinton Jones coined the phrase 'Forty for sixty.' I had been with some of these guys for ten years, but I'd never felt such unity and rapport as at that moment. We shutout the Rams in the second half and won, 24-17. When quarterback Joe Kapp received the MVP award from the league, he turned it down, saying it belonged to the whole team. That's the kind of oneness that enveloped the Vikings."

BENEFITS OF COMPETITION

Bill Bradley, remembering the night in Madison Square Garden when the New York fans honored teammate Dave DeBusschere, his roommate, on his announced retirement—" 'De-fense, de-fense, de-fense,' they chant. Memories of a hundred games come to mind; memories of last-quarter surges to victory and perfect team communion; memories of the road and years together; memories of defeats and rebirths; memories of aspiration fulfilled and challenges met.... My eyes water. 'Why am I crying?' I wonder. It's his night. But it's not, really. It's our night."[3]

Sport competition can bring the participant further toward Christ's commandment to love one another. John said in his epistle, "We know that we have passed from death to life, because we love our brothers.... This is how we know what love is: Jesus Christ laid down his life for us. And we ought to lay down our lives for our brothers" (1 John 3:11, 14, 16, NIV).

When Jesus steps into the competitive team concept, the possibility then exists for the relational circle to be completed.

Bill McHenry, athletic director, Washington and Lee College—"In the first college football game I ever coached, John Zola came off the field, complaining of a headache. He went into convulsions and we rushed him to a hospital. He died thirty-six hours later. To that point football and coaching had been my life. We took a secret ballot among the players to see if they wanted to continue the season. They voted to do so. I wasn't so sure. It all seemed so worthless. But we had team leaders who were Christians. A spiritual bond formed on that team. The death had nearly shattered my faith. Those kids and that season restored it again. Ten years later we held a team reunion. We agreed it was our faith that brought us through. I never questioned competition again."

Tom Woodall, cross country coach, Eastern Illinois University—"Practicing for the Pike's Peak Marathon, I was jogging at 11,000 feet when I heard a woman singing 'Jesus loves me, this I know.' I stopped and saw below me a woman and her two children sitting in the rocks, singing choruses. I ran on, thinking it a bit unusual.

"On race day I was in seventh place 1,000 feet from the top when I experienced the worst cramps I've ever had. I couldn't go on and I couldn't go down. I just stood there in tears, watching people pass me. Then a fellow stopped, asked my trouble, and gave me the best massage I'd ever had. After finishing, I sought my friend and discovered he was a professional masseur. He introduced me to his wife—the lady I'd heard singing in the mountains! His stopping had cost him several places in the race. It was the most meaningful Good Samaritan act I'd ever had happen to me."

"I sought my soul—but my soul could not see; I sought my God—but my God eluded me; I sought my brother—and I found all three." This loving of spiritual teammates is more than infatuation, more than a mere modular relationship based on the competitive common denominator, more than an emotional locker room high, more than a closeness generated by time together in work, sweat, tears, and contesting. It is a love based on a faith that is the most giving love of all.

Reuben Welch wrote in *We Really Do Need Each Other*—"The point is—Christians are not brought together because they like each other, but because they share a common life in Jesus and are faced with the task of learning how to love each other as members of the family. . . . It isn't 'Jesus and me,' it is 'Jesus and we.' "[4]

The kind of love the competitor can begin to fathom from the relationships of a competition that is ultimately completed in Jesus is illustrated in this letter, signed by eleven players, which was distributed on game nights to fans attending Garden Grove, California, high school football games:

"We, a group of athletes at Garden Grove High School, would like to tell you about an outstanding occurrence that has taken place in our lives, an event which has reshaped our entire attitude and perspective toward sports and life. Each of us who cooperated in composing this letter has individually accepted Jesus Christ as personal Lord and Savior. We are by no means perfect people, but we have found that there is a process going on in our lives—a process of change. Jesus Christ is changing each of us from the inside out, helping us to become the best people that we can possibly be.

"We are thankful that God has allowed you to be here this evening. We hope that victory will be the result of our efforts on the field. We realize that the most important result of this game is not how many points we score but whether or not we win with Christ. We can, by playing our best and being good witnesses of his Word. It is to Jesus Christ our Lord, Coach, and Friend that we dedicate this football game and entire season. Whether we win or lose, we will strive to do our best because God has done his best for all of us."

Life says "me."

Athletic competition says "you and me."

Beginning faith says "Jesus and me."

Maturing faith says "Jesus and we."

11
THE HEALING
POWER

We stood on the topographical high point. To the north the fields ran in lines of corn to the trees bordering the Missouri River. Paralleling the river labored a freight train, its mournful whistle proudly denoting its determination. It moved east to someplace, anyplace. Had there been no fortress-thick stone walls and stoic guards superintending from gun turrets—there would have been a stampede of freedom-starved men chasing a whistle. To go someplace, anyplace. The Marquis de Sade could not have devised a crueler torture.

"You get used to it," my companion said. "I don't even hear it. I see the same thing you do, but it's a painting to me. Some guys lie in their bunks or sit out here street trippin'. They get like vegetables. Sometimes the guards carry them out of here in sacks."

We were at "the walls," the ancient, scarred, and saddened hulk of stone in Jefferson City that serves as Missouri's maximum security prison. I was part of a prison ministry. A dozen athletes from various sports brought the sport/faith community to area institutions. We put on sport clinics, held rallies and chapel services, and ate and slept in the joints. We followed up, corresponding, and then helping men when they hit the streets. To quote a cliche of a different coloration, some of my best friends are cons.

We toured the yard. Men stood in clusters, talking, smoking, sunning. Others walked. Walked in long, straight lines and back again. Walked in circles, flesh leaning against and directing flesh. Walked in squares and rectangles, like figure skaters carving out precise patterns in a compulsory routine.

Others played. Roller skating to music. Doing dance steps while getting a workout. Playing handball, sweating and grunting while palming the ball against pockmarked walls. They wore dark glasses and bandannas and tattoos and faded T-shirts and torn tennis shoes. Hardly the facilities and dress one sees where the suburban mascara-and-touch-of-gray devotees dabble.

We stopped at the baseball field. No game today. At second base a group was diligently doing calisthenics in front of a solemn leader who led an earnest cadence. "They'll be in shape," I noted. "Those are Muslims," he said. "They're getting in shape to kill white men." Two days earlier, in a remote hallway, a con had been found . . . in nine pieces. I studied the muscled bodies wet with sweat, looking for suspects.

We passed a deteriorating shack. He pulled out two coupons and bought soft drinks. We sat in the stands and watched a group of laboring figures run the track. Actually, it was nothing more than a worn rut circling the baseball field. The men ran single file. If one wanted to pass, he edged up the side, went around, and came back in again.

"I run every day," my companion said. "Eight times around is a mile. I run eighty times around.

"Over there," he pointed, "is a bad rut. I stutter-step around it so I don't twist my ankle. I can run this course with my eyes closed, telling the turns by the way the sun plays across my face. I know where the sand will be loose under my feet and where it will be firm, where the water will stand when it rains.

"There's guys in here who can't run even one lap," he

continued, trying not to appear proud or smug. "I see how fast I can run it every time. I pass guys; then I catch them and pass them again.

"When I'm done I go to my house and lie down, totally exhausted but feeling so good—you know?—and I can sleep and do it again the next day. It keeps me going. Running and the Lord. If I couldn't run and I didn't know Jesus, I might be in one of those sacks."

My guide at the "walls" was Billy Joe Taylor. He had the liveliest eyes I have ever seen. They shimmered; no, they danced; no, they did the cha-cha. Jesus, through the sheriff who captured Billy the last time, cast them that way. Billy is on the streets now, an evangelist in Missouri. Jesus rescued him. Sport kept him going.

There is a sublime healing power operable in both play and competitive sport. And there is healing power released through the platform competitive sport offers. Many men and women find their identity, their self-worth, through sport.

This is not to say there aren't those whose self-worth and identity are shattered through bad experiences with competitive sport. But the subversion comes through other forces operating in the name of competitive sport—pressuring parents, maniacal coaches, societal inducements. But for the person who has the gift for sport, there is often great healing power found and loosed through the opportunities to test skill in the competitive sport arena. Sport is an outlet, an avenue of grace, to help complete us as total people. And when Jesus is part of it, the healing is lofted to its highest plane.

I met Catfish in another Missouri prison. He could sing beautifully. And he could do it all on the basketball court. "When we're on a break," he asked me, "do you know how it feels? There's a rhythm, a flow. And when I slip open and they get me the ball and I make my moves and then float toward the hoop, I'm flowin', man; I am flowin'. It could be Madison Square Garden. I don't even know I'm in this joint. I love that flow, man. When the game's over and I'm in my house I can feel that high, and I know I'm OK. Catfish is somebody. Catfish can do things with that ball other dudes can't do. You dig?"

At the same prison there was a stocky blond kid who followed me through the baseball and fencing clinics. During free time one afternoon he walked over, fingering a hard, black ball.

"How about some handball?" he asked, smiling.

Racquetball is my game. I never saw the sense in badgering your nerve endings when one can let a racquet bear the brunt. Of course, there are no racquets allowed inside the joints. So I agreed.

I started easy. My first inclination was to let him win—not make it obvious, of course. How best to do it? The question was academic. Tuffy was good. And it had been so long since I'd played handball that the first few times I went to my left, instead of using my left hand, I reached across and hit the ball with the back of my right hand. It skittered away. "Never saw that shot before, did you?" I joked.

The game wore on. It was his court. No ceiling, side walls or back wall. Just a perpendicular slab of concrete he knew like the front of his hand. He knew how to hop the ball, when to change speeds to keep me running, how to lay the ball soft in the cracks so it would trickle out of my reach. Knew it all. Enough to beat me easily. He was quite satisfied with the whole affair, and really, so was I.

Tuffy had stood off to the side in the other sport clinics. But handball was his game. "Tuffy?" the other cons said. "You played him? Hey, he's good. About the best in here." Tuffy and I wrote each other for several months after that. He was released on parole, and I lost touch. I hope he made it. If he's still playing handball, I think he might have.

The only other time I have seen competitive sport mean as much is in the Special Olympics. I saw a little boy stand for minutes, his eyes on the ground, sucking his finger, while two judges tried to convince him to make a try in the standing broad jump. Finally he made a token half-effort, hopping a few inches. He looked for approval and was applauded and hugged. He clasped his hands and laughed. And he jumped again. And again. And again. They could not get him to stop. Only a game of work-up among the angels could have been any happier. Jesus said, "Let the little children come unto me." Let the little children run unto me.

The big children, too. After my divorce, I moved to an apartment in midtown Kansas City. There were no magical remedies to my hurt; time and faith were the ultimate healers. But, surprisingly, there was one thing that initially helped. A silly thing, really. But God often uses inconsequential things to keep us going.

There was a park across the street. Every day after work for the first few weeks I took a football to the park and would punt the ball and run wind sprints after it. I would return home after a half hour of this, and a two- or three-mile run, exhausted and calmed.

It was a healing factor in that trying time of my life just to punt a football well. It was play, a diversion, a physical release. But also a personal competition. How many kicks could I kick and wind sprints sprint in thirty minutes? And the punts had to be good. Not the playground spiral off the side of the foot, which curves right to left like a boomerang. No, a high, deep projectile that mortars from the instep with good hang time.

It was healing to watch that spiral bite into the sky, pause at the apex, stall out, float down, and take that end over end roll for another ten yards—and then race after it. Silly? Only if you haven't been there. To know that I could kick a ball well and could still run and feel my body and do things physically helped me believe that I was still a person of some worth.

Sport can help heal that way.

Competition, especially individual competition, has the capacity to get us in touch with ourselves and convey us beyond ourselves. There are many purely spiritual experiences discovered at unintended and unexpected moments by the athlete. Runner Mike Spino describes one in the book *The Athletic Revolution:*

"In the last half mile something happened which may have occurred to me only one or two times before or since. Furiously I ran; time lost all semblance of meaning. There was myself, the cement, a vague feeling of legs, and the coming dusk. I tore on. Jack (Scott) had planned to sound the horn first when a quarter mile remained, and then again at the completion of the six miles. The first sound barely reached my consciousness. My running was a pouring feeling. The final horn sounded. I kept on running. I could have run and run.

"Perhaps I had experienced a physiological change, but, whatever, it was magic. I came to the side of the road and gazed, with a sort of bewilderment, at my friends. I sat on the side of the road and cried tears of joy and sorrow. Joy at being alive; sorrow for a vague feeling of temporalness, and a knowledge of the impossibility of giving this experience to anyone."[1]

And there is the release of being in touch with all of life, including sport, by being in touch with the source of life. Darrell Imhoff, former pro basketball player, commented, "On a Sunday morning in 1961, while playing for the New York Knicks, I was baptized at a small Episcopalian mission church on Long Island. That afternoon

I played the best game of my life. All my burdens seemed to be gone, and I had a lightness on my feet I'd never before experienced."[2]

The crux of being Christian is to be freed from the bondage of trying to be religious.

And the crux of sports is that anyone can be athletic without being a skilled athlete.

Seeking perfection as a Christian is facing a twenty-foot barrier; we'll never vault it. But when we rest in Christ's grace and strength, we discover we don't need to. And in sports you may never be good enough for one team or good enough for another group but you are always good enough to enjoy the sport at your own competitive pace, in your own way and time, with your own friends, and to your own level of satisfaction.

The beauty of Christianity and athletics is that both are for everyone just for the taking.[3]

And this freeing process further means that healing is available for the taking. One reason people compete, among the many conscious and subconscious causes, is to feel good about themselves and to know themselves. It was said of Willie Loman in *Death of a Salesman* that he "never knew who he was." We want to know the who and what of our existence.

Inside of us resides "the person we've always wanted to be"—a person of ideals, of courage, of conscience, of ethics, of higher qualities and capacities than we sometimes evidence; a person above all the mundane pettiness and squabblings; a person who is healed and becomes a healer.

I am a Gregory Peck fan. I need to believe there is an Atticus Finch. I am convinced there are fathers like the man he played in *The Yearling*. I would like to meet the Jim McKay he played in *The Big Country*.

Challenged in front of the cowhands to ride Old

BENEFITS OF COMPETITION

Thunder, McKay declines and his reputation as a coward is born. Later, alone, he subdues the horse and no one, except stablehand Ramone, knows about it. McKay says, "I'm not responsible for what people think. I'm only responsible for what I am."

Challenged to a fight in front of the cowhands, McKay again declines. Later that night he rousts his antagonist from sleep, they repair to a field and bloody each other to a moonlit draw, and then McKay asks, "Tell me, Leach, what did we prove?"

Self-worth, personal security, and spiritual health are not engrained simply by risking dares in front of a taunting crowd. They come from knowing who we are and being content with that. Competition can point the way. Faith is the tape at the finish.

In thinking about self-worth and the healing balm competitive sport can provide our personal identity, the word *prove* kept running through my mind. "We had something to prove," the victorious manager says. "He had to prove himself," it was said of the champion.

We "prove" ourselves. We "disprove" others. We "re-prove" ourselves or others. We seek and need "approval."

The athlete with a strong sense of self, whose inner-being has experienced healing through his competency in competitive sport, has nothing to prove to anyone but himself. When "I'll show them" becomes "I'll show me and be satisfied with that," healing has begun.

"As I mature and have more self-worth, I view competition differently," said Tim Foley, defensive back for the Miami Dolphins and one of the more articulate pro athletes. "The true sense of competition is to develop our potential to the fullest. You have to know yourself and be honest with yourself to do that. This 110 percent jazz some coaches still dish out is nonsense. If we perform to the capacity that our inner-self recognizes and feels good about, that's all we need ask of ourselves."

"I believe the athlete in an individual sport gets to know himself best," said LSU track coach Bill McClure. "The team athlete can hide in the team. The individual athlete is in a fishbowl. He must know his goals, his capacity, his limitations. People who aren't knowledgeable about sport may wonder why a runner can finish sixth and feel good about it. The athlete must resist outside pressure, know himself, and be content with the inner wins and satisfactions."

In the final analysis, the only ones we have to prove ourselves to is ourself and Jesus.

Many people have a habit of reproving themselves. Life gives us ample opportunity to feel badly about ourselves. Watch TV to see just who is "pretty." Check the crowd to see who is "popular." Study the economy to see who is "wanted." Just be. You can feel put upon and put down any time you so desire.

Competitive sport says, "Come, try me, seek your level of enjoyment, test yourself to whatever height. I will not turn you away." Mrs. Hazel Wightman, after whom the Wightman Cup tennis match is named, once said of her teaching, "I have a special feeling about the awkward and shy ones. By doing something well that other people admire, they can gain confidence and poise. It can be the difference between a frustrated and full life."[4]

Two statements indicate where the individual can go in his search for self-worth through competition. Famed concert pianist Paderewski wrote, "There have been a few moments when I have known complete satisfaction, but only a few. I have rarely been free from the disturbing realization that my playing might have been better."

In contrast to a maestro who perhaps exists in melancholy because he cannot achieve the unachievable, a student at Stanford University said, "I didn't get away from the (academic) competition games by finding a lower level of competition, where I would obviously be 'best.' I got out of them by going higher, to a level where I couldn't be the best. I had to accept who I was and be happy with it.

"I think the Body of Christ is like that. In the first place, God tells us we're all uniquely valuable and accepted by him (much higher acceptance than Stanford's!). We don't have to prove and reprove our worth. We're worth something because God says so. We can relax."[5]

Jesus said in John 8: 36, "So if the Son sets you free, you will be free indeed." Free to know ourselves, free to feel good about who we are, free to continue competing—rather than run away from it—and free to feel our self-worth and identify in the process and relax with the results.

As to the approval and disapproval of others, consider the sport phrase "court sense." It's imperative in basketball, especially among post men who play with their back to the basket, to have this court sense, this "sense of where you are" when you make your fakes and turn to drive for the shot.

Jesus gives us a sense of where we are in relationship to God—"I do not receive glory from men. . . . How can you believe, who receive glory from one another and do not seek the glory that comes from the only God?" (John 5: 41, 44).

Competitive sport can teach us this sense of *where* we are. Faith teaches us, ultimately, after competition may have initiated the process, the sense of *who* we are. The two complement each other.

There is another healing factor that both sport and faith provide, healing that adds fuel to the eternal flame of peace and assurance that burns in the soul.

I was a freshman at Michigan State, trying to decide which physical education class to attempt that first semester. For a kid off the farm who still had straw in his Sunday shoes the class marked "Fencing" sounded glamorous—Errol Flynn, the Three Musketeers, all the swashbucklers.

I eagerly signed up.

The instructor was MSU fencing coach Charles Schmitter, a stern, no-nonsense taskmaster. He scared the life out of me. He loved fencing as an art form and had no time for those taking the class as a lark.

He snapped instructions, denounced our ineptness, intimidated us with sharp glances. While I was as coordinated as a baby calf on ice, I did begin to appreciate the subtle movements, the challenge of man and foil alone on the strip with the opponent, and the courtesy and refinement of the sport.

At the end of the semester there was an all-college intramural tournament. We only had masks, gloves, and plasterons—no fencing trousers or jackets. Unwisely, I wore gym shorts, and through the series of bouts my legs—not a target area for scoring—became covered with cuts and welts from opponents whose wild charges and slashes seemed intent on maiming while I tried, with limited skill, to fence instead of joust.

I finished fourth and sat dejectedly in the locker room rubbing my legs and arms and thinking of the three more aggressive but not necessarily better fencers who finished ahead of me. Then I felt a hand on my shoulder.

It was Coach Schmitter. It was the first time I could recall him smiling at me. "Mr. Warner," he said, "you fenced like a fencer and a gentleman."

The Lord blesses our lives with unexpected pleasant interludes—moments that come as total surprises and are quickly gone but leave a comforting glow in the

memory bank. Athletics is filled with pleasant interludes—healing interludes:

A laugh and pat on the back from a coach that lances
the nervousness and tension.

The look of respect from an opponent, which heartens
our sense of worth and accomplishment.

A word or a look or a touch from a teammate that
conveys the togetherness and loyalty one finds best in
both athletics and the sharing of faith with Christian
brothers and sisters.

And there are so many more.

Scripture is also filled with these pleasant interludes,
these healing interludes, of the faith life that add to our
assurance and settle us in the Lord's peace and presence.

Acts 3: 1-10 is the story of a lame man at the Beautiful
Gate healed by Peter and John. When they approached
the Temple, he asked for something from them even as
he begged from everyone else who passed. He expected a
coin, a handout. Instead, he received healing.

In Acts 8, an official is reading Isaiah but before his
pleasant interlude with Philip is over he has found Jesus.

In the pleasant interludes—the healing interludes—of
sport and faith we usually receive far more than we ever
expected.

Several years ago I was in a Missouri prison for an
evening chapel. Something special was going on. The
inmates kept asking, "Have you seen Paul yet?" And
when Paul came in, his smile was ear to ear. He ran
toward me.

Paul's love was softball. He played on an institution
team. I had watched him in previous clinics. He was
lacking in fundamentals and natural skill. His swing was
too fast, too hard, too full—the kind that misses the ball
nine times and hits it out of the park the tenth time.

"Here," he shouted as he got closer. "This is special."

116

I unwrapped the box. It held a softball. On it was scrawled, "This one is for Gary. A three-run homer. July 19, 1974."

I thanked him. The ball rests in my youngest son's room among his trophies and model planes. It will never be tossed or hit. It is not for that.

It is for realizing the worth of every person. Paul and I never wrote or visited after that but what he would mention the homer. I would tell him it must have been quite a hit. His eyes would shine, and he would agree . . . and tell me about it again.

I imagine Jesus walking up to me and giving me a gift. On it is written, "This one is for Gary. A homer. Calvary."

Healing from the Healer who uses all means to heal us, including competitive sport.

PART

3

THE DANGERS
OF COMPETITION

PRIDE

When playing racquetball competitively, I often worked out alone, practicing shots and rethinking court strategy. It was a refreshing diversion and an opportunity for some contemplative physical solitude.

A player or players waiting for another court would occasionally sit above my court to converse while watching me hit shots. I not only noticed them, but I would cater to my apparent need for recognition and approval.

If I was doing something relatively uninteresting at the moment, it was amazing (and amusing!) how I could remember that I needed to hit a few more forehand kills from front court where the ball would pinch into the corner and roll out, sometimes in rather impressive fashion. I would sneak a look at my "fans" to see if they were sufficiently attentive. If not, I would come up with some innovative effort to rekindle their enthusiasm.

If I held their attention away from the other courts— or would overhear one say to the other, "Hey, this guy is good"—I would radiate.

At times I would stop my performance, dismiss myself as a "hotdog," and go about my practice. But it would happen again. I started to question myself. Why such silly behavior over something so meaningless?

Reviewing my athletic career, it was not hard to find other such situations. It was a pattern, a pattern I'm sure exists, in some degree, in all athletic competitors. As a high school athlete I could not wait to get the newspaper before and after games. Did it mention my name? How many times? If it ran your picture, that was really special. (Years later I would recall a quote from Bishop Fulton J. Sheen—"A proud man counts his newspaper clippings; the humble man his blessings.")

I had a tryout with the Detroit Tigers as a high school senior, one of scores of such tryouts given aspiring players. If people did not question me sufficiently about it, I would venture all the details. The first time I pulled on the college baseball shirt that read State across the front, I felt a surge of deep feeling. I was special. I was someone very important.

I was quite proud.

It was easy to determine which "vice" to use as the lead to the tail's side of the competitive coin. Pride is the first of the seven cardinal sins. All other sins run in the face of God; pride stands firm in opposition. And God opposes in return. Three times in Scripture—Proverbs 3:34, James 4:6, and 1 Peter 5:5—we find that God resists the proud. Pride is the core malignancy from which other vices flow.

The finest description of pride I have read is by C. S. Lewis in *Mere Christianity*—"The essential vice, the utmost evil, is pride. . . . It was through pride that the devil became the devil: pride leads to every other vice; it is the complete anti-God state of mind."[1]

And why does the athletic competitor have such a struggle with pride? Lewis continues, "Pride is essentially competitive—is competitive by its very nature. . . . Pride gets no pleasure out of having something, only out of having more of it than the next man. . . . It is the comparison that makes you proud: the pleasure of being above the rest."[2]

Before proceeding, let's be sure of our semantics. Self-worth is on the plus side of the competitive coin. I am not tampering with the mandate of Jesus' second commandment that we know, love, and respect ourselves before we can truly love others. Jesus validates the need for a firm realization of our self-worth and "OKness" before him.

But self-worth marches to the point of wholeness and halts. It says, "God has said I am all right. Therefore, there is no need to bad-mouth myself or indulge in self-flagellation. By the grace of God, I am a person of gifts and merit and worth because God says I am."

Pride does not stop there. Pride barges impudently through to conceit by adding, "Hey, everybody, look at me. I am really something." March on further and you arrive at haughtiness, only a few steps removed from arrogance.

Athletically, we think more in terms of *ego* than *pride*—the "big head," the "braggart." This crowning self king and allowing self to reign in our lives ultimately comes from the competitive sin of pride. So for this chapter we'll disregard the other kindred expressions and concentrate on *pride*.

The antonym of pride is humility. And the scriptural imperatives concerning pride and humility are beyond dispute. The whole matter is crystallized by Jesus in Luke 14:11: "For every one who exalts himself will be humbled, and he who humbles himself will be exalted."

Our goal is humility, a goal that demands a choice. "There are two kingdoms," says Earl Jabay. "The Kingdom of Self and the Kingdom of God. If God's Kingdom becomes established in the human heart, it is hardly noticed at first, because we allow God only the smallest control over our wills. King self surrenders by degrees. Ego-slaying and obedience are terribly painful, and yet afterward there is a quality of inexpressible joy which the presence of God generates in us."[3]

And the way to humility? A pure heart. "Who is pure in heart? Only those who have surrendered their hearts completely to Jesus that he may reign in them alone. Only those whose hearts are undefiled by their own evil—and by their own virtues, too. . . . The pure heart is pure alike of good and evil, it belongs exclusively to Christ."[4]

Humility by way of a pure heart. Simply stated but difficult to attain, especially in the athletic world, which so readily encourages pride. Competitive sport presents a threefold problem of pride:

1. Organized competitive sport encourages pride because having "pride in yourself" is often regarded as part of what it means to be a "competitor."

Appealing to one's pride is a typical coaching technique: appealing to pride as a man (or a woman); as a performer; pride in the team, the school, the sport one represents. It is another way of authoritarian disposition to keep the troops in line. In war men die proud and unquestioning (until recently, thank God!). In sport they play proud while the spirit dies, suffocated by the Marley chain that pride wraps us in, link by link.

Again, to the sport's cliches: they were defeated but "they can hold up their heads and be proud." They have "too much pride to quit." The pro team played this one for "pride" (last game of the season and thirty-seven games out of first place). Stoic in pain, unconquered in defeat . . . pride.

As C. S. Lewis writes: "Pride can often be used to beat down the simpler vices. Teachers, in fact, often appeal to a boy's pride, or, as they call it, his self-respect, to make him behave decently: many a man has overcome coward-ice, or lust, or ill-temper by learning to think they are beneath his dignity—that is, by pride. The devil laughs. He is perfectly content to see you becoming chaste and brave and self-controlled provided, all the time, he is setting you up in the dictatorship of pride."[5]

In his book *Rip off the Big Game,* author Paul Hoch observes, "It is obvious that college and professional footballers would not go through endless hours of agonizing calisthenics and brutalizing scrimmages under the yoke of fascist coaches for money alone. Nor do hockey players crack each other's bones with their sticks for 'love of the game.' Nor do boys run themselves ragged to play on varsity teams because they like 'clean living.' None of this could happen without the spur of intra-male competition—the endless dog-eat-dog struggle to be the biggest jock on the block. Sports is one of the central arenas in which this struggle—with all its physical and, especially, mental brutality—is carried out. . . . This is the competition behind the competition. 'This,' we are told, 'is where they separate the men from the boys.' "[6]

And separating the men from the boys often rotates around pride.

One of the young leaders at an FCA conference was a wrestler/football player from Northern Illinois University, a scowling brute of a lad who played under Pat Culpepper, the much-maligned figure of Gary Shaw's book *Meat on the Hoof.* While an assistant coach at the University of Texas, Culpepper was accused by Shaw of conducting brutalizing drills in practice designed to run off scholarship players who were no longer of use to the team so Texas might recoup the scholarship for incoming freshmen.

I asked the young man about this. Were the charges in the book true? What was it like playing for Culpepper?

This Christian athlete looked at me quite defensively, his eyes narrowing. "Coach Culpepper is a great man," he said. "Sure, he's tough. But it's tough on that football field. Those who are toughest survive. They win. And that's what it's about." Then his eyes widened and he smiled, "We like to believe we're real men and the toughest team in the country." He returned to his impressionable high school group members to implant his concept of who and what Jesus was. I'm sure Jesus was a "tough guy." A Savior who had a "lot of pride."

2. *The sports competitor performs in the spotlight and all the accruing pressures encourage and stimulate the sin of pride.*

Vanity is commonplace in sport. A runner said, "People wish to excel in things other people take seriously. They wish to be noticed. Not every competitor has illusions of grandeur, but they all seek to carve out a place for themselves in other people's estimations, and they would not be competing were they seeking self-satisfaction only."[7]

Pastor/athlete Donn Moomaw said, "Athletes to be good have to have a lot of ego needs and ego strengths, because it's rather foolish to do all they have to do to play a game when they could play a game without all they have to do."

And sports psychologist Dr. Thomas Tutko adds, "Most people compete to feel worthwhile. In our society there are very few ways to feel a sense of importance. If we were all brought up in a way to feel worthwhile and capable, to have self-esteem, I don't think there would be the insanity there is about sports. But as it is, there is no end in sight. You even have people like Evel Knievel willing to kill themselves for the attention."

An important distinction must be made. Again Lewis writes: "Pleasure in being praised is not pride . . . the saved soul to whom Christ says 'well done' is pleased and ought to be. . . . The trouble begins when we pass from thinking, 'I have pleased him; all is well,' to thinking, 'What a fine person I must be to have done it.' "

Perhaps as long as one does not go as far as killing himself for attention, vanity is a form of pride that has an

acceptable price. Lewis, however, goes on to point out a
far worse form of pride that infects the sports community: "The real black, diabolical pride comes when you
look down on the others so much that you do not care
what they think of you . . . the devil loves 'curing' a small
fault by giving you a great one. We must not try to be
vain, but we must never call in our pride to cure our
vanity; better the frying pan than the fire."[8]

"Black, diabolical pride" begins in the small-fry leagues
and grows until one has the arrogant, imperious professional whose whole attitude is "I will be who and what I
want to be and if you do not like it, drop dead." And as
competitive sport begins and intensifies in younger age
levels, this attitude becomes accentuated in college, in
high school . . . and even earlier.

One especially sees it in the attitudes of those affiliated
with various loyalties in sport. Consider the story of the
Oklahoma City newspaperman, who, doing his job, uncovered recruiting violations in the University of Oklahoma football program. Was he praised, appreciated,
thanked? Hardly! He was denounced as high as the state
legislature. Why? Because he had the audacity to tamper
with state pride.

To some, Oklahoma football is larger than morality.
Oklahoma, nearly blown away by dust and Steinbeck,
rallied to survive. Rallied around football. As University
President George Lynn Cross quipped in seeking addi-
tional funds from the legislature after World War II,
"We'd like to build a university of which the football team
could be proud." This kind of pride, too often evidenced
at all levels of competition, says, "We'll do what we please,
whatever it takes to win, whatever it takes to be on top."

*3. Since the nature of both organized sport and pride is
competitive, the only sure way to health is to work through
competition and not remain apathetic about it or refute it.* As

DANGERS OF COMPETITION

Lewis writes: "If anyone would like to acquire humility, I can, I think, tell him the first step. The first step is to realize that one is proud. . . . If you think you are not conceited, it means you are very conceited indeed."[9]

We mentioned in our discussion of the plus side of the competitive coin that all is not cut and dried. A plus can, at times, be a minus. And vice versa. Such is the case with pride. Those who advocate eliminating all competition in favor of play would destroy one potential plus for competition: that competition itself can be a strong force in nullifying pride.

Competition shatters illusions. If one always opts for play, he may become a victim of self-delusion and self-inflicted pride. One can fantasize himself to any height of excellence, and there is no danger. One never has to prove himself if he always plays.

In competition one continually puts his pride and ego on the line. Over the years I have been praised by the unknowing or the mediocre as an outstanding racquetball player. I could bask in that were I never to compete again. But I know the levels of the game. And I know where I fit. I have played those whose skill and pace are superior. So I acknowledge the compliments and then explain, gently so as not to disparage their game, that I am really quite average. They do not always comprehend, but I do. There is no kidding myself. It would be folly, which is another description of pride—folly before God.

Some competitors may continue to find means to fool themselves and others, remaining proud by rationalizing or alibiing or excusing or compromising. When one remains proud in the face of competitive facts, he is truly entwining the chain of black, diabolical pride around his soul.

Before offering two remedies of pride in competitive

128

sport, a word about the most deadly pride of all—spiritual pride. During my years with the Fellowship of Christian Athletes, this pride was evident among those in leadership capacities (including myself), in the in-fighting and competition between the various sport/faith groups, and within individual Christian athletes and coaches.

The game of spiritual one upmanship is called "out-humbling." My all-time, hands-down winner is a former pro quarterback who had played on a 1960s World Championship team. A bulwark of fundamentalist Christianity and a very decent, giving man at heart, he is the supposed epitome of humility. He is humble, humble, humble . . . and quite proud of it.

The more a person assures you he is nobody, the more you can be sure he believes he is somebody. As Samuel Taylor Coleridge wrote, "And the Devil did grin, for his darling sin is pride that apes humility." Or as Lewis wrote in *Surprised by Joy,* "But til the end, give me the man who takes the best of everything (even at my expense) and then talks of other things, rather than the man who serves me and talks of himself, and whose very kindnesses are a continual reproach, a continual demand for pity, gratitude, and admiration."[10]

The "out-humblers," however, are usually recognizable and, therefore, relatively harmless. The insidious danger comes from a pride that masks as legitimate humility and is recognized as such by both the extender and the recipient. Two cases as a contrast:

For years I have known a well-traveled major college, assistant football coach. He and his family are pillars of the faith and of the FCA. He is a churchman, an FCA spokesman, a highly regarded clinician, a leading sports/faith exponent.

And a man of acute spiritual pride.

DANGERS OF COMPETITION

He is a small man, soft-spoken. As a boy he had to work to survive, had to be big to overcome being small. He admits as a player he would do anything to win, even injuring opponents. Then he became a Christian. He not only leads FCA groups and recruits under rigid Christian standards, but opens and closes each practice with prayer. He would quit a job were his right to gather for prayer at the drop of a hat ever called to question.

He follows the Athletes in Action approach—you get more attention if you win. He labels Jesus "a winner." His goal, simply stated, is "to have a head coaching job at a major university, to have the top Christian coaching staff in the nation, and to win the national championship to prove that it can be done in a Christian way by Christian people."

He calls the stadium his pulpit. He wants to win with "class and character." He calls losing worse than death because "you have to live with losing." Defeat is like "losing one of my family." He does not eat or sleep after a loss. He calls competition "overcoming obstacles." His kids are quietly but ferociously competitive. Life is extremely serious business, and winners face it with "intensity." After all, looking good, showing class, is important. He knows where he is going. He has the answers, football or spiritual. It is only a matter of time. Only a matter of pride.

I have another coaching friend, Thom Park, assistant football coach at The Citadel. He is a shouter, a screamer, an intense fighter in competition. But he has a gift that disarms pride—he has the ability to laugh at himself.

"I got married recently," Thom says. "Married into a family of two little girls. I've seen a shift in me. I don't grit my teeth as much any more. I'm more open and sensitive to life. Maybe that's why the great world leaders are usually sixty or older. They've had time to sort out all the meaningless stuff and can concentrate on what is vital. I know my limitations, my capabilities, and can honestly quit playing silly games about who and what I am. If we coaches just teach kids to be their best and to rise to their level, I think we can impart self-respect without leaving the competitor to struggle with the blinding sin of pride."

The antidote for pride for the Christian athlete and coach? First, I would advocate the balanced life. It has long troubled me that too many athletes and coaches are one-dimensional people. Sport is all. They have no other reference point, no other source of self-worth or identity. Therefore, a fixation, a ferocity of singlemindedness sets in that too often leads to pride.

Fortunately, more and more athletes (still not as much with coaches) are diverting from the pattern and becoming people of diverse interests. Sport is only a part of their lives, not the whole. As one broadens, becomes more knowledgeable and experienced, pride is dissipated by awareness and openness.

A decade ago I was surprised and pleased to read that Duke football player Jay Wilkinson, son of the famous coach Bud Wilkinson, was studying to become an Episcopal priest and then would enter politics. He was a forerunner.

Today such an athlete is not the exception. Pat Haden, Los Angeles Rams quarterback, studies in the off-season at Oxford as a Rhodes Scholar. Says Haden, "Football players are always getting patted on the back and called celebrities, and sometimes it's hard to keep your feet on the ground. The Rhodes has made football seem less important to me; it brings it down to earth. Most kids my age grew up with a tremendous social conscience because of Vietnam. And when you think about things like that, football doesn't really mean anything. In the universal sense, it's just not that important, and it shouldn't be."[11]

Say his colleagues of Haden. "The guy doesn't have a pretentious bone in his body."

Along with the balanced life, I would advocate another antidote as a key to the mature Christian life: we must learn to relax the tempo of our lives, laugh at ourselves, and not take sport life, or ourselves too seriously.

Frank Deford, in his three-part *Sports Illustrated* series on faith and sports, wrote that most "Sportians" are "humorless and persevering." He explained, "That's exactly what I found in talking with many Christian athletes and coaches. Oh, there were jokes and laughter but nothing spontaneous or really freed-up. The humor was contrived or had an edge to it. People were afraid to let down their guard, even just to have a silly laugh."

I would, in large measure, agree. Henri Frederic Amiel said, "True humility is contentment." The laughter of contentment is not evidenced in the sport/faith community as it ought to be."

Billie Jean King said, "When you are playing good and hit a difficult shot, you want to grab the microphone and say, 'Hey! Look what I did!' " The attitude and motivation behind this may be the key to establishing our self-worth through competition without crossing the tenuous line into pride. If I am saying "look what I did" while puffing my chest, pride has its curse on me. But if it's a moment of laughter and happiness prompted by a deep joy of contentment and satisfaction at just being able to hit such a shot and nothing more, then I have found the joyous wholesomeness competition offers.

13
LIFELONG ADOLESCENCE

The single-engine Piper banked into the final approach and slid impatiently down the asphalt runway. It taxied to where I was standing, and the pilot emerged, dressed in a red and white Cleveland Indians uniform. Legs spread, arms akimbo, he disinterestedly surveyed the flat, corn-impregnated countryside, stuffed his dark glasses into his back pocket, and jumped to the ground.

"Hello, I'm Bob Feller," he said, shaking hands without stopping as we moved toward my car, the bored expression set in granite.

"Yes, it's nice to have you here."

"That's all right. How long will this take?"

"Not long. Can you stay?"

"No. Need to get back to Cleveland. We may get some weather," he said, keeping his eyes from the cloudless sky.

Bob Feller. Hall of Famer. Retired strikeout artist. All dressed up and no place to play. He'd flown to Adrian to help dedicate our newly lighted baseball stadium. As sports editor who had editorialized for the lights, I was given the privilege of being his escort.

I tried, rather nervously, to make small talk. He answered "yes" and "no," finally leaning his head against the window and closing his eyes. His profile was fleshy, gray, and deeply lined.

The crowd was not as large as I had hoped. It did not matter to Feller. All such nights were the same, the towns the same, the words the same. He studied his fingernails as the lights were turned on and he was introduced, strode to the mound and waved to the fans, threw a couple of "first pitches," spoke briefly into a microphone that whined back, signed several token autographs . . . and we were enroute back to the airport.

"Do you have the money?" he asked.

"I'm sorry. They'll send you a check."

"I was afraid of that," he sighed. "Tell them to hurry, will you?"

"Yes. Thank you for coming. It was nice to meet you."

"That's all right."

I waited until the plane had slid back up the runway and was enveloped by the thickening haze. A man-child had come and gone. It had been more a matter of minutes than hours. For years I had continued to indulge in self-pity over not becoming a major league baseball player, nursing the emotion like an all-life sucker. I took one last lick and threw the stick away.

It is widely heralded that sport can make men out of boys. Conversely, sport can also make boys out of men. "The perennial high school jock," said Georgia Southern College basketball coach Larry Chapman, "is the guy who's forty years old and still believes in Santa Claus." Said All-Pro George Sauer in a statement that could apply to other sports, "The way football is structured today, being an athlete is like being kept in perpetual or prolonged adolescence."[1]

The faded athlete, this aging child (be he or she twenty-two and out of college sports, thirty-five and finished as a pro, or sixty-two and no longer able to function recreationally) has been depicted in song and verse—from John Updike's Rabbit Angstrom in *Rabbit, Run* to the tennis player in Paul Petrie's *The Old Pro's Lament*, "Playing in an empty court under the dim floodlights of the moon with a racket gone in the strings—no net, no ball, no game—and still playing to win."[2]

Writes Pat Jordan in his exceptional baseball book, *A False Spring*, "And on the day I finally took the mound in the same semi-pro league in which five years before I had struck out batters at will, I was unable to retire a single man. The fans loved it. They laughed and hooted each time my poor catcher (some high school boy I have never seen again) scrambled back to the screen to retrieve another of my wild pitches. . . . I left the game in the first inning. . . . Baseball was such an experience in my life that ten years later I have still not shaken it, will probably never shake it. I still think of myself not as a writer who once pitched, but as a pitcher who happens to be writing just now."[3]

It begins early, as early as we first make heroes out of those who play games, convince them it is all right to be a man-child forever, then turn our backs when they take us up on it. It often culminates at the high school level when the athlete makes the decision, premeditated or subconscious, whether to begin the pursuit of life's vocation or continue playing the player.

Peter Lowry was an All-American soccer player at the University of Maryland. He was honored by the Atlantic Coast Conference as a "scholar-athlete," and taught in Maryland's intellectual history department.

Lowry defined his version of the typical campus competitor, "In general, athletes don't get involved with ideas. There is a reliance on purely physical or material things. There's a locker room mentality, a virility and masculinity hangup. They don't have the sensitivity for the world around them. They don't ask the question 'why?' "

Any wonder there has been a boom in counseling services to prepare the aging pro athlete for his trip into the adult world? John P. Palsios, a psychologist and personnel consultant, states, "Football players and many other athletes find themselves living through a period of enforced adolescence. For years they are both pampered and bossed like rich little children. Consequently, they often find it difficult to make decisions about themselves because they really don't know who they are. . . . At age twenty-five or thirty or more he may have to face for the first time the realities of the adult world and standards from which he has been shielded.

Even the church conspires against the growth and maturity of the athlete. In a classic example of sports baby talk—not at all uncommon among the nonathletic suddenly given the opportunity for a prayer or sermonette in the sport spotlight—Miami's Roman Catholic Archbishop Coleman F. Carroll invocated at a Miami-Atlanta game, "Your Son is our quarterback and You are the coach. We sometimes get blitzed by heavy sorrows or red-dogged by Satan. Teach us to run the right patterns in our life so that we will truly make a touchdown one day through the heavenly gates as the angels and saints cheer us on from the sidelines."

(In reporting the notable invocation, *The National Catholic Reporter* added, "And when that final gun goes off, dear Lord, lead us out of the parking lot of life through the interchange of Purgatory, on the freeway into Heaven, with our fenders undented, our spirits undaunted, and our metaphors untangled. Amen.")

The care and keeping of the man-child is all so facetious one is tempted to brush it aside with a laugh as Ogden Nash did:

The hunter crouches in his blind
'Neath camouflage of every kind.
And conjures up a quacking noise

To lend allure to his decoys,
This grown up man, with pluck and luck,
Is hoping to outwit a duck.[4]

But there is nothing humorous about the thirty-five-year-old man-child.

The Scriptures put considerable emphasis on growing to spiritual maturity. Paul wrote in Hebrews 5:11-14 (NIV), "We have much to say about this, but it is hard to explain because you are slow to learn. . . . You need milk, not solid food. Anyone who lives on milk, being still an infant, is not acquainted with the teaching about righteousness. But solid food is for the mature."

And in 1 Corinthians 3:1-2 (NIV), "Brothers, I could not address you as spiritual but as worldly—mere infants in Christ. I gave you milk, not solid food, for you were not yet ready for it. Indeed, you are still not ready."

Emotional and intellectual growth is, to some degree, a parallel course with spiritual growth. In some situations involving the man-child, spiritual growth is not possible without the prerequisite of the emotional and intellectual hard look. Once the man has seen the child, has dealt with his emotions and reasoning process, then the resulting spiritual maturity to the solid food level can take him eons further along toward wholeness.

The sports world is populated with gray-hairs, including Christian athletes and coaches, who have yet to be weaned from the milk offered the man-child from an endless group of star-struck suppliers.

Roger Kahn wrote, "Yes, it is fiercely difficult for an athlete to grow old, but to age with dignity and with courage cuts close to what it is to be a man."[5]

To avoid a lifelong adolescence, the athlete must *face up to what he is involved in*. Moby Benedict left pro baseball after a couple of seasons when he attained the understanding that "the ball player is only as good as his last game. No one remembers him after that." He helps his players understand this today as the highly successful baseball coach at the University of Michigan.

"I was booed in crescendos my last season at St. Louis," said former pro quarterback Gary Cuozzo. "It made me realize how little all the years of cheering meant. People cheer for themselves as much as for you. The boos helped me know I could give up the adulation. And I loved the game so much it took those boos and the kids riding my little girl on the school bus about her daddy throwing 'those stupid interceptions' to make me realize just what it was I was involved in."

The athlete has to *face up to whom he is involved with.* Former pro running back Ron Burton remembers, "You can be a cutie when you're on top but that won't get you anyplace when the party is over. You better be a decent guy and make friends who are friends."

The athlete has to *face up to himself.* Ross Fichtner was a defensive back with Cleveland before he moved into coaching and later to the FCA staff. He recalled the indecisiveness that was a part of his man-childness: "I had a chance to invest in some land in Cleveland. I didn't, and it became a shopping center worth a fortune. I'd moan about 'if I could only do it over.' Then a similar ten acres of choice property became available . . . and I passed again. I had to examine myself. I was a child. I could be that way forever or change. I wanted to change."

The wanting to change is vital. In John's Gospel, fifth chapter, Jesus encounters a man at the pool called Bethesda who had been an invalid for thirty-eight years. Jesus' question seemed cruel but was pertinent: "Do you want to get well?" If the man-child wants to get well, he can get well. Or he can choose to lie by the competitive sport pool all his life.

"Happy is the man who finds wisdom, and the man who gets understanding, for gain from it is better than gain from silver, and its profit better than gold" (Prov. 3:13-14).

More athletes are coming to that understanding of what it is to grow up.

Tom Goode was a standout lineman in the NFL for ten years. "You've got to understand what pro ball meant to me," he said. "We still didn't have running water in the house when I was eighteen; I studied by a kerosene lamp. And then to be a pro? To play and get paid for it?

"One day in Baltimore I stood by Johnny Unitas on the sidelines. He'd ripped an Achilles tendon; everybody knew it was over. I asked why he didn't get out. He didn't say anything, just looked at the ground and mumbled. I didn't want to hang on that way."

Jim Carroll played for Notre Dame and then five years as a lineman in the NFL. "I'm a bad fan," he said. "When I quit, I quit for good. It takes you years to build a name and weeks to lose it. There's nothing deader than yesterday's hero. I saw guys who weren't equipped to make a living being carried by businessmen. I determined never to be that way."

Wes Parker and Maury Wills had significant careers with the Los Angeles Dodgers . . . and went out with Kahn's "dignity." Said Parker, "I love baseball, but I (also) love reading, writing, bridge, movies, concerts. Major league baseball is a game for single men in their twenties. . . . If you're in it too long, you're trapped."

Said Wills, "With night games you go to bed late, you get up at noon, by four you're on the way to the park, and you haven't done anything with your life. (Wes and I) used to talk about how nice it must be to get up at 7 A.M., before the air is polluted. I'm doing that now, and it's beautiful."[6]

DANGERS OF COMPETITION

Another former major league pitcher came to Adrian. Ned Garver was a standout hurler for the St. Louis Browns and Detroit Tigers in the 1940s and 1950s. He retired to a farm near Alliance, Ohio, and traveled summers with the town's semi-pro club.

A large crowd was attracted by the "name." Our team was eager to face the former star. The exhibition was, instead, ludicrous, pitiful. Ned lobbed the ball plateward. We hit line shots. Baserunners scampered like ducks across a shooting gallery. The crowd laughed and catcalled. The kids on our bench rode the old timer; juvenile jackals in on the kill. The older players quieted them. It had become embarrassing.

Afterwards I sought out Garver. "Why?" was all I could summon up. "Oh, don't worry," he laughed. "I'm not a guy trying to make a comeback or living on memories. I farm all year and this is play. I don't care if I get hit. Heck, if some kid gets a hit, it might be a story for his grandchildren. People won't understand, but that's OK.

"I don't have anything to prove. My record speaks for itself. I love the game, like to have a good time."

Years later I would understand and appreciate Ned Garver. He was one athlete who knew both how to play and how to compete. He was an adult in the land of the man-child.

The opposite of lifelong adolescence is true manliness . . . and that involves Jesus. Jesus spoke of being whole, being free, being pure, being God-led. You don't get that in a protein supplement or from the catharsis of the cheering crowd.

"When I was a child I spoke and thought and reasoned as a child does. But when I became a man . . . I put away the childish things"—1 Corinthians 13:11 (TLB).

It's like getting up in the morning, before the air is polluted.

14

HERO WORSHIP
AND IDOLATRY

*My main objection to football and all professional sports is a
personal one. They prevented me from becoming a millionaire.
As a boy, I estimate having spent an average of three hours a day
reading or talking about my various heroes on the Cubs, Bears,
and other big league teams.*

*Like most kids I memorized all the averages, all the statistics of
the all-time greats as well as the all-time clunks. Ask me anything
about Lenny Merullo. Go ahead, just ask.*

*What good was all this knowledge? Once I waited outside the
Cubs' park for the autograph of a hero. I knew all about him. I
could have told him what he hit 11 years earlier, how many
career doubles and triples he had, how often he spit during a
game, and what he ate for breakfast (Wheaties). I knew more
about his career than he did. When he came out he stepped on my
foot and was gone.*

*Looking back, if I had spent all those hours reading about the
stock market, bonds, real estate, and so on, I could have become
rich. I could have had my own yacht. You can bet that Aristotle
Onassis never memorized Lenny Merullo's fielding averages.*

*I might have become a Chicago tycoon, maybe another insur-
ance millionaire like W. Clement Stone, although I wouldn't
have grown his sneaky mustache. Then, even without that sneaky
mustache, I could have been a big man and given millions of*

DANGERS OF COMPETITION

dollars to elect Nixon and Agnew as Stone did.

On second thought, maybe Lenny Merullo wasn't a bad idea.
Mike Royko
Chicago Daily News

Not a "bad idea." Perhaps that's the most appropriate way to define the place and value of hero worship in competitive sport. An idea latent with dangers but also containing the genes of, as a friend of mine is apt to say about most anything, "The constant possibility of goodness."

It would so simplify matters if Andy Warhol's prediction were true: everyone in the world is going to be a hero for fifteen minutes. Perhaps that would suffice and then all of us, knowing our fifteen minutes was to come and we were at the same station in life as everyone else, could get on with just being us.

Life, however, is not this tidy. There are leaders and followers, heroes and hero worshipers. People need someone to emulate. We do not like ourselves very much. To make a buck, today's hustlers and money changers point out all our faults and the readily attainable remedies through waves of advertising propaganda. Inwardly there is the compulsion to be more, to be better, to be somebody. For whatever reasons, our eyes search the masses for a person, a quality, an idea, a belief, an answer we can revere.

Play will not produce heroes. But with all its potential of good and harm, competition will. Hero worship is listed as a minus on the competitive coin because, without restraints and a spiritual perspective, there is little nobility in it. Giving homage to another person too easily degenerates to blind admiration and idolatry. What begins with seemingly harmless hero worship often leads to the harder stuff, the creation of false gods.

Hero worship, however, can be a great plus of competitive sport. If the hero or heroine becomes a road marker pointing to superior qualities and virtues that can be incorporated into the lives of the adherents, better people are produced. And, taking the potentiality to the ultimate step, if this adulation leads to a worship of Jesus Christ, then hero worship becomes a strong grace of competitive sport.

We are turning the corner from a time when heroes were somewhat out of fashion to a period in which a yearning for the return of heroes is evident. Wrote William J. Bennett, executive officer of the National Humanities Center in North Carolina, in *Newsweek*, "It's hard to have convictions without ideals. Heroes instantiate ideals. Real heroes, not the bionic types who do it with wires, may be fictional or factual as long as they embody character, as long as they possess qualities that we instantly recognize as true to human life and worth human attention."[1]

And the subjects of hero worship appear to be changing. In the open season on heroes of the mid-1960s to the early 1970s, the debunkers attacked with a "take no prisoners" mentality. This put-down, however, may be the redemption of authentic heroism. We need more common, human, real-life heroes. We don't need idols—we need models.

There's a wide diversity of athletic heroes. Some are pampered prima donnas who, outside the spotlight, are nothing more than pompous phonies. Others are gut-level men and women who are willing to have their frailties exposed for public consumption. As long as frankness and vulnerability are genuine, I prefer the latter breed of hero.

143

DANGERS OF COMPETITION

Pitcher-author Jim Bouton (*Ball Four*) has been labeled a debunker of heroes. He responds, "I didn't set out to destroy heroes. Anyway, it all depends on what your idea of a hero is. Why do our heroes have to be so perfect and unflawed? I believe there are enough real heroes in America so that we don't have to kneel to fake ones."

Why do our heroes have to be so perfect and unflawed? One reason is the American tendency to project unto others what we cannot be—and then take great delight in tearing these idols apart and pointing out they are only like us after all. It's an escape mechanism. We know we'll never be what we are projecting our hero to be. (We also know, deep down, that our hero cannot match those expectations, either.) So we set up our heroes for the kill, like children laboring long to build sand castles and then getting the most pleasure out of instantaneously kicking them down.

When we construct our sand heroes, why do so many resemble the sports competitor? Why the attraction to the world of athletics?

Is it physical? Don McClanen, founder of the Fellowship of Christian Athletes, a movement built on the concept of utilizing the hero worship of athletes as an avenue to Christ, said, "The athlete has the added blessing of physical prowess, an endowment to use as his pulpit of influence. Strength in any form is a tremendous persuader for good or evil."[2]

Or is it the charisma the spotlight often births? An Associated Press report stated that Olga Korbut was "the biggest problem in Russian sports history." Said television gymnastics commentator Gordon Maddux, "The Soviets really would have preferred it if she had never surfaced. . . . Her presence there (1972 Olympics) came by grace of a teammate's broken wrist. . . . She and her coach decided early on not to gear their performances

144

for the judges, but for the audience (hardly Marxist mentality) . . . there she was, doing a back somersault off the uneven bars. It was something I had never seen a human do before. And the charisma . . . she just glowed."[3]

Perhaps we identify with the amplification of our small successes. William F. Buckley, Jr., writes in *Execution Eve,* "Joe DiMaggio is up at bat not necessarily more often than Toscanini, but the results are easier to chart, and they appear in the next morning's newspapers and the next year's almanacs. . . . And we have all hit home runs at some level of competition, in Little League or in stickball or one-on-one against the little sister's knuckle curve: these small successes can be magnified, the crack of the bat simulated by a popping tongue, the home run follow-through held, frozen, like Discobolus' sculpted approach. Few of us, on the other hand, have conducted a kid sister's chorus."[4]

And maybe it is nothing grand at all. Writes former Dallas Cowboys wide receiver Pete Gent in *North Dallas Forty,* "It was always surprising to me to see respected businessmen who deal in millions of dollars and thousands of lives giggling like pubescent school girls around a football player. I could never figure out if it was worship or fear. Probably just confusion."[5]

Whatever the reasons, the hero worship of sports competitors has been, and will be, with us in some form and fashion. And there are several crucial points to consider in this context.

There is little rationale in hero worship; none in idolatry. People are simply going to believe what they want to. New York Yankee Reggie Jackson said, "I have to be careful. What I say will be quoted week after week, year after year. People are going to write stories and magazine articles in the future of all the things I say today. People are going to write books of collections of my quotes."

One is tempted to snort and dismiss this as the tongue-in-cheek babbling of a professional man-child. But the peril is, first, that the media would seriously report it; second, that Jackson, should he repeat it enough times, might actually start believing it; and third, that a considerable segment of the reading public might even—does even—believe such nonsense.

I have always been amazed that when a competitor, who may have barely eeked out a high school education, attracts attention through his athletic performance, he suddenly becomes an instant authority on everything from the state of our national defense to politics and the economy. And not only is he asked his views by the media, he is often given more authenticity by the adoring masses than experts in those fields.

It's obvious that many a Joe Fan is a curious conglomeration of gullibility, little boy, Monday morning quarterback, frustrated jock, and stubborn protagonist for whatever side of a player or team he happened to get up on. Don't confront him with reality. Life is hard enough as it is, and sports is one facet of life in which he can grab his blanket, implant thumb firmly in mouth, and crawl into his bed of fantasy.

Consider the Western hero. Authorities tell us Billy the Kid was a yellow runt who sulked around and shot his victims in the back. Yet many people make heroes of the Kid, Jesse James, and the like.

In the same way, some sports heroes are above reproach. The guy down the street may be justly thought of as an immoral, libertine scoundrel, and avoided because of it. But if the pro athlete brags about the same thing, he's a "swinger," the anti-hero become hero. When former Detroit Tiger pitcher Denny McClain blew his life apart with most every conceivable stupidity and then begged forgiveness with an "I haven't grown up yet," his fans put signs on their cars pledging "Remember '68" (last time Detroit won the World Series) and even donated funds to help a once wealthy man avoid bankruptcy.

It's nothing new. When it comes to picking heroes there will always be those who choose a Barabbas over a Christ. The former is off-beat, to be sure, involved in revolution and a little murder. But he's doing his own thing and doesn't really make demands on our personal lives. But the Christ, well, he's something else. He sets up high standards, issues strong challenges, and lays down some tough disciplines. It simply costs a lot less to give three cheers for Billy (or Denny) the Kid than to pledge allegiance to Jesus Christ.

There is great responsibility involved in being the subject of hero worship. Will Rogers said, "Heroes are made every little while, but only one in a million conducts himself afterwards so that it makes us proud that we honored him at the time." The historically proven insight only further confirms the need for responsible modeling. Said Olympic decathlon winner Bruce Jenner, "When kids ask me a question, I know whatever I tell them will be taken seriously."

Wrote Dr. Richard C. Halverson in *Perspective*, "The larger the rock you drop in a quiet pool—the greater the ripples that radiate out from the splash. . . . And the bigger the man—the greater his impact. Good or bad, it influences those around him. His sin moves out to cover the crowd—just as much as his righteousness. . . . Whether a man likes it or not—if he's in a place of leadership—he will be influencing others. He has no right just to consider himself. He must think in terms of influence. This is part of the price of leadership. Not just the man himself—but what happens to those who follow in his footsteps—is the serious responsibility of the leader—the big man. This is inescapable! As Jesus said, 'To whom much is given, much shall surely be required.' "[6]

Just what does this rippling effect, this influence of the "big man" on those who would follow him, involve? For years in sports it was thought of merely in terms of availability—to give radio interviews, to be accessible to reporters, to sign autographs, to visit hospitals, to speak to clubs. A word, a smile, a pat on the head.

And it was apparently easy to tell the responsible hero from those who were not responsible: "Any ballplayer that don't sign autographs for little kids ain't American. He's a Communist." So stated the astute baseball great Rogers Hornsby.

For the Christian athlete, there is more to it than signing autographs and not being a Communist. Paul Anderson was known for years as "The World's Strongest Man." He has opened several youth homes and long been a spokesman for the faith. But he rues a time when he missed a chance to be a responsible subject of hero worship: "In 1955 in Russia I put up 402.41 pounds in the two-hand press lift to win the world title, and I broke two other world records that same night. The astonished announcer called me 'a wonder of nature.' For days I toured Russia, lifting weights and meeting people who flocked to see me.

"What an influence for God I could have been. But, unfortunately, at that time I was not living for Christ and a once-in-a-lifetime opportunity for personal testimony behind the Iron Curtain went by the wayside."[7]

The Christian who is an object of the hero worship that competitive sport provides has a chance to function, not as a "to" but as a "through." The profound German author Hermann Hesse wrote a young Japanese student after World War II in *If the War Goes On . . .*, "The author who has awakened you or given you an insight is neither a light nor a torch-bearer; he is at best a window through which light can shine on the reader. His distinction has nothing whatever to do with heroism, noble intentions, or ideal programs; his only function is that of a window: not to stand in the way of the light but to let light through. Possibly he will long to do noble deeds, to become a benefactor of mankind, and just as possible such a longing will be his ruin, preventing him from admitting the light. He must not be guided or spurred on by pride or by a frantic striving for humility but solely by love of light, by openness to reality and truth."[8]

The advisability for those seeking a model (a hero) is to seek light. The responsibility of those serving as a model (a hero) is to let the light shine through. In this way hero worship has the savor of nobility.

But what seems elementary is often the most difficult to attain. Most hero worship crumbles to idolatry. Most heroes want to shine themselves rather than let a light shine through. An exchange between two of my favorite cartoon characters goes this way:

Bullwinkle: "You mean you have a hero, Rocky?"

Rocky: "Sure, Bullwinkle, you're my hero. Don't you have a hero? Everyone has a hero."

Bullwinkle: "Sure, I have a hero, Rocky. Same as yours. Me!"

Too many idol creators and worshipers will flitter to the light like moths in the night and seldom question its value. Said a lady from Memphis at the funeral of Elvis Presley, "I wonder what people will do now that he's gone? What will they have their hopes, their dreams on? I know my dreams have just gone. It's just like someone just snatched the world from under me."

DANGERS OF COMPETITION

God warned against such idolatry when he said, "You shall not make for yourself a graven image, or any likeness of anything that is in heaven above, or that is in the earth beneath, or that is in the water under the earth; you shall not bow down to them or serve them" (Ex. 20: 4-5). And Martin Luther was so correct when he said, "We easily fall into idolatry, for we are inclined thereunto by nature, and coming to us by inheritance, it seems pleasant."

The trap of idolatry is perpetually baited, and we are often caught before we have become aware of the danger.

The FCA and other sport/faith organizations depend heavily on the influence and activity of the sport hero to make their thrust workable and marketable. And while they decry idolatry, they are often guilty in whom they project, how they are projected, how they are catered to. What growth is encouraged for those in the spotlight? Not much when it is more marketable to keep them center stage spouting inane testimonies rather than moving into serious nurturing in the faith, which might lead the testifier to a change of venue.

Such ex-FCA heroes as Fran Tarkenton, Bill Bradley, and Bill Curry, while guilty of overlooking the foundational faith and inspiration FCA brought to their young lives, nonetheless may be justified in their feelings of being paraded and manipulated for the FCA cause. And if FCA stumbles here, on occasion, Athletes in Action, because of its overburdening win ethic, and Pro Athletes Outreach, because of its involvement only with a limited number of pro athletes, fumble the ball more often.

Lip service is paid the "unsung hero" by all the sport/faith movements, which is fine as long as the unsung hero is quite content to remain unsung. He will not be signing fund-raising letters, giving addresses at major banquets and rallies, or holding a place of leadership and influence on boards. These are reserved for the "name" heroes of sport or finance—even those heroes who have yet to become windows to reflect a higher and truly honorable light.

The Scriptures make several clear points concerning hero worship and idolatry. We are to keep from idols (1 John 5:21, 1 Thess. 1:9). Coveting, into which hero worship often deteriorates, is idolatry (Eph. 5:5, Col. 3:5). Idolaters will not inherit the Kingdom of God (1 Cor. 6:9). Idolatry is a work of the flesh (Gal. 5:20).

And in a verse that says it all about false and empty sports hero worship, Paul writes, "an idol has no real existence" (1 Cor. 8:4). When we make a god, an idol, of something or someone, we are actually giving ourselves to something that has no life, no existence, no light.

There is only one to be lifted up, exalted, followed, believed, loved—the God-man Jesus Christ, to whom all is to be given. And there is only one accurate criteria for determining genuine heroes among Christian athletes and coaches—to whom does the individual point with his or her words and life? To himself or to Christ? Consider John the Baptist. He claimed no status other than that of a poorly designed advertisement, a forerunner of Christ. But how did Jesus appraise this common man? "In all humanity," Jesus said, "there is no one greater than John" (Luke 7:28, TLB). When a Christian athlete is himself, when he admits his shortcomings and points only to the perfection of Christ, he becomes a true hero.

And the plus side of hero worship means not only looking to Jesus but also looking to ourselves. Rosemary Cobham wrote in the *Christian Science Monitor* concerning personal maturity, "Grownuppery can happen at any age. It is simply a realization that what excites your admiration need not trigger your imitation. It is most gratifying to appreciate a Tolstoy without wishing you had written *War and Peace*, to watch an Olympic gold medalist glide across the ice without rushing out to buy a pair of skates, to enjoy Queen Elizabeth's Silver Jubilee without craving to ride in a gold coach and wave at crowds."

Growing up in Michigan, Detroit Tiger outfielder Barney McCoskey was my hero, and my younger brother, Ron, liked first baseman Rudy York. If they'd have walked into a tornado, Ron and I would have done the same.

We'd sit in front of the radio, pounding our fists into the pockets of our dilapidated baseball gloves, pulling for our Tigers and hating those villainous Yankees and Red Sox and Indians with the fervent passion of youth. And it never failed that after the game Ron would say, "Let's play catch. You be BaCoskey and I'll be 'ork."

There was a time when I wanted more than anything to be Barney McCoskey. I'd have traded home and mother for left field in Briggs Stadium. Then I evolved through a stage where I wanted to be just like a McCoskey or whoever was my hero at the moment. Today I am coming toward a fullness of peace in just being me.

Many experience this three-stage existence. Some spend a lifetime in the first stage. This is emotionally, mentally, and experientially paralytic. Many others stagnate in the second stage, frustrated and empty.

The hazards of such immature responses to life are obviously apparent in the sport/faith movements. If adherents are allowed to camp in either the first or second stage, the Lord has been shortchanged. If participants are moved to the third stage— personal awareness and acceptance of their individual identity and worth— the movements have presented God a valuable gift.

A couple of summers back Ron and I were in Michigan for a family reunion. Again we listened to the Tigers, but there was more of a difference than just thirty years in time. We didn't pound our gloves and didn't cry when Detroit lost, and when the game was over Ron looked at me with a knowing smile and said, "Let's play catch."

I laughed and stopped him, "OK, but one difference: you be you and I'll be me."

GREED
AND EXPLOITATION

Found inscribed on a cowboy hustler's grave:
> As you lay me
> down to sleep . . .
> Leave one hand free
> so I can fleece the sheep.

In competitive athletics today, both hands are free. Label them "greed" and "exploitation." And each hand knows exactly what the other is doing. It's quite a tandem—the one grasping, counting, hoarding; the other manipulating and deceiving.

These hands are spin-offs of competition. Where there is only play, the necessity for and the chances of rapacious self-interest are minimized. But introduce levels of ability, an emphasis on winning, play for pay, and the natural selection of the competitive arena, and greed and exploitation begin to emerge.

Remember this scene? It's a comedy classic: Jack Benny accosted by a hold-up man who demands, "Your money or your life." Ah, the insoluble dilemma! Hand to cheek, Benny turns to the audience, the look of helpless indecision prompting laughter and identification.

Certainly identification. We understand greed. We should. It has been with us long enough. As John Steinbeck wrote in *America and Americans*, "Every single man in our emerging country was out for himself against all others—for his safety, his profit, his future."[1]

Greed infects and affects us. Byron wrote, "So for a good old-fashioned vice, I think I must take up with avarice." But greed is not treated so flippantly by Mr. Webster, who uses such synonyms as grasping, ravenous, voracious, and gluttonous. And it is not given kid-glove treatment in the Scriptures, either, being listed with immorality, indecency, and lust (Col. 3:5) by Paul, and being defined as an anti-God devotion by Jesus (Luke 16:13).

No strata of sport is immune to greed: society communicates its illnesses to its offspring. When we outfit a team of ten-year-olds in the finest uniforms, put them in the best sport facilities, and toast them at banquets, where do we go next? Why, to flashier equipment and more sumptuous banquets. And we wonder why little Johnny and Mary aren't properly grateful. They are surrounded with greed, not gratitude, so how can they express a virtue foreign to their makeup—and ours?

Of all the vices apparent in collegiate sports, none has a deeper grip on the jugular than greed. Greed plays a major role in recruiting: the coach who will get up whatever it takes to land a prospect or who will overrecruit just so an opponent won't get a player; the player who has been told for years how wonderful he is and is now demanding the top dollar for his services; the parents who can get that new car or color TV if junior or sissy can get a "full-ride."

Where you find high stakes and a premium on producing the bucks, you'll find greed. In 1978 Notre Dame became the first school to clear one million dollars from a bowl appearance. The athletic budget at Ohio State University annually exceeds $8 million. And when eager alumni are assured, "As long as you support us we're gonna have the best sports program possible," greed begins to salivate in anticipation.

DANGERS OF COMPETITION

At the college level, the coaches, the players, the alumni have long stood indicted and found guilty as charged on a multitude of sins, including greed. But there is one group deserving special mention: the university presidents and the boards of regents. Were they to say, "Stop!" to all the nonsense presently infesting intercollegiate sport, and mean it, many of the ills could be rectified. But theirs is the greater hypocrisy—the imploring looks of innocence, the washing of the hands, the hidden presence that approves all it takes to win and put the school in the headlines and suck in the funds and the students . . . until the athletic department is caught. Then the coach is fired and the administration absolves itself under a banner of high ideals. But this flag of idealism and purity is bloodied by greed.

"If you want to win," a Midwest university hockey coach says, "You'd better build some dorms and fill 'em with booze and broads, like we did."[2] Like the college administration did—the Pharisees of competitive sport.

And, of course, there are the pros. Boxing has always played for the big chips. In 1976 alone, Muhammed Ali grossed (double meaning intended) over $13 million for four title fights and a bizarre exhibition with a Japanese wrestler. But, then, mayhem always draws a crowd. We enjoy a bit of sadism in the name of sport. The Pilgrims finally halted bear-baiting, not because of the pain to the bear but the pleasure it was giving the spectators.

What about legitimate sport? Consider a few of the figures. Baseball's Larry Hisle, who earned $47,000 for Minnesota in 1977, signed with Milwaukee in 1978 for $525,000 a season; football's O. J. Simpson made $2 million in three years; and the average salary in the National Basketball Association is over $100,000 a year. Men with a skill to bounce and shoot a ball, who may be the tenth man on a ten-man squad, earn $100,000 while social workers, teachers, and others must leave their professions because they cannot afford to continue. And these figures do not even contain the additional money a pro earns from appearances and endorsements. It is a madness—a madness that is, in part, greed created and greed perpetuated.

In every segment of the competitive sport rat race there are those out to get all they can get. Including:

The player: Arnold Palmer said, "If you're the best at what you do, I think you're worth what you can get."[3] Quarterback Fran Tarkenton, estimated at being worth over $8 million, stated, "Who is to determine what any group of people make? We make what the market bears."[4] Said basketball star George McGinnis of the Denver Nuggets who makes $3.2 million on a five-year contract, "I know what it's like to get up hungry, to go to bed hungry, not to have any clothes, not to have spending money. I didn't like the feeling at all."[5]

Said Marvin Miller, executive director of the Major League Baseball Players' Association, "The fallacy of comparing athletes' salaries with other professions is that it makes a stupid assumption. If a ballplayer made less, would a teacher be paid more? Absolutely not. If a ballplayer makes less, then the rich owners will make more."[6]

The owners: ego, greed, childishness, and pride are the Four Horsemen of the pro sport ownership Apocalypse. When a man or a group of men can afford a professional team as a toy, greed flows.

In 1977 before the All-Star break, owner George Steinbrenner entered the Yankee clubhouse after a loss and knew just the right formula to buck up his crestfallen New Yorkers: he gave everyone $300 in cash and told them to go out and have a nice time. How do the players react to George's apparent generosity? Well, on a flight to

DANGERS OF COMPETITION

Los Angeles during the World Series, Yankees Thurman Munson and Reggie Jackson threatened not to play in the next game unless the club came up with better complimentary seats for their friends and family. "These tickets are a disgrace," stormed Jackson. "I won't put on my uniform until I get better seats. I'll sit in the clubhouse until Bowie Kuhn brings me tickets."

But the game went on . . . and so do the Steinbrenners, Jacksons, and Munsons.

One entrepreneur's success pricks another's greed. California Angel owner Gene Autry and Texas Ranger owner Brad Corbett both traveled the road of unprecedented spending in 1977-78. Sixteen of the Rangers earn over $100,000 a year. Journeyman pitcher Doc Medich was given $200,000 a season and will be paid $50,000 a year for four years after his retirement as a medical consultant. Richie Zisk, a twenty-nine-year-old slugger with lead in his bat and in his feet, was given a ten-year pact worth $3 million. Asked about his good fortune, Zisk stammered, "I find it difficult to put into words."[7]

All such folly must eventually be transmitted to the fan. In the pyramid of competitive sport, the bottom level must always pay the price of greed. So ticket prices soar. Most pro hockey and basketball franchises are subsidized by the block seat buying of the expense account crowd. With ticket prices at six to twenty dollars or more a seat, the average family cannot attend pro hockey or basketball—also, to some extent, pro football—except on special family promotion nights. And the general admission ticket, which has helped keep baseball the people's game, may one day be only a memory.

Here television takes over. Pro sport has greedily used television to remain afloat financially. Baseball's minor league system was ravaged years ago by the oversaturation of the majors on television. And because the average fan finds it difficult to impossible to get into the stadium and arena, he turns to television. And television, not missing a beat in the melody of greed, can gobble up fat revenues from advertisers and palm off such fiascos as celebrity trash sports on a public hungry for any kind of sport it can afford to view.

Proverbs 15:27 says, "He who is greedy for unjust gain makes trouble for his household." There is trouble in the competitive sport house because greed is running amuck.

The pro football strike of several years back was especially interesting. It was a showcase of greed with Christian athletes in lead and supportive roles. Part of the demands were outlandish and gave little credence to the platitude often espoused by Christian pro members, "I don't play for the money; I play because I love the game." What seemed more factual and relevant was a statement by Charles Horton Cooley, "It is partly to avoid consciousness of greed that we prefer to associate with those who are at least as greedy as ourselves."

In all my years of relationships with Christian individuals in play-for-pay sports, I have found few willing to do more than give lip service to the problem of greed.

Said Roger Staubach, quarterback for the Dallas Cowboys, "I definitely don't want to be paid a ridiculous figure, but as long as a sport is drawing people and making money an athlete deserves his fair share."[8]

While not the case with Roger, the problem is that "fair share" usually turns out to be "all I can get."

Said Cleveland Brown Don Cockroft, like Staubach an avid spokesman for the sport/faith community, "Pro football's a business, an entertainment. There's no reason we should just play for the so-called love of the game. Don't sell yourself short just because you are a Christian. Know what you deserve and go after it."[9]

DANGERS OF COMPETITION

Problem is, "Knowing what you deserve" usually means "all I can get."

The sport/faith organizations have not been noted for being overzealous in trying to eliminate greed. Their major concern about the pro athlete and his salary is getting a portion of it. To be fair, a number of the pros do give generously to their church and the organizations. Not a lot, but some. The sport/faith movements would advise the athletes to use their money as the Lord directs (hopefully, our way), but little attention is given the whole matter of greed and high finance in sports.

I have seen it attempted. Sitting in on a Chicago Bears Bible study with FCA staff member Bruce Bickel, who has a sensitivity about the alternate life-style and how Jesus views our use of money, it was almost embarrassing to hear the pros and their wives fumble with the subject. They had little concept of their own greed and the alternate approach to money that a commitment to Jesus might well entail. But they were starting to think, a step few others have made.

Diogenes wrote, "He has not acquired a fortune: the fortune has acquired him." Your money or your life? Your greed or your soul?

Greed is an insatiable hunger in a nation that has an endless hunger for anything "bigger and better." "Bigger and better" results from greed and leads to more greed.

The sport palaces of Rome and Greece were symbols of national hedonism, but one is accused of crying wolf if he dare suggest we could learn from history. Cities have entered a crash course of outdoing each other in extravagant stadiums. The New Orleans Superdome is the Eighth Wonder of the World—until the Ninth Wonder comes along.

Sometimes I get stabbed in the gut by pangs of common sense. I know the rationale about "all those people" and "all that money" boosting the local economy. The trouble is that the money exchange bypasses the areas of critical need. People only blocks away from new stadiums, who live in wretchedness and end each day hungry, are seldom affected by this money flow. They sure can't get a ticket to the game!

The problem is that what is "bigger and better" is often not "bigger and better" for people.

The problem is that sophisticated towers of Babel that lure crowds also help generate a commercialism that saps the spirit of fun and competition.

The problem is that we build an unappeasable appetite for the glamorous and the extraordinary that can never be satisfied. When the attractiveness of the container overshadows the sport it contains, we've lost the essence of competing and watching.

Jesus talked about this in Luke 12:16-21. A man had abundant crops and no place to put them. So he built "bigger and better" and entered the good life at the expense of his soul. Jesus didn't mince words. He said God calls such a man "a fool."

There is some encouragement in competitive sport. Some of the athletes have exhibited a courage rare among their peers: the courage to say no to money or to being affected by the greed around them. Ray Goff played quarterback at the University of Georgia and had a tryout with the Denver Broncos. When he failed to make the team and went back to Moultrie, Georgia, to open a gas station, he astounded pro sport by giving back his $1,000 bonus, saying simply, "My dad always taught me not to take something for nothing." Understated Bronco General Manager Fred Gehrke, "I've never seen a player quite like him."

In 1977, Philadelphia Phillies slugger Greg Luzinski, a giant, soft-spoken man, spent $22,500 of his salary for a block of seats in left-center field to be used by kids. He has contracted this arrangement for five years. Other than Dave Winfield of the San Diego Padres, it has not started a trend in pro baseball.

In Luke 17:11-19, Jesus heals ten lepers, yet only one returns to give thanks. There's a definite parallel in competitive sport today. Forget those outside a faith perspective. Of the *healed* lepers in the sports world, it is rare for even one of ten to forsake his greed and return to the Lord in thanksgiving. And this is the only way greed will be conquered in sport—for Christian men and women to start the trend.

While the right hand of greed is picking our pocket, the left hand of exploitation is patting us on the back and setting us up for another fleecing.

Exploitation is not the singular domain of any group or individual in competitive sport. It is apparent among players, parents, coaches, fans, and ownership. It is nothing new. Jesus ran into it a number of times. One interesting situation is in Matthew 20:20-28 when the mother of the sons of Zebedee asks that her sons be given favored positions among those who follow Jesus. She'd have made a great Little League mother!

As for explicit instances of exploitation, there are five areas that require close scrutiny. The first is *coaching*. Because the coach is the pivotal figure in organized competitive sport, he or she is also in a position to use others for their personal gain. And the trait is passed along to the competitor.

During the 1978 NBA playoffs, Boston Celtic General Manager Red Auerbach spent a television halftime talking about coaching at the pro level: "The idea is to win. That's all. And you do anything to win. You scream, you plead, you talk sweet, you use sarcasm; you mix it up. Whatever it takes to motivate."

Jack Scott commented on such a mindset: "Lombardi would tell his team, 'If you come off the field defeated, you've lost your manhood.' The satisfaction is taken out of competition with that philosophy. To me this manhood thing is a very crude motivational technique."[10]

The coaching profession too often reeks of crude motivational tactics. Anything to psyche up. Anything to win. Anything to make the coach look good.

And when a coach is heard from on the plus side, it is often to brake someone else's exploiting. The coaches of the Southeastern Conference voted 10-0 against a post-season basketball tournament. The conference administrative and faculty board voted the tournament in. Said Kentucky coach Joe Hall, "It's an exploitation of the players, mainly for financial reasons."

The second primary area of exploitation is *college recruiting*, perhaps the most immoral aspect of competitive sport in America today. It is a national disgrace, a corrupted machine with greed and exploitation as the generators that make it run.

"I'd like to get rid of sport's recruiting and big-time football," one Southwest Conference president admitted, "but I couldn't stay in this state for two days if we did."[11]

University of Michigan athletic director Don Canham said, "Recruiting is a necessary evil. If we did not recruit and have a great football team, we wouldn't have anything going. We wouldn't have any money."[12]

The exploiting comes from the school. Tennis pro Sandy Mayer recalls being recruited by Rice University. "They put on a fantastic show for me. At a basketball game, a tennis team member motioned to the cheerleaders and said, 'Which one would you take if you had a choice?' I picked the prettiest one and was told, 'she's yours.'"[13] Mayer fell in love with the cheerleader but, on his father's advice, enrolled at Stanford.

The exploiting comes from influential alumni. When Steve Spurrier, former pro quarterback, was recruited by Vanderbilt, he said, "I flew up to Nashville in the Governor's helicopter, then visited him in the Governor's Mansion, and we shot some pool."[14]

And then the athlete begins to exploit in return. Said John Stark, Western Amateur golf champion in 1976 who played for the nation's "golf school," the University of Houston, "I try to keep away from the books. But grades aren't all that easy to come by, nor is graduating. Coach (Dave Williams) doesn't have the pull he once did."

And not only does the competitor exploit by taking advantage of his position to get all he can off the field, but the obvious exploitation rampant throughout organized competitive sport at all levels makes it almost impossible for the athlete not to feel perfectly justified in taking this mindset and attitude into his play during actual competition. Why not bend a rule or push it as far as the officials will allow? Why not intimidate or undermind in whatever way possible—physical violence or psychological abuse—an opponent or someone vying for your position? After all, isn't everyone else? So sporting competition receives another black eye, not for what is intrinsic to competition but for what people do to each other in the name of sport competition.

In attempting to get some foothold in the morass of recruiting ills, I've spent hours with Christian athletes and coaches. I've come away frustrated. The ability of Christians in sport to rationalize their behavior or shrug off the recruiting problems as if they were minor irritations rather than a cancer at the heart of sport is simply amazing.

Still there are those with deep concerns. Tommy Limbaugh was formerly assistant football coach at Texas Tech University. One story he told of recruiting intrigue and deviousness makes James Bond sound like Mr. Peepers:

"In 1977 we were recruiting a great running back from Beaumont, Texas. Joe, let's call him, and his family and I got to be close. All along he had indicated he was going to Tech. Then toward signing day he called and said he wasn't sure; Southern Methodist University was pressuring him.

"I headed for Beaumont. We drove into Louisiana and spent the day together. He was set on Tech. It was two days before signing day, so I thought I'd just stay there.

"The next day I drove to his house and found two Cadillacs out in front. I called Joe from a pay phone: it was SMU people. I told him to go to bed and let them sit in their Cadillacs. He did and they left. I sat in front of his house until 1 A.M. when I went for coffee. I came back about 3 A.M. and sat there through the night. At 5:30 I went to the house to have coffee with Joe's folks and sign Joe. Three cars drove up and the SMU coaches walked in with me.

"We laid two letters-of-intent on the table. For thirty minutes we sat there—the coaches, the parents, me, Joe—without saying anything. There was nothing more for me to say. I knew Joe and his parents both wanted Tech. The SMU coaches told Joe their jobs were on the line, that he could 'save the program.' Finally Joe signed the SMU papers. I shook his hand, wished him well, went to the kitchen with his folks, and watched them cry. I later found out SMU had promised Joe that his best friend, an average athlete, would get a scholarship if Joe signed.

"What goes on in recruiting makes my stomach churn. If I cannot recruit as a Christian I will leave coaching. I believe Christians can change the system if enough of us want to and will pay the price to do it."

And then there is the exploitation in *pro sports.* But this is a little easier to deal with if one simply keeps in mind that this is basically entertainment and business. As Leonard Schecter wrote in *The Jocks,* "Around the simplicity which most of us want out of sports has grown a monster, a sprawling five billion dollar a year industry which pretends to cater to our love of games but instead has evolved into that one great American institution: big business. Winning, losing, playing the game all count far less than counting the money."

Which might even be plausible except it's the tax-payer's money being counted. The more than fifty-three new sport stadiums and arenas built in the past few years have committed unsuspecting taxpayers to spend more than $6 billion. Consider: the New Orleans Superdome was to have cost $35 million and ended up costing up-wards of $300 million; Yankee Stadium in New York was advertised at $24 million and wound up costing more than $100 million. And in 1977, because of a special maintenance clause in the contract, the Yankees paid the nearly bankrupt city only $150,000 in taxes rather than upwards of $1 million. Said Mayor Ed Koch of this problem-plagued megapolis, "It's legal but not equita-ble."

Nothing is equitable in pro sports. The fans use the spiraling price of a ticket as justification for violence, a major problem in American stadiums today. Players es-tablish unions, hire agents (prime candidates for the Exploitation Hall of Fame), and go to court. Owners milk and bilk cities for all they can get, then jump the fran-chise.

The fourth area of exploitation is *business,* which has always been at the forefront of knowing what is good for self-perpetuation. And sport is good for business. Sport sells. Ask the television advertiser. Ask Sears and others who promote the AAU Junior Olympics, not because Sears has a burden for young athletes, but because young athletes buy sporting equipment by the millions of dollars worth and can also sell them through their performance. Wheaties, a breakfast cereal proven to have minimal nutritional value, is another classic case in point.

With business, winning and losing isn't all that important in the competitive arena. Sometimes losing can be even better. In 1977 the Denver Bronco defense was nicknamed the "Orange Crush," and the soft drink of the same name started selling incredibly well. Was there sadness at Crush International, Inc., in Toronto, after Denver lost in the Super Bowl? Far from it: "The promotional aspect of the loss is much better for us," said Donald Ottaway, executive vice-president. "In losing, it means the Broncos are still the underdog team, still the favorite of fans throughout the country. It is much better promotionally."

And often business, whether involved in sport or elsewhere, is so engrained with intimidation and exploitation that folks can switch sides daily. It's the way the game is played. The head of Buffalo, New York, recreation industry wrote the *New York Times* on an article the paper had carried titled "The Greatest Enemy of Cross Country Skiers: Snowmobiles": "I was amused by Allan Pospisil's article. We manufacture all-terrain vehicles and used to sell snowmobiles. Guess who was the advertising copywriter on our account with the advertising agency? Allan Pospisil. I guess Allan has changed his mind since he took up cross country skiing. Lord help General Motors if he takes up street crossing."

Business is filled with Allan Pospisils. After all, they're just playing by the rules.

The last stop on our exploitation walk brings us to the

sport/faith community, a glass house where few stones should be thrown. In the mid 1950s both the Fellowship of Christian Athletes and Campus Crusade for Christ were in their fledgling stages. And a darling of both organizations was Donn Moomaw, three time All-American at UCLA, and later on the Fellowship's national board. He now pastors Bel Air Presbyterian Church in California. In an interview in *The Wittenburg Door,* he talked about his feelings of being exploited as a star college athlete:

"I was used to build an organization . . . I don't think the organizational leader felt, 'Let's use Moomaw.' But I think the nature of their position at the time and my vulnerability to be liked by Christians led me to fall right into exploitation. The wounds didn't come until years later as I began to look in retrospect at how I was not really appreciated for being me. . . .

"I was drafted by the Los Angeles Rams as their first choice in 1953. What better way to dramatize the fact that you're a good Christian then by turning down the draft? So the day I was to tell the Rams that I had decided to go into the ministry, Bill Bright (Campus Crusade) suggested that I have a press conference in his home. I didn't foresee at that time that I was being used. I was getting a lot of pious advice. But I wasn't getting a whole lot of earthy, loving support. . . .

"I've never had an athlete in the pulpit. I have scars all over from people inviting me, saying, 'We want you to come because we know you can get a crowd.' And they'll be frank to say that. . . . When people call wanting an athlete to speak in their church I'll ask, 'Do you want an athlete who may not be able to say very much but who may be a star athlete? Or do you want one who can say something but who may not be a star?' Very often they can't answer that."

Exploitation of athletes and coaches in the name of Christ is not just a scattered and individualized phenomenon. Perhaps it is difficult for sport/faith organizations to deal realistically with the subject of personal competitiveness when these movements themselves are guilty of violating Christian ethics in their inter-organizational competitiveness.

While all is serene on the surface and the leaders and movements salute and praise each other, there is an undercurrent of frenzied grasping for names and situations to make the movements go. For instance, the sports arm of Campus Crusade for Christ, ardently orthodox and triumphalistic, has long held suspect the established veteran of the sport/faith area, the Fellowship of Christian Athletes. FCA's theology is termed "evangelism through Fellowship" and does not produce enough pelts on the salvation barn door to satisfy the Crusade zealots. Crusade has long considered FCA soft-sell and felt no qualms about moving in on FCA programs.

The most disastrous situation was at the University of Kentucky. The friction between the two groups was so severe, and athletes were going to different meetings every night or being tugged between the two, that finally the Kentucky coaching staff and administration resolved the problem. It ousted all the religious programs from the campus.

This same kind of intermovement rivalry has surfaced among the pros. While the various movements—FCA, Pro Athletes Outreach, Baseball Chapel, Inc., and others—have done better here, some of the individual sport "gurus" that the chapel program has produced have used sport to exploit themselves into the limelight. Check the roster of sideline chaplains and locker room "pray-ers." Some Christian leaders know the best route to self-promotion is as a team's spiritual trainer.

DANGERS OF COMPETITION

To the credit of FCA President John Erickson, the exploitation, at least publicly and as a practiced philosophy, has lessened between the two organizations after he met with AIA's leader Dave Hannah and put the cards directly on the table. Because Erickson has been concerned and up front about this, the leadership of other organizations is at least aware of the past exploitation and know they'll be called on it in the future. And, in many local situations, the movements have worked well together.

But where there are conversion scalps to be taken and big bucks to be gathered by putting the right people in the limelight to make the movements go, exploitation will go on, competition will go on, even at this supposedly sanctified level of sport. So what chance have the people themselves who are struggling to apply their faith to their competitiveness?

The only chance, for either organizations or individuals, is to confess their greed and exploitation. Only then can they be forgiven and shown a better way.

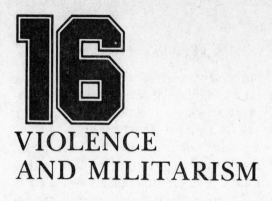

VIOLENCE
AND MILITARISM

The true mission of American sports is to prepare young people for war.

General Dwight D. Eisenhower

In Guatemala City, five persons are hacked to death at a soccer match when hometown loyalists, bitter over a defeat, descend on the winning team with machetes.

I had a license to kill for sixty minutes a week. It was like going totally insane. The best linemen were all sadistic.

Alex Karras
Former Detroit Lions defensive tackle

In Florida, an argument at a football game ends when an assistant high school principal is shot and killed by the rival school's business manager.

I've started dreaming about Merlin Olson. I see myself breaking his leg or knocking him unconscious, and I see myself knocking out a couple of other guys . . . in my dreams I see myself as the hero.

Jerry Kramer
Former Green Bay Packer offensive lineman

America wasn't built on going to church. It was built on violence. I express America in the ring.

Ron Lyle
Heavyweight boxer

171

DANGERS OF COMPETITION

Three persons in a Denver bar wanted to turn on the juke box in the final moments of the televised Denver-Baltimore football game. One was shot to death and the other two wounded by an irate Denver fan.

The dogs of war and the dogs of sport too often prowl together. And the mongrels, yelping and dragging foam-specked tongues, feed on the same fare—violence. One of the more obvious evils of competition is its tendency to evoke and perpetuate violent behavior.

We have no official puberty rites in America, but war and sports definitely have an unofficial sanction. Both deal with artificial realities. We have a romantic naivete about athletic competition and war. To the uninitiated both seem a parade of heroes. Too late young men learn that war is only hate and carnage and death. There are no winners, only those who lose less. What an overwhelming sadness when sport becomes the same.

Tom Tiede wrote, "A man pays seven dollars to see a hockey game and purchases a war. The only difference between the players and the soldiers is they don't wear bandoleers on ice. Some of the game's survivors have grown rich doing things outlawed in Geneva fifty years ago. Blood flows, bones break, eyes are blackened, flesh rips. Some time after the second period they should evacuate the wounded by helicopter. This is sport? What goes on in America's arenas today must be defined as mayhem.

"Football is organized destruction, professional basketball has become an aggregate of mercenary huns, auto racing is the sport to see who enjoys the odor of roasting hair, watching a boxing match is often the same as watching someone kick his dog.

"Some fans in the realm enjoy anything with stench, as long as there are odds. If a tiger kills a man, as Shaw says, it's terrible, but if a man kills a tiger, it's sport. It is these fans, as much as anything else, who demand the worst from athletes. They are morbid voyeurs.

"No other people but we have so institutionalized broken teeth as a sacrifice to manhood. Kids as young as eight in this sovereignty are taught to demolish the guy in the different color jersey. By the time they weigh 250 pounds, many of them are walking weapons. Athletic stitches have become a mark of achievement, like kill counts on an F-105."

In the film *Battle of the Bulge,* a German panzer commander says the goal of his existence is "to wear the uniform just one more day." And in our language, our strategy, our unquenchable thirst for victory, we too often approach athletics with this militaristic mentality. When we exchange the playing field for the battlefield, when the arena becomes a caldron of invective and hatred instead of a setting for entertainment and enjoyment, we have prostituted the role and value of competition.

Sport, like war, has its superpatriots—dogmatists who either cannot or do not want to see sport as anything but 99 and 44/100 percent pure, and war, by our side, at least, as always "necessary." These are not usually the people who fight wars, but those who send boys off to fight them.

At the other extreme in sport are the superliberals who spread nonsensical verbiage like a lawn sprinkler gone mad, ready to condemn everything occurring in the name of competition without giving competition its due.

There's considerable distance between the anticompetitor and the sportsmonger. One must be open to and strive for the common sense and reason that lie at the balance point.

What creates the sportsmonger, who loves a good game or a good war with equal passion and can never get enough violence? One can uncover a plethora of sociological and psychological reasons, symptoms, excuses, rationalizations, and justifications. But Australian Leon Morris, writing in *Christianity Today*, cut to the heart of it:

"A sports commentator interested me by claiming that in this country over a wide area sport is being ruined by a 'win-at-any-price' attitude. This led him to a reference of Scripture. He was reminded of the destruction of Sodom when Abraham pleaded that the city be spared if fifty righteous men could be found in it, if forty-five, if forty, and so on down to ten. He ended by suggesting that we are heading for a situation in which we will not be able to find even the barest minimum of people who know what sport is all about.

"The games we (Australians) play are for the most part different, but they are marred by the same ugly features, the same 'win-at-all-costs' philosophy, the same readiness to use physical strength to excess, the same cynicism about those quaint souls who play games for the fun of it. Modern athletics can be a fierce and hate-filled thing.

"Why do people adopt tactics like those I have been deploring? Deep down it is surely because of the truth that theologians have enshrined in the doctrine of original sin. The trouble is that deep down in the heart of every human being there is a tendency to do evil and this is finding an outlet on our sporting fields.

"The doctrine of original sin is often caricatured and is widely dismissed as quite untenable in a thoughtful age like our own. But I doubt whether any age has offered more widespread illustrations of the truth of the doctrine. There is a flaw in human nature, and unless this is recognized there is little room for optimism."[1]

One can detect this flaw in every element of competition. It is readily discernible among the spectators. For years we Americans have self-righteously looked over our noses at those barbaric "foreigners" who forced their competitors to play soccer behind barbed wire fences and inside moats to keep them away. But we overlook the nastiness here.

For years few prep contests in metropolitan areas have been staged at night. Fan violence in the form of knifings, rapes, and property destruction drove the games into the sunlight and, eventually, in many situations, into police-cordoned arenas with no fans allowed.

Players in all sports at all levels are open targets for bottles, darts, ball bearings, and other savage missiles. Whatever happened to the days when the most serious episode was a fish tossed on the ice at a hockey game?

At Churchill Downs several years ago hundreds of drunken youths broke through a barrier in the backstretch and pelted the horses with beer cans. In Cleveland at "Beer Night," the worst incident in the 105-year history of baseball sent hundreds of drunken, marauding fans on a rampage to assault players, umpires, and each other.

Sporting competition in America has become the true opiate of the masses—the power elite and the powerless alike. We use sport in America to act out our sexual maladjustments, our aggressions, our identity crisis, and our fears. While the phenomenon of fan violence has been explored and dissected by experts, it does not take a genius to understand some basic underlying factors for the excessive and unrestrained behavior.

Permissiveness in spectating was a forerunner of the increasing permissiveness in society. There is a license allowed the fan that he would not receive in other sectors of society. We condone his actions in the name of "sport." And when "the tendency to do evil" is given an inch, it is not long until the miles are stretching out.

Once it was a matter of tearing down the goal posts or

cutting down the net after a big victory. But why go for the goal posts when you can destroy the whole building?

Americans are party lovers. It takes little excuse to have a party. Mix in competition, add people with opposing views and favorites, give them alcohol or other stimulants, and let them know that if they get carried away it's not that big a deal. Our culture creates highly volatile mixtures in the laboratory of competition and then wonders why explosions happen.

So hockey players are cursed and spit on. Baseball fans strip sod and whatever else they can carry from a stadium. Football fans overturn cars and school buses. Mobs lurch through streets destroying property while police smile along the curbside; and, in Zaire, Muhammad Ali fights George Foreman while sixty-thousand fans chant "Ali, *bomaye,*" which means in Lingala "Ali, kill him."

It is madness. But a madness that is condoned and often, by management, intentionally stimulated. Minnesota North Stars defenseman Tom Reid said that several years ago the NHL Players Association proposed stringent rules to eliminate the flagrant fighting in pro hockey. The owners turned it down. At the same time they were promoting ads in warm weather U.S. cities emphasizing the physical excessiveness and violence of hockey to attract the new breed of fan not familiar with the sport. Conn Smythe, one of the pioneers of NHL who managed the Toronto Maple Leafs in an era when a poorly skilled ice bully would have been scorned by knowledgeable Canadian fans, set the official attitude for the league when he stated, "Yes, we've got to stamp out this sort of thing (violence) or people are going to keep buying tickets." The right price covers a multitude of sins.

The blessing of sport spectating is that for many

people being a fan and having a team builds community. But when violence enters the picture the results destroy peace, and men, and ultimately community.

"The flaw" is well entrenched in the vaporable and pressurized profession of coaching. Too many men blend a sport and military ideology into a warped sort of patriotic, pseudoreligious authoritarianism. The result is that lives of young athletes are permanently scarred by prolonged contact and the emotions of rabid crowds are whipped to a fever by a sportsmongering charisma.

Consider Hank Stram, the dapper little egotist who led Kansas City to the Super Bowl and New Orleans to mediocrity. "The defensive line players are like the infantry," said Stram. "The secondary corresponds to the air corps, protecting the front against an aerial attack. And the linebackers are the tank corps. They must be mobile and able to strike against both land and air."

This romantic coupling of competition with violence and war, this ludicrous injecting of sport and competition with military analogies and language (politics through the ages is, of course, filled with it, including Nixon's dubbing the blockade of Haiphong as "Operation Linebacker") makes one wonder if coaches, athletes, politicians, fans, and others who participate have ever been to war or if they are patently ignorant of just what a war does to flesh and bone. One hopes the latter is the answer. If the former is true, God save us from such coaches. If the later is correct, God bring a wisdom and healing.

Several years ago Jack Scott's book *The Athletic Revolution* brought howls of protest from the athletic community. Yet his words about authoritarianism are irrefutable:

"Because of the rampant authoritarianism that permeates the administrative and coaching ranks of the

DANGERS OF COMPETITION

American sports world, athletes who themselves are not authoritarian are usually quickly filtered out of sport at a very young age. This filtering process begins as early as Little League baseball, Pop Warner football, and age group swimming where the 'correct' attitude is often as important as athletic skill.

"Mindless obedience seems to be the most essential ingredient for success in many American sports. . . . Non-authoritarian or 'free-spirited' athletes find it difficult to stomach American style athletics; and if they choose to continue competing rather than quit, these individuals are usually branded 'uncoachable' or 'troublemakers.' Not surprisingly, given the nature of the American sports scene, a very large percentage of American athletes are quite authoritarian, and these athletes will usually only respect an authoritarian, 'hard line coach.' "[2]

It is these kinds of coaches who foster violence as a promulgated aspect of the "game plan." A Southeastern Conference basketball coach sent me the book *Aggressive Basketball* written by Robert M. Davis, head coach at Auburn University. Here are excerpts from the book:

"Unparalleled coaching success has always necessitated aggression. The meek shall not inherit the championship trophies of the basketball world. . . . I have taken some 'lambs' and turned them into 'tigers.' . . . The aggressive coach is a stern disciplinarian . . . does not like weakness . . . must despise losers and losing. . . .

"Make a boy bold, forceful, domineering to the point of hostility; accomplish this by persistently injecting this spirit of aggressiveness into the teaching of the most minute details. Little things are important—mean, tough little things. They develop big, hard men who win. . . .

"Never let up when a competitor shows a weakness. Hit them where they are hurting and pour on the steam. . . .

178

Don't show mercy on the basketball court. If you have an urge to be kind to your fellow man, join the Peace Corps."[3]

Davis resigned several years ago.

Why would coaches knowingly perpetuate violence? Perhaps my good friend University of Michigan baseball coach Moby Benedict, in a moment of candor, unknowingly crystallized it: "On the double play I tell my infielders to come across the bag and aim at the runner's forehead. He'll get down. If he doesn't he has something else in mind, like taking advantage of me. And I can't let him do that."

No, that would be unthinkable. When winning is the essence of sport competition, one must not be taken advantage of. One must go for the edge, whatever the means, whatever the cost.

So how does one curb violence and its outright instruction or, at least, toleration in the coaching profession? Sport psychologist Dr. William Beausay says, "I'd eliminate all authoritarian people from coaching. Our educational system is extremely poor at preparing men and women to be coaches. They are taught rules and technique but nothing about people and how to relate and communicate. Any man or woman with an authoritarian personality should not be a coach."

Porter Miller, assistant football and head track coach at Otterbein College (Ohio), found another way to temper his violence: "As a non-Christian I taught my players it was important to put the opposition's quarterback out of the game in the first quarter, and I didn't care how. I should not have been coaching then. I was a vicious person. I don't think about such things since I've become a Christian."

Vicious people coaching produce vicious people competing. "The emotion of the game sometimes controlled me instead of my controlling the emotion," said former Baltimore Colt lineman Bob Vogel. "I could not wait to get back to the line to punish the guy across from me. When this happened, I was ineffective because, being a small lineman, I needed control and intelligence to out-perform others."

In January, 1975, Boston Bruin winger Dave Forbes sat in the penalty box in Bloomington, Minnesota, unable to wait to get back at North Star Henry Boucha. When their penalties were over, both men skated across the ice toward their benches. In the next few nightmarish seconds, Boucha lay bleeding on the ice, the victim of Forbes's stick. And Forbes became the first pro athlete in the United States to be tried in a court of law on criminal charges resulting from action in a sporting contest.

Before the trial, Forbes committed his life to Jesus Christ. The trial resulted in a hung jury. The case was dismissed. But Dave Forbes, now skating for Washington, will carry a special cross born of violence the rest of his life.

"For a long time I had this sick feeling of guilt," said Forbes. "I believe the Lord is easing that guilt. There will always be people who hear my name and think, 'Oh, yeah, Dave Forbes. Wasn't he the guy who . . .' There's nothing I can do but play the game I love hard and clean and be the man God wants me to be. I believe one day God is going to heal every hurt and answer every question."[4]

Dave Forbes is not the only Christian competitor with questions about violent play. "It's a paradox," said Chicago Bears defensive back Doug Plank. "As a Christian I learn to love, but when the whistle blows I have to be tough. You're always walking a tightrope."

"A coach instructed me in a team meeting to put a crack-back block on a linebacker and put him out of the game," said New York Giants wide receiver Walker Gillette. "I refused and he went nuts. Violent play is such an accepted thing he couldn't understand my attitude."

"I was in the press box eleven years," said Cleveland Browns head coach Sam Rutigliano, "and now that I'm back on the sidelines the sound of contact is an awesome, frightening thing. The best hope for a violent game is the respect a player has for his opponent. When that is undermined, well . . ."

And there is another hope: that competitors are saying no to this juxtaposition of competition with war and violence. Whereas once the jocks could be counted on to be in the corner of the administration during any war venture and would bust a few heads if things got uptight on campus, in the latter stages of Vietnam it was the athletes who rose up to protest our further involvements. Bob Gailus, Columbia University basketball player, became coordinator of the Pennsylvania Action for Peace; Ivy League team captains meeting at the Heptagonal Games issued a statement condemning our Cambodian adventure; and sixty-six of sixty-eight Columbia football players followed suit. This consciousness-raising was filtered down from the collegiate ranks and also reached upward to the pro level.

If only this concern about violence can be internalized into the actual practice and game aspects of our competitiveness as well as the peripheral visage of sport.

Physical violence is not the only, or perhaps even the worst, form of competitive violence that must be curtailed. Psychological violence—the using of people, the putdown, the verbal intimidation of coach to player, player to player, fan to player and coach—is a more accepted, more widespread, and more debilitating form of violence than the physical use of our fists.

"We violate the personhood of an individual in all

kinds of ways," said Morehead State University football coach Tom Lichtenberg. "If a boy comes to school, makes All-American, but doesn't get an education in the process, he has been violated."

"Physical violence gets the headlines," said Bethel College (Indiana) basketball coach Homer Drew, "but psychological violence is much more damaging. When one is in the insecure position of player or coach—and winning is a must—we'll do what it takes to win. And this means using, shaming, embarrassing, and humiliating others."

Psychologist Beausay defines psychological violence as "anything that detracts from my sense of well-being and my respect for others.

"I like to see the cerebral, the psychological come into play in competition," said Dr. Beausay. "That's smart. If it's done within the confines of the rules and decent human living, that's anticipated. Outmaneuvering, out-skilling, out-thinking somebody is fine. Putting a person down, inside or outside the rules, is wrong.

"Remember, we're dealing with a defective creature, man. Violence will always take place in some form. I'd rather see violence within sports than outside it. People can understand and deal with occasional forms of physical violence in sport. It's better in sport than between nations, in labor unions, between husbands and wives, in the church, or on television.

"I'd rather see a fight in a pro hockey game than a coach violating a youngster in Little League through his words and actions."

Violence, both physical and psychological, in sport competition can be restrained. It may take more than the solution proposed by Snoopy in a "Peanuts" cartoon. Asked by Lucy how he would cut down violence in sports, his answer was "more kissing."

We have, however, been kissed by a loving God. We have been visited by a loving Savior. Violence accompanied Jesus' life. He died a violent death. Yet Christians are to aim for those things that bring peace and strengthen others (Rom. 14:19).

As Psalm 11:5 so acutely states it, "The Lord . . . hates him that loves violence." However one slices it, Christianity is incompatible with the authoritarian abuses of sport competition.

Yet while the teachings of Jesus and the Epistle writers are clearly against violence and toward the bringing of peace to all men, and while the church has maintained a seeming attitude of outrage against violence per se, there is a persistent itching just beneath this respectable ecclesiastical veneer that won't go away. And when one scratches and probes at the itch he discovers that the church is almost a coconspirator with a number of other self-righteous forces in condoning a curious mixture of patriotism, sport, militarism, and violence.

When competition degenerates into bread and circus—ala the Super Bowl with its gaudiness, its fighter planes flashing overhead as the "Star Spangled Banner" is sung by a former beauty queen, its mom and apple pie coloration before the bones start to snap—the church has been right there with its sanction and blessings: pregame prayers, sideline chaplains, a ready pulpit for the superstar.

Rather than the church denouncing physical violence in competition, the use and abuse of people in the name of sporting competition, the warlike language of sport, the church has too often gratuitously played the giddy child, begging an autograph from its hero.

The sport/faith parachurch organizations have done little better. Most are composed of athletes, coaches, staff members, and devotees whose religious, political, and philosophical viewpoints either rest firmly on or are tilted toward a rigid, conservative, legalistic foundation. In this context, sport, violence, and militarism have seldom had an unhappy marriage.

The Fellowship of Christian Athletes' posture on violence and militarism typifies the stance of the para-groups. In 1971 *The Christian Athlete* magazine published an article titled "Sports and War." The article and the photographs—pairing athletes and soldiers in similar war and competition poses—touched off the largest reader response in the history of the magazine.

The vast majority of letters were positive.

"It appears the magazine is coming of age. You have made an important statement."

"People have turned athletics into a training ground for their warriors. The degeneration of sports into mere warfare is all too common in my athletic experience."

"To believe in athletics is not to justify blindness to those evils that would creep in and destroy athletics."

"You have helped me clarify my own witness."

"Congratulations on your continuing effort to affirm sport while resisting romanticizing it. Sticking our heads in the sand and refusing to recognize the dishonest and unhealthy aspects of the sporting scene is certainly not becoming of any intelligent person, especially one committed to Jesus Christ. There has been a false idolatry connected with sport that is harmful to Christianity as well as the sporting movement."

There were rebuttals. Here's part of one from a Texas golf pro: "A Christian athlete who won't do everything possible within the rules of the game to win is a slacker and out of fellowship with God. The same holds true in war. Every Christian soldier should strive to be the very best killer in his outfit. Anything less is a sin. . . . I am uninterested in a balanced viewpoint. . . . I want dogmatic answers that I can use in a crisis situation . . . answers taught dogmatically in the Scriptures. God's word is dogmatic and does not have any double meanings. . . . You have done great harm in trying to show several sides to an issue that doesn't have several sides. . . . Liberalism is a great tool of Satan. . . . I have decided to cancel the FCA Pro-Am golf tournament. Sending young and impressionable boys off to a conference where they could be misdirected . . . is something I want no part of."

This kind of mentality won. The FCA Board of Trustees slapped the hands of the editorial staff, established an editorial watchdog committee, restated that the magazine was to be a "house organ" (stories of athletes who win trophies, not articles dealing with touchy subjects). Over the years this mentality remained inflexible. The magazine was published in a state of conflict and tension—the editors pressing to the limits, the leadership attempting to suppress anything that would muddy the waters, spark thoughtful dialogue, or be at all controversial. As a final solution of the matter, an issue dealing with violence in sports scheduled for January, 1978, was drastically altered and watered down to the point of being largely unintelligible.

As long as the church and the parachurch groups, out of apathy or fear, remain unwitting cohorts in this distasteful competition/militarism/patriotism blend that breeds the tumor of violence, then physical and psychological violence will continue to grow. Denouncing the excesses will not be popular with sport leadership, the fan in the pew, or those who donate to respective coffers. It will be much simpler to pray to the "great Quarterback," dismiss church early so everyone can get to the big game, or be a locker room guru and give a folksy little talk, than to denounce man's inhumanity to man in the name of competition.

DANGERS OF COMPETITION

I have heard it all called a matter of "perspective." Once you get things in the "right perpective," violence will be comfortably controllable. This is self-delusion. The matter is, instead, one of "priority."

The difference must be understood. Perspective is a specific point of view in understanding or judging. Priority is a precedence in time, order, and importance. One's perspective is not much of an antidote to violence if it is not of the highest priority. As long as success, winning, and being number one are the priority, then violence will be a by-product. Perspective, in this sense, becomes the proverbial tail to wag the dogs of war and the dogs of sport.

Every level and segment of competitive sport has always maintained an antiviolence perspective. But it has seldom been a priority. The Pharisees had a religious perspective. But love was not their priority. Jesus called them a pile of dried, white bones. When it comes to violating the personhood of others physically, psychologically, and spiritually, the competitive athletic community, at times, resembles a mountain of dry, white bones.

PART 4
THE MODELS

17
JESUS
THE COMPETITOR

When I was growing up, I thought of Jesus as a man who hung around with lambs and children. He wore a long, white, always detergent-clean robe and had sad eyes. In all the Sunday school posters I saw he was depicted as emaciated and effeminate. Sometimes he had a red heart that I was positive glowed in the dark like a reflector light on the back of a bicycle.

Women hung around Jesus, also. I don't know why. He wasn't much of a "man's man." But there they were, clinging to his robe, stroking his hands; chunky, middle-aged nymphs gazing up at him with doelike eyes. And Jesus always did a lot of gazing up, too, with a half sigh, as if imploring God to give him some peace.

As a young man I gave this no thought. Church was not a part of my life and Christ was just the second half of an expletive.

Then my use of the name Jesus became motivated by adoration rather than anger. I gave my life, in a questioning, searching, wondering fashion, to this mysterious God-man sent to communicate to me that there was life in life . . . and life beyond life. And I began to investigate just who the physical Jesus was, receiving counsel in abundance from people who were as unenlightened as I.

My church's ignorance in helping me understand the man Jesus was paralleled by its ignorance in helping me grow spiritually. Within a few weeks after becoming a Christian, I was assigned a Sunday school class. I was told it was the "best way to learn." I was also young, eager and available, which nary a church retreading its worn-out veterans can resist.

I figured I could handle third graders. But instead, I was deposited in the high school and college class. A Bible illiterate trying to instruct kids who had Bibles with pages wrinkled from apparent use. Some even had passages underlined, and all I knew was that the New Testament was on the right!

To add to my discomfort, I had a slight lisp. Words with *th* and *s* gave me a problem, especially if I was rushed or nervous. I felt myself naked before the world trying to pronounce *Thessalonica*. I searched for other words. But there was no way to totally avoid *th* and *s*. I would stumble; the kids would avert their eyes and giggle into their Bibles. I wanted to attack but, being a newspaperman, knew the headline "Sunday School Teacher Goes Berserk" would not be good for the church.

In my frustration and embarrassment I tried to follow another dictate of the church: in any situation try to think what Jesus would do. Well, the Jesus I knew would look at them with his sad eyes, look up to heaven again—and start to bawl. He wasn't any help. This Jesus was not a competitor by any stretch of the imagination.

I was wrestling with so many images. The essence of the faith was so lofty, so overpowering, so incomprehensible. The Trinity, the incarnation, the creation, life everlasting, a God who loved to the point of death and can, of all things, forgive sin and love us when we are so untidy and unworthy. That was magnificent! It was truly the greatest story ever told, and it gave me goose flesh just thinking of whom I was attempting to follow.

And then the physical Jesus of lambs, children, and middle-aged nymphs would come to mind. Somehow, the image didn't fit.

In bits and pieces I came across the masculine Jesus. I read Bruce Barton's *The Man Nobody Knows* and reacted as had basketball coach Homer Drew: "When I read that book I knew I'd found the Jesus I always prayed was there. It was a relief that the one I worshiped was a man in every sense of the word. He was competitive. He had goals. He was strong physically and didn't back down from mental and spiritual competition. It made me feel I was all right and that following Jesus meant I was following a competitive man as well as the Son of God."

I listened to men I respected: pastors—men of the Word and former athletes. Nelson Price played basketball at Baylor before pastoring Roswell Street Baptist Church in Marietta, Georgia. He wrote, "Competition means to have an opponent or adversary. The title 'devil' means adversary. Jesus and the devil went head to head. Their teammates still do.

"Jesus, like all good competitors, mastered the fundamentals. The fact that he had a working knowledge of the Rule Book is revealed in his frequent quoting of the Old Testament texts. . . . Jesus knew his opponent's game plan and made him play his game. . . . Jesus psyched himself. He got up for the game. . . .

"The 'Wilderness Games' (the temptation) showed Jesus to be a competitor of discernment, diligence, and dedication. Today's competitors need to emulate his example. Be discerning. Jesus was a thinking competitor. Three elements must play in harmony with each other—mind, muscle, and morals. Jesus out-thought his competition.

"Be diligent. A competitor has to consistently stick to his assignment. A competitor has to use his instincts. The head, heart, and hand must be attentive and responsive.

"Be dedicated. Know what you want. The competitor has to have a burning desire. Be committed. The intellect, emotions, and will must be consecrated to the competitive intent.

"Jesus was a competitor par excellence. Numerous encounters revealed different competitive qualities. His confrontation of the money changers in the temple showed him to be a gutsy competitor. . . . His clash with the intellectuals who sought to trap him with a complex question revealed him to be a gritty competitor."[1]

Even though I recognized the rah-rah in all this, I was comfortable with Christian athletes and coaches who believed and who followed a strong Jesus in this belief. It was a breath of fresh air. My faith was confirmed. There was a solid, tangible man to follow as well as an omniscient, omnipotent God to try to fathom. I believed Jesus to be a man whose jaw was set, whose eyes could drill through you, who could laugh and slap you on the back. At last, a Jesus I could relate to.

By the time I found the Fellowship of Christian Athletes, my new Jesus was in full uniform and ready to play the game. The first time I heard a recording of the gravel-voiced, baseball immortal Branch Rickey, an FCA founding father, saying "this is no namby-pamby Jesus we follow," I was the All-American Jesus' cheerleader.

In speeches across the country I would share the Tom Skinner Jesus who had "sweat in his armpits and gravel in his sandals." Old ladies would wince but the kids would be pop-eyed. A spiritual Superman to follow. The revolutionary, competitive Jesus.

I was only a step away from turning Jesus into "the great Quarterback in the sky." As the excesses became obvious I had to get my head straight again.

It was not God's intent to provide a press book on Jesus. The Bible is not a bio sheet on the Son of God. In our interpretation and amplification, we can make whoever we want of the physical Jesus. This, to a large extent, is what the sport/faith movement has done.

It is easier to follow a "fiercely competitive" Jesus. We make him just like us. He understands why we lose control, get angry, and do whatever it takes to win. After all, he's just like us; he's gone through it all. He knows how tough it is to play the game. He got upset in the Temple, didn't he? He trained and sacrificed, didn't he? He bled and suffered and cried, didn't he? Jesus knows.

This is a Jesus you can keep at arm's length. This is a Jesus we can carry like a rabbit's foot but who won't infringe on our manner of playing and coaching. Jesus becomes the patron saint of sport. We don't suction his statue to our car's dashboard to ward off accidents. We stick this plastic Jesus in our locker and on chains around our neck and on the front of our Bible to keep him from really entering into our competitive world.

In his book *On God's Squad,* Norm Evans, Seattle Seahawks offensive tackle, a long-time FCA member and a founder of Pro Athletes Outreach, says, "I guarantee you Christ would be the toughest guy who ever played the game. . . . If he were alive today I would picture a 6-6, 260-pound defensive tackle who would always make the big plays and would be hard to keep out of the backfield. . . . I have no doubt he could play in the National Football League. This game is 90 percent desire, and his desire was perhaps his greatest attribute. Yes, he would make it . . . and he would be a star in this league."

Childish? Certainly. But this is the juvenile level to which sport/faith hero worship too often declines. The fallout is spread as the sport/faith leadership tolerates, even encourages, this mentality. And the church leadership, men who should decry this and strive for a full measure of spiritual growth, are often too busy primping for their invocation at the big game to consider the offensive depths to which the human Jesus has been relegated.

MODELS

In a telling response to this sport/faith baby talk, free-lance writer Kay Lindskoog in a *Reformed Journal* article quoted Evans, and also quoted from Isaiah 52 and 53 on the suffering of the coming Messiah, and concluded, "I don't know. I'm a positive thinker. But if Christ were an overgrown Miami Dolphins defensive tackle instead of the Morning Star, I don't think I'd have a chance in life. I have no doubt he could play in the National Football League. I have no doubt he could be the world's toughest jet fighter pilot. I have no doubt he could make billions in big business. I have no doubt he could be the greatest tap dancer the world has ever seen. More significantly, I have no doubt he could turn stones into bread. It seems a bit beside the point."[2]

Beside the point. And I was searching for the point. Jesus the man. Who and what is he? A competitor? And I began to consider the point that should Jesus pay us a return call tomorrow, he would not consent to be some combination Norman Vincent Peale-Billy Graham-Joe Namath for the Oakland Raiders. He might just say, instead, that pro football had gotten to be a little much. He might just say that organized sports for our children is detrimental to the health and growth of our children. He might just remind us that there is more to life than throwing a ball or watching it be thrown.

He might not play our game.

I was not alone in my quest for the authentic God-man. Some have explored alternate approaches. Their views must also be weighed for their merit and contribution.

Rev. Loren Young, a former 440 runner from Duke University, spent a decade on the FCA staff, and is a much traveled motivational speaker. He espouses the theory that was adopted by many of the young people during the Jesus Revolution of the late 1960s and early 1970s—Jesus was not a competitive person.

"I believe Jesus was so secure he didn't have to compete" is the gist of what Loren believes.

"My brothers were football players," Loren explained. "Mother wanted one son who was not 'an athlete,' so football was out. But track was not a sport to mom. So I got to run. I ran out of insecurity. I got my self-worth from track. I needed the applause; I had to win. I believe Jesus was so secure he didn't have to do that.

"I am much less competitive now. As we develop self-worth, as we mature, as we become more loving, giving, caring, sacrificial Christians, there is less need to compete, less need to prove ourselves. The competitive person usually takes himself very seriously. I no longer take myself so seriously. I no longer deal with everything on a win-lose basis. It sometimes doesn't matter. In sports we may believe our only strength is competitive strength. As we mature we major on qualities other than aggression.

"Can the Christian athlete and coach change roles from a 'fierce competitor' on the field to a loving, giving person off it? Perhaps. But it's hard. The contradiction is too severe. Maybe competitive sport can be a healthy outlet. But it's hard to be a Jekyll and Hyde. Aren't we better off if we can mature beyond this? Maybe this is the key question as to what being Christian and being competitive is all about. Can we become secure enough we either don't have to compete or could care less about the outcome of our competing? Jesus was concerned about much more for us than for us to remain children."

Loren has experienced the gamut of emotions and change on the sport/faith competitive spectrum. We agree on most points. Yet I believe there is one crucial area of difference: I don't believe Jesus was so secure he *didn't have to* compete. I believe the Jesus of the Gospels was so secure he *could* compete—compete as the Son of God and not some manufactured "sportianity"

195

superstar, compete in all the right ways and for all the right reasons as a model for our competitiveness.

If one wishes to point a finger at God for leaving anything out of the New Testament, it could be in the area of play. The Gospels are a pretty serious proposition. While books have been written about the humorous Jesus and the playful Jesus, this requires an abundance of speculation, conjecture, and deductive reasoning, as well as more than a pinch of wishful thinking.

But one can find a competitive Jesus on every page, in most every confrontation, in most every parable. If Jesus is to be our model, it is evident that the way to wholeness is by being willing to compete and not by trying to extract ourselves from the competitive process.

Jesus competed in strong, emotive ways, like his physical action in the Temple. What he also wants us to understand is that we compete just as hard when we wash feet and wipe away tears.

Jesus called his followers to compete, to "fish for men." He taught them how to compete; then he commissioned them (Matt. 28:19-20, Acts 1:8) to compete.

Jesus told stories about competitors: the shepherd who had ninety-nine sheep but went searching for the one that was lost; the persistent widow who kept coming back, coming back; those who aggressively pursue and use their gifts (talents) instead of fearfully allowing them to stagnate; the follower who puts his hand to the plow and does not turn back; those willing to give up father, mother—all—to follow Jesus.

Jesus evidenced competitiveness in his life and not just in his parables. The temptation, Gethsemane, the trial and crucifixion. A quiet, steellike resilience and commitment borne of inner peace and strength that competed at the highest rung on anyone's standard of excellence.

He said those who followed him would wear a yoke. One does not yoke himself up to play. You put on a yoke to get on with a task. We put on the yoke of Christ to bear his name and lift his message. But he said the yoke would be easier to wear than we might understand. It is only after one submits to the yoke and agrees to compete that he finds it does not chafe.

Jesus once opened the eyes of a blind man because "your faith has made you whole." Only as one competes with himself and against evil in the process of Christian growth are our spiritual eyes opened to the depth and virtues of the competitive faith procedure.

Jesus asks two crucial questions in the Gospels: "Who do you say that I am?" and "Do you love me?" He asked the second directly to Peter and the first in Peter's presence with Peter eventually answering. It is interesting in as much as Peter, from the Gospel narratives, is perhaps the one disciple who might most closely match the physical and emotional makeup of many competitive men and women.

Jesus addresses these same two questions to competitors today. It is as we answer them and live out the expression of our answer that we come to grips with what it means to be competitive and how one should model his or her competitiveness both in and out of sport competition.

If we say and believe that Jesus is Messiah, and if we love him as our personal Messiah, then our competitive theology must evidence this. If not? "If we say we have fellowship with him while we walk in darkness, we lie and do not live according to the truth" (1 John 1:6).

The best example of Jesus' competitive theology is found in the mini-Bible, the Sermon of the Mount. If one were to read only the Beatitudes and stop there, one might get a picture of a noncompetitive Savior. Only as one reads all of Matthew 5, 6, and 7 does amplification come. How does one find the strength and courage and security to be a peacemaker, to mourn, to take on a manly meekness, to be merciful, to be pure in heart, to hunger and thirst for truth? A noncompetitive person would not have the experience, the understanding, the heart, the foundation for this highest apex of loving, sacrificial living.

But as one becomes salt and light, inner-fortitude and assurance come. As one learns to discern instead of judge, to relate and communicate in openness and honesty, self-awareness and wisdom are appropriated. As one experiences love for enemies and sharing with those in need, a balance of velvet and steel is perpetuated. As one begins to ask, seek, and knock, confidence and boldness are established.

When we compete as Christians the fruit of Matthew 7 appears on the tree—fruit that ripens only as we, as followers, are committed to competing as part of the world order on a standard above the world order.

In 1972 I visited Israel with a group of writers and editors. We spent time in Nazareth, and one afternoon, while wandering through the streets, I came to a bare, dusty soccer field behind a school.

I wondered how many layers of dust had been lifted away by the Galilean breeze since Jesus the boy may have played some sort of game on this or a nearby field.

I wondered what play had meant to him? Probably the same as to any other boy. And what sort of competitor was he? Was he a star? Was he a talented athlete? Was he clumsy and awkward? Was he the team captain or the last one chosen? Did he go home and dream about the goal that won the game or did he brood over the goal he let in that lost the game? Did he ache to play again or didn't he really care? What sort of sports competitor was Jesus?

The Gospels do not tell us. Perhaps because it is all beside the point.

But the Gospels do tell us about a competitive Jesus in the arena of life and death. Because that is the point.

A competitive Jesus is the point, the bull's-eye, the center from which all else revolves.

18

PAUL
THE COMPETITOR

Paul, the chief architect of the New Testament letters, is the subject of considerable conjecture and analysis. There is no shortage of opinion and speculation as to who and what he was. One can deduce from his letters that he had some knowledge of and feeling for sports. One can also deduce that the man had an interest in soldiering, business, the arts, and other professions and avocations. He was a man of considerable personal experience, and the Holy Spirit spoke through him to offer further insight, advice, exhortation, and wisdom.

Paul is, of course, a father figure of the sport/faith community. In Romans, 1 Corinthians, Philippians, and the letters to Timothy, Paul pens specific references to athletics. If one were to erect a scoreboard and illuminate it with all the autographs ever signed by Christian athletes and coaches, one would discover the apostle to be the chief collaborator: the athlete's name and then "Philippians 4:13," or "Romans 5:3-5" or "1 Corinthians 9:24-27," or one of many others.

Over the years thousands of young men and women have used these Scripture passages to get their initial grasp of what being Christian entails. In "huddle" groups they have discussed fighting the good fight of faith. In quiet times they have sat alone beside the ocean or in the mountains or under southern pines or northern maples, closed their eyes and envisioned themselves picking up the baton for Christ, stripping off all encumbrances, putting their eyes on the goal, and running the race for Jesus.

And because of the few, simple, specific references to sports competition by the apostle Paul, thousands of athletes and coaches have made commitments of their lives to Jesus Christ and started running this race, surely "the power of God unto salvation to all who believe."

As the apostle has been enshrined by the sport/faith community, his motives for using athletic examples have, at times, been extrapolated and distorted. It is hard to figure how one could conclude that Paul was using sporting illustrations to glorify sport. But people do. Paul does urge the Christians in Corinth to "glorify God in your body" (1 Corinthians 6:20)—a throwback to the Greek ideal.

At the same time, as his instruction to Timothy indicates, he repeatedly calls for temperance and self-control in our activities and desires lest we become enslaved: "Every athlete exercises self-control in all things" (1 Corinthians 9:25); and "Do you not know that if you yield yourselves to any one as obedient slaves, you are slaves of the one whom you obey" (Rom. 6:16). To understand Paul the competitor, it helps to know what the athletic arena meant to him and why he would allude to it for illustrations.

Paul was a proud, high-born Pharisee, a persecutor of Jewish believers who was struck down, turned around, and set upon a new road—a road that took him throughout the known world, into the lowly places and before emperors. One hears him describe his background, plead his guilt, abhor his sin, and set his face toward martyrdom. One watches him scold, exhort, inform, persuade, and share his joy and faith. One senses his fear, uncertainty, frustration, discouragement—but always his assurance of the way he goes and the Lord he follows.

MODELS

One sees, hears, and watches Paul, and sees, hears, and watches himself.

Coinciding with the life and times of Paul were the life and times of athletic competition that helped shape the way he looked at life and expressed his hope and faith.

Paul's exposure to competitive sport life had its distinctive Greek and Roman sides. The Greeks embodied all sport can be; the Romans give us lurid evidence of what so-called "sport" can become.

The chief ideals of the Greeks were freedom, beauty, and wisdom. Beauty and virtue were inseparable. If something was beautiful, it followed that it must also be good. The Greek life of sport served the ideal that the beauty of mind and strength and bodily dexterity should be developed and directed in harmony.

As early as the poet Homer (900 B.C.) it was considered an unthinkable disgrace not to be experienced in gymnastics. Gymnastics flourished among the Greeks. It was practiced naked in the open air, and *gymnasia* were developed.

Paul often refers to running and wrestling in his sport analogies. The Greeks built special covered wrestling sites called *Palaestra,* and race courses were built in the *stadion.* Later gymnastic schools were developed called the *Academy* after the legendary hero Akademos. It was only a short time before all the activity and interest culminated in national games.

There were three chief national games in Greece. The first competitions were arranged at military triumphs, harvest festivals, and the dedication of temples. As a pagan religious influence was an integral part of each event, we can see that our modern sport/pseudo religion/patriotism excesses are really nothing new.

Culminating from these minor games were the Olympian games at Olympia every four years in honor of Zeus;

the Isthmian games near Corinth (the direct reference of 1 Cor. 9: 24-27) in honor of the sea-god Poseidon; and the Pythian games near the foot of Mount Paranassas in honor of the sun-god Apollo. These games became the flower and chief impetus of Greek sport. They were sites of fairs and festivals and orations. There were music competitions, and later, chariot races.

Olympia became a national shrine. It was granted permanent freedom from war. No armies were allowed to cross its borders. When the Olympian games were in progress, hostilities had to cease all over Greece.

In the Roman Empire, it was the other way around. When sport began, hostilities began. Sport and war were interchangeable.

Instead of freedom, beauty, and wisdom, the Romans idealized and idolized right and power. All the competing and spectating violence one sees in American sport today, sordid as it may be, is child's play compared to the brutality and degeneracy of Roman sport.

The horror of Colosseum events has been well cataloged. No need to dwell on details. But some of the statistics give an overview of the prominence of this sort of "sport" in Paul's time.

The ampitheater and the circus were the chief sites. Roman sport was also characterized by pagan worship. The competitors prepared themselves days before events through prayers, sacrifices, and adorning the altars. There was often a parade before the chief games to honor the gods with statues of the gods being carried on magnificent chariots or on the shoulders of slaves.

The word *circus* is from Latin, meaning circle. But the interior was a long, oval race course rather than a circle. The largest circus was the Circus Maximus in Rome, the place where "bread and games" began being demanded of the rulers and by the rulers in a bored society that looked to the excitement of the arena to satiate its senses. The turnouts were spectacular. By the fourth century the seating capacity of the Circus Maximus had risen to 385,000, and it was continually filled. The largest U.S. sporting crowds, by comparison, run about 105,000 for certain football games.

And the events! What had begun as foot races, chariot races, and boxing and wrestling matches turned into bloody exhibitions of sadism. Beasts fought with beasts; men fought with animals; gladiators fought for the thumbs up or thumbs down; Christians were martyred before cheering crowds.

Water was even rivered into special basins, and the spectators could see an actual sea battle with whole flotillas contending. This was not mock war but real battles in which thousands were killed or drowned.

In the 120 days of the games at the dedication of the Colosseum, twelve thousand animals and ten thousand gladiators lost their lives.[1]

Greek sport and Roman sport—Paul had seen both the joy that fulfilling athletic competition could be and the terrible depths to which competition could be taken.

Rather than glorifying sport for sport's sake, Paul seems to have had two main reasons for his use of athletic terminology:

1. To communicate with people in language they understand. In Paul's day, just as in ours, sports competition was a major part of community life. Just as Jesus talked to people of the land about seeds and sowing, Paul talked to people of the *gymnasia, Paleastra,* and *stadion* about running the race and fighting the good fight.

2. Paul seemed to believe that the lessons learned through athletic competition can have carry-over value to the competition involved in the Christian experience.

Paul was involved in serious business—"spiritual warfare" is what he called it. Whatever sport may have meant to him in his days B.C., it is apparent that as a follower and proclaimer he had little time for fun and games. Someone else would have to be the advocate for play. Paul is surely an advocate for competition—teeth-gritting, back-bending, leg-pumping, mind-setting, heart-willing competition.

And in his quest for followers who will compete in the world and against the world for this fledgling faith of "Christ in us, the hope of glory," Paul gives us a parallel to the athlete who also knows what it is to train and suffer and endure—not as one who is playing for exercise or for relaxation, but who is playing to win.

"Do you not know that in a race all the runners compete, but only one receives the prize? So run that you may obtain it. . . . I do not run aimlessly, I do not box as one beating the air; but I pommel my body and subdue it, lest after preaching to others I myself should be disqualified" (1 Cor. 9: 24-27).

"Not that I have already obtained all this, or have already been made perfect, but I press on to take hold of that for which Christ Jesus took hold of me. Brothers, I do not consider myself yet to have taken hold of it. One thing I do, forgetting what lies behind and straining forward to what lies ahead, I press on toward the goal for the prize of the upward call of God in Christ Jesus" (Phil. 3: 13-14).

"I have fought the good fight, I have finished the race, I have kept the faith" (2 Tim. 4: 7).

There is obvious danger in contextualizing Paul's athletic remarks. Were one to do so, Paul could be accused of applying the stereotyped "winning is all that counts" philosophy to athletics. But Paul is using the sports references to illustrate what it means to enter the real world as a Christian, especially Paul's real world with its blatant and widespread physical persecution. In his world, winning and losing meant literal life and death. So one "runs to win." This may well result in death, but a death for which one has fully prepared, striven to the end of one's physical and spiritual resources.

If the athletic competitor is willing to assume this posture for a laurel wreath that soon dies, how much more should the followers of Jesus be willing to compete at the highest plane of competition for their Savior?

In other passages Paul speaks forcefully of the attributes and qualities that are most honored and cherished in life, which should mark our every activity as a follower: the "fruit of the spirit" in Galatians 5: 22-23; the "still more excellent way" of love in 1 Corinthians 13; the attributes of God's "chosen ones" in Colossians 3: 12-17. Not to apply *all* of Paul's principles and guidelines into our activity as Christian athletes, coaches, and spectators is to misinterpret Paul and fragment the Scriptures.

But Paul does lift up the athlete as an example. So one can take the fruits of the Spirit and the still more excellent way of love, wear it like a uniform, step to the starting line as a believer, and compete. Compete to win. Paul, in laying out principles, reiterates that the principles must be actualized in the running of the race to have value.

One can step book by book through the New Testament and follow Paul as he relates the competitiveness of sport to the competitiveness of Christianity:

Romans—Throughout this letter of instruction touching upon the main truths of the gospel, Paul works in numerous references to athletics for an audience well aware of the abuses of sport in the Roman games.

Paul's main athletic emphasis in this letter or series of letters to Rome is the need to "keep on." Paul had followed the training and sacrifice required of an athlete preparing for the Greek games, sometimes as much as ten months of intensive physical and mental preparation in a sober, Spartan atmosphere. Paul speaks of character, hope, and endurance in 5:1-5, and the living sacrifice in 12:1-2. He knew the athlete's continual struggle to persevere, speaking of his personal distress about discipline and self-control in 7:15-25.

But the reward, whether competing at the apex of one's ability and winning the laurel wreath as an athlete, or gaining the crown that never perishes as a Christian, is always worth the battle for, "I consider that the sufferings of this present time are not worth comparing with the glory that is to be revealed to us" (8:18).

1 Corinthians—In this practical letter with its emphasis upon the life of the local church, Paul issues his most quoted athletic passage in 9:24-27. The Isthmian games, in which the foot race was a major event, took place in Corinth's backyard. They were a subject of pride among the city's residents. The believers would readily and easily relate to such an example.

Paul is simply saying, in strong imagery, that competing is a part of the Christian life. One must prepare fully and compete totally. There is only one way to run for Christ as his earthly model—to win. In 6:20 (NIV) Paul instructs the church to "honor God with your body." One does this positively through proper training and conversely through abstinence from those habits and forces that weaken it. And one also honors God with the body by hurling one's body and mind and spirit into the competition for the message of Christ crucified and raised from the dead.

Through the chapter Paul lays out the facts as they are. In 4:13 he talks of the Christian being "the refuse of the world." Perhaps that is why fellowship and the team unity concept stressed in 12:12-26 are so important. For it is in our diligence, in our fellowship, in our faithfulness, in "running in such a way as to get the prize," that we can say with Paul in 15: 57, "But thanks be to God, who gives us the victory through our Lord Jesus Christ."

2 Corinthians—In chapter 12 Paul refers to his "thorn in the flesh" and spends much of this letter relating his experiences and sufferings for the sake of the gospel. He again takes us to the race course and tells us to compete by fixing our eyes not on what is seen, but on what is unseen (4: 18).

Galatians—Paul gets intensely personal in this letter, having used it to set forth the nature of his apostleship to squelch opponents who were questioning the truth and authority of his message. He ends the letter by restating what the gospel is and what is involved in living it out.

Several passages give us insight into Paul's competitive nature. In 1: 14 he terms himself "extremely zealous." In 5: 7 he says, "You were running well; who hindered you from obeying the truth?" and talks about being "cut in on" and diverted from the goal while running a good race. And he could easily remember the marks of the competition evidenced on his own body—"the marks of Jesus" (6: 17).

Ephesians—Written from Rome in his first imprisonment, Paul is anxious to restate to believers in Ephesus that the church is the body and Christ is the head. To be with Christ for eternity is a high and sacred calling, and Paul stresses the position and blessedness of the believer and encourages him to live in accordance with this high calling.

Again, the team concept appears in 4: 1-6, and the need for a commitment, which is required of any athlete preparing for competition, is suggested in 4: 22-24.

Paul ends by switching from the analogy of competitive sport to the analogy of combat, 6: 10-18. The Roman soldier, already too familiar to Paul, dons his armor to go to war. The Christian puts on the armor to stand for Christ in peace. It is interesting that in Paul's writings this is one of few references to putting on battle gear to fight. The usual reference is to the athlete rather than the soldier, that one competes in the competitive sport framework for Christ by *stripping off* to run rather than *putting on* for battle.

Philippians—In this letter of personal attachment and joy, Paul issues another noted athletic reference in 3:12-14. Paul "forgets what is behind," "strains on" toward what is ahead, to "win the prize." "This one thing I do" has been the motto of many an athletic competitor in describing his competitiveness. Paul says it also applies to the Christian striving toward the perfection of Christ.

And his words in 4:8 may well have been written while contemplating the grace and beauty and competitiveness he recalled in the Greek gymnastics, running, and wrestling games . . . the pure, the true, the noble, the right, the lovely, the admirable, the praiseworthy—"Think about these things."

1 Timothy—This letter to a young friend was perhaps written from Corinth, the site of the national games. In 4:7-8, as previously noted, Paul does put in proper perspective the place of sport and physical exercise. And in 6:11-12 he again characterizes the Christian life and the crown of righteousness offered for eternity as goals to be pursued. And in this pursuing, in this competing, one "fights the good fight" as does the athletic competitor.

2 Timothy—Paul uses an identical passage, 4:7-8, in this letter to contrast his own life of competing for Christ with that of the athlete. He has "fought the good fight," he has "finished the race," which is what is involved in "keeping the faith." And then the reward. And it all begins for the Christian and competitor in the words of 1:7—not from "a spirit of timidity" (neither the athlete nor the Christian would get far that way), but from a sense and a spirit of power, love, and self-discipline.

The Colosseum where Nero sat and Christians died still stands. Only there is one key difference today. About 1300 a cross was erected in the very center, directly in front of the royal box, in memory of the martyrs. It was lost for a time but erected again by the Italian government in 1927. And on its base is written, "Hail to thee, O Cross, the only hope!"[2]

The cross. The only eternal hope worth competing for. Or as the competitor Paul would put it, "I count everything as loss because of the surpassing worth of knowing Christ Jesus my Lord" (Phil. 3:8).

PART 5

WHERE IT MAKES A DIFFERENCE

YOUTH SPORTS ...
WHERE IT ALL BEGINS

"All a person has to do is spend an hour here," the young man beside me casually remarked, "and he would understand why there are riots and wars."

The observation came from number one son, Jeff, a collegiate gymnast and criminal justice major. We were watching number two son, Gregg, play baseball. We had been buffeted by the raucous and sometimes vile interaction of the crowd in the compact bleachers. Jeff had survived the youth sport rigors. Little wonder he had been subsequently intrigued by a profession dealing in law and order.

Organized sports for boys and girls five through fourteen may be, albeit sophisticated, the last legalized form of child abuse sanctioned in America. And I offer that advisedly, knowing the programs are not without benefit.

In a "Peanuts" strip, Charlie Brown says to Linus, "Life is just too much for me. I've been confused from the day I was born. I think the whole trouble is that we're thrown into life too fast. We're not really prepared." And Linus responds, "What did you want . . . a chance to warm up first?"

Laws were passed to outlaw the sweat shops and mitigate against the exploitation of children in our labor market. No one would claim youth is overworked today. But they may well be overplayed. Will it take legislation to absolve the youth sport sweat shops? Doesn't a young person deserve the right to warm up first?

"Little league this and little league that." A monster roams at will, but it is such a fuzzy, cuddly monster of our own creation that we never really contemplate destroying it. Instead, we are prone to rationalize and compromise for it, and find ourselves in a paradoxical love/hate relationship.

In analyzing the beginnings of the competitive sport life-style, one must focus on the youth leagues and individual youth sports. No longer are we a nation of corner lot, choose-up games, backyard scrimmages, and street and playground ball (except in metropolitan areas where there are few programs, coaches, and facilities other than the hoop at the school's asphalt playground). Spontaneous, unsupervised play is actually in some cases an anomaly on the youth sport scene. Some parents and coaches discourage play. It will "tire you before practice"; you'll "learn bad habits"; someone "could get hurt"; and so on.

For those who have passed through several eras of play and competition, it is mind-boggling.

Stepping back and taking a detached, objective look at the kid sport phenomenon one will, at some stage, ask, "Just how did we come to this?" Its spurious and harmful encumberances are numerous.

"I strongly believe that when we force competition prior to the child's capability of handling pressures involved . . . the long-term detriments will outweigh any supposed benefits," said noted sport psychologist Dr. Thomas Tutko. "Consider the typical scene at a youth league baseball game. Bottom of the ninth, two out, bases loaded. A little boy comes to bat. The bat's heavier than he is, he's afraid he'll get hurt by the ball, he doesn't even know if he'll hit it—he's just praying for a walk.

"We tell him this is for his own good, it is building

character. Once again we have applied an adult model to a growing child."[1]

"Kids get started in sports because they are playful, but they get caught in a system where they are playing for other rewards," said Bill Harper, philosophy professor and director of intramural sports at Emporia State College (Kansas). "Any time you have games in which the participants have less control than the organizers about how they play, who they play, when they play, then it is not really play."[2]

"Just as play, games, and sport have the capacity for positive socialization, they may also breed deceit, hatred, and violence," said Dr. Rainer Martens of the School of Human Kinetics and Leisure Studies at the University of Waterloo in Ontario, Canada. "It is the interaction with parents, teammates, and coaches that determines if sports help the child develop morally or immorally."[3]

Of course, you say. Off with the youth sport head! But there is a Catch (and Throw) 22. Get caught up in youth sports. Have a child who plays well. Try coaching. Have a winning—not successful, necessarily, but winning—season. Youth sports are spawned and sustained by the pride, ego, and youth and sport mania of adults. And when good things happen to you, brother and sister, you are hooked. While you may see the speck in the eye of another parent, coach, or participant, you'll easily blink away the beam in your own.

One fact must be faced: "little league this and that" is here to stay. Over thirty organized sports involve, depending on whose statistics you believe, between 4 million and 20 million of the nearly 40 million children in the United States between ages five and fourteen. As the major sport expressions of children, work-up and two-hand touch are gone with the Edsel. Gasoline will be back to twenty-five cents a gallon before kid play returns.

WHERE IT MAKES A DIFFERENCE

The youth sport bureaucracy is so entrenched that to change it would be like trying to balance the national budget. Little League baseball alone encompasses over ten thousand leagues in thirty-one countries. Add to this Pop Warner, Cub Scout, YMCA, and recreation department football involving hundreds of thousands of youngsters; Biddy Basketball and the collection of roundball circuits; organized hockey in which six year olds practice at 4 A.M. because the facilities cannot keep pace with activity; and the exploding interest in the individual sports of running, tennis, figure skating, swimming, and gymnastics.

Augment this with television coverage. Add to it newspaper saturation, which has hyped sales of weeklies, small dailies, and suburban papers as youth sports provides one of the press's strongest local selling points. And surround it with the multi-million dollar business of producing equipment, uniforms, and shoes for youth sport participants. If something is good for business—and youth sports definitely is—it is here to stay.

Sporadic banana revolutions are not going to topple this empire. As long as Americans salivate every time the Pavlovian bell of sport is rung, and as long as the Valium to the American dreamland is "bigger, better, and sooner," youth sports will infest the land, regardless of the psychological, physiological, and sociological dangers.

The youth sport scene is one of tremendous ambivalence. As a high school athlete told me about his youth sport experiences, "It made me a better person, I guess." Christians find themselves in this same shoulder-shrugging, "it's a pretty good deal, I guess" attitude. Where can the Christian—who is confused, who wants to be involved as a coach or parent, who wants his children to participate and yet not be damaged—stand while awash in a sea of uncertainty about this form of competitiveness and its ramifications?

Realize, first, that there is a plus side to competitive youth sports. "I see many children benefiting from athletics," said Dr. Creighton Hale, president of Little League International, the largest youth sport organization. "The numbers turned on by the program far exceed those being turned off. And I see the extension of something unique to America—the volunteer movement. When you see thousands of adults giving their time for nothing, it's an admirable quality to continue."[4]

Organized competition does give kids something worthwhile to do and keeps them occupied in an age when the work ethic and opportunity are eroding in urbanized America. "Give a boy a bat and a ball and a place to play and you won't have a juvenile delinquent" an oft-quoted playground slogan reads. I'd add "and keep the adults away."

This early competition does produce better athletes for higher levels of competition. But, as Dr. Tutko asks, "How many kids are we sacrificing along the way so that ten players can entertain us at a pro basketball game?"[5] If our goal is to produce skilled professionals and Olympic champions at the expense of play and fun, youth league sports are on target. If our goal is to produce a nation of playing, active, sport-involved-people-for-a-lifetime, then the youth sport concept needs overhauling.

Youth sports do give some youngsters who will not be good enough to play in junior and senior high school a time and place to play organized, competitive team sports. The goal, then, should be to make the initial experience such a joyous remembrance that they will continue to seek—and shall find available through their adult years—other avenues of competitive sport play at their level of expertise.

WHERE IT MAKES A DIFFERENCE

It can give families a rallying point—maybe provide the glue for some tottering relationships. Perhaps furnish a dadless (whether or not the father is around) son with a coach to serve as a father figure. "We've had letters stating it was the Little League experience which gave some parents a common interest and held families together," said Dr. Hale. "That certainly makes the program worthwhile, even if it happens only minimally."[6] To a larger degree, however, one finds "youth league widows" of compulsive volunteer coaches, family life scheduled around games and practices, and numerous other disruptions organized sport can bring.

An appreciation for sport play and competition does add to the balance of life. Commented syndicated columnist Sydney Harris, "Knowing my strong feelings about the insane emphasis on sports in American society, a friend expressed surprise at seeing me at a school basketball game with three of my children. . . . The mistake most of us make lies in assuming that because someone is against overemphasis, he is against emphasis. . . . I think it important that my children be exposed to athletics and understand its beneficial value. . . . What is desperately needed is a sense of appreciation of other modes of life, and of the excellence that goes into every phase of doing and becoming. Without this sense we become rigid, narrow, dull, and intolerant of other modes. Then the society suffers an imbalance which can only injure it—for every kind of skill and interest must be fostered in our complex type of civilization."

Yes, to many things. Youth sport programming *can* provide good coaching, *can* provide healthy learning exposures, *can* provide earlier skill attainment. Grade all these a tentative *can*. Because when *can* is not the priority, disaster may well be the result to young bones and psyches.

Minnesota Vikings offensive guard Ed White, pro football's arm wrestling champion, waved the caution flag: "Let's treat the little ones as people."

When we treat the little competitors as people, this means we loosen up, allow for mistakes, don't take ourselves so seriously, maybe even have a good laugh. Laughter is in short supply on the youth sport front.

Think not? Attend a gymnastics workout for seven-year-old girls; observe a "tennis mother" watching her ten year old practicing; see the nine year old doing compulsory figure eights on the ice for hours at a time; see the eight-year-old swimmer doing laps at 6 A.M.; listen to the agony of two-a-days in the August heat for six-year-old footballers.

Serious business. Diabolically grim business. Yet there is hope as long as we can laugh and keep our children from being automated. A manager in one youth league had to stop the baseball game, call his infield around him, and explain, "Boys, you don't razz the pitcher when he's on your own team!"

The team, the fans, the umpires all had a good laugh over that. But the sound of giddy, high-pitched laughter is a vanishing sound on the fields and courts of America.

There are sounds. Violent sounds. Frightening sounds, hanging like a curtain ready to be drawn over any youth sport complex. In my years of watching, coaching, and reporting, I thought I had seen all the ugliness: coaches in fights, players and coaches tangling, coaches and officials fighting, mothers literally doing battle, coaches and fathers in fist fights. Now we have progressed, in the patented inventiveness of war, from fists to guns. Keep a close eye on the daily paper. We are digging a graveyard in the name of youth sports.

But the physical violence is still incidental to the psychological violence wrecking havoc with our children through the intense pressure of organized competition and the never-sated win syndrome.

To celebrate his birthday, Steven Butler swam a half mile—with two toy boats in his hands. "My son's a real star," said his father in Miami, Florida. "I don't plan to set any immediate goals for him," said Steven's first swimming coach, Fleet Peeples. "His potential depends on how much interest he shows."[7] Steven is two years old.

There are national championships for minibike racers at age six; hockey leagues enlist four year olds; three year olds compete in baton twirling Olympics; and swimming and track and field groups include those as young as one. What happens to the Steven Butlers when they become old men of ten?

Burn out. This is the inevitable result of what we have done to our children in the name of competition. Fortunately, many matriculate to leisure and individual sports and carry on a lifetime of activity. Others gravitate to beer, pretzels, and television, and get out the scrapbook occasionally as a catharsis. Others—bored, pampered, indulged—drift, lost on a sea of faded dreams and misled aspirations.

Check out most any organized sport complex. The stands will be packed with parents and friends when the six to twelve year olds play. When the kids have reached high school age, a few parents show up, a couple of girlfriends stop around, coaches have to coax athletes to practice and play to form just one league let alone the B and C leagues of earlier days. A blasé, jaded tint envelopes games now featuring one or two players still seeking stardom and the rest who are playing out the string.

"I'm concerned with how many good athletes have been scarred by injury or burned out psychologically by the time they were unable to meet the insatiable needs of their parents, their coach, their fans or their own personal obsession," said Dr. Tutko.

The compulsion for winning at the youth league level has been covered in volumes by the psychologists. Strains of winning above all else can be found in most of the other disadvantages of organized competitive sports. "Belonging and contributing are normal needs which can be fulfilled by all of us," said Dr. Tutko. "But they are being subverted at the childhood level by a gilt-edged emphasis on winning and competition. Fierce competition should be the last step in the development of young athletes.

"Anyone who has ever taken up a sport knows the frustration—almost impossibility—of trying to pick up a skill while being under pressure to perform that skill. But we expect this of children all the time. The average person might feel differently if he himself were once thrust into a pressure situation while being evaluated by his peers and his superiors. For example, how would a mechanic feel if he were suddenly shown a totally new type of engine, given a box of tools, and told to repair the engine while a gallery consisting of his neighbors, friends, and opponents from a competing garage cheered or booed, depending on how he fared with the engine?"[8]

One of the earliest and foremost critics of organized youth sports was Robin Roberts, the Hall of Fame pitcher, who wrote in *Newsweek* concerning the formation of Little League, "For the life of me, I cannot figure out what they had in mind."

Others have taken up the cry. Quarterback Fran Tarkenton wrote, "I sense that kids today are getting tired of structured sports, of playing the foil to adults. Kids want to be kids. I hope my boy is allowed to be a kid. I know I won't get in his way."

WHERE IT MAKES A DIFFERENCE

Hal McRae, known for his aggressive play with the Kansas City Royals, leads a growing list of pros who say quite frankly, "My kids will not play youth league sports."

Other pro athletes moderate it with "they can do what they want, but I won't push them." The emphasis on winning, however, is the one area that sets teeth grinding: "If you never do anything but win, you'll have shattering experiences when you lose later in life," said Willie Lanier, former Kansas City linebacker.

Another area of frequent controversy is that of physical injury stemming from early organized competition. A distinguished panel of physicians brought together to dialogue on youth sports in *The Physician and Sportsmedicine* magazine concluded that "making weight," encouraging young competitors to gain or lose pounds, was the only obviously detrimental physical aspect of youth sports. Their conclusions were backed by other doctors and trainers.[9]

"With over one million people dying annually from degenerative diseases in this country, over 400,000 of which are heart attacks and strokes, any participation is great for the body," said Michigan physician Lou Radnothy.

"I see so many advantages as to conditioning, variety of play, and physical development that I cannot name them all," said Central Michigan University trainer and assistant professor of physical education Bill Podell.

Hold on, caution colleagues. "The big problem is contact sports," said orthopedic surgeon Dr. Buddy Whitesides of Gastonia, North Carolina. "I get sick when I see a knee injury that will limit a boy for life."

"While youth sports can aid physical development," said James Conboy, head athletic trainer, Air Force Academy, "there are physical problems peculiar to this age that may be amplified unless care is exercised."

"More than ever I am seeing chronic injuries that relate back to youth sports," said Leo Hamel, trainer, Trinity College (Connecticut).

But probably the worst danger of youth sports is summed up by well-known former Olympic trainer Ducky Drake, "The only disadvantage to youth league sports is adults."

And you find this "disadvantage" in the most crucial of all positions—the coach. The Athletic Institute estimates that there are five million volunteer youth sport coaches in the United States.

They come with various labels and functions. Some of our children—upon the tacit agreement of the parents and a special tutor coach—are professionals by ages four or five. This primarily includes the sports of ice skating, swimming, gymnastics, long distance running, and tennis. Some children do not attend school. They are tutored at home. And they practice. The goal is to be a Janet Lynn or a Nadia—Olympic champions, professionals. This is not fun and games. It is business—for child prodigy, parent, and coach. The roles are clearly defined and understood—by at least two of the three partakers.

But the vast majority of youth sport participants are the team members who perform under volunteer coaches. Unfortunately there are few men or women who coach these youngsters for the sheer reason of teaching skill and opening avenues for kids to have fun.

Some have a child they want to guarantee the chance to play. The Athletic Institute estimates that 85 percent of all volunteer coaches have a child on the team. Some need this one area of expression in which they can experience winning. Some quest for authority and power. Some need an excuse to get out of the house. Some are reliving days when the world was brighter and the days ahead held more promise. Whatever the reason—and not all are negative—there are men and women ready to coach. Youth sports cannot survive without them. And some youngsters—too large a percentage—cannot survive with them.

Jim Martin lives in La Mirada, California. He was the tenth of twelve children and has seven of his own. He coaches the La Mirada Lords football team of nine to eleven year olds. Between 1970 and 1977 they were unbeaten. "What's the name of the game?" "Winning!" "What do you like to do?" "Hit!" This is what the Lords yell before each game.

Martin screams at everyone—his players, referees, the opposition. Practices are hard and sometimes kids cry. But they don't talk back. "I get them so, if we're going to play a team wearing blue, they don't like blue. We hate blue. We'll tell them this guy said this or that, get little things and start harping on them. When they come out on the field they want to mow the other team down—and they do. It's good for a boy. Before you can learn what love is, you've got to know what hate is.

"The first year I coached we lost to a black team. There was parent dissatisfaction. They brought me before the board. They said I didn't play enough boys, that winning was too important.

"And I said the word *nigger* when we were playing the colored team. One parent didn't think that was right. The board put me on probation a year. The next year I started from scratch. We were 7-4, and then the winning streak started. The same people who voted against me then said I was too quiet on the field. They started badgering me to get on the kids a little more. When these teams start winning, it just turns the whole theory around."[10]

The Jim Martins are not atypical in the youth sport

coaching fraternity. They are legion. And there is concern.

Dr. Hale reported that the major innovation in Little League baseball in the mid-1970s was the opening of training centers for the preparation of volunteer coaches. A primary emphasis of the Youth Sport Program of the Athletic Institute is instructing youth sport coaches. A new program under way by the American Alliance for Health, Physical Education, and Recreation is to have the educational arm of U.S. sports—the school system coaches—provide leadership and training for volunteer coaches.

All laudable plans, but at the national level, still more theory than practicality. What must be developed is such intensive, careful screening and programming of leadership at the local level.

For example, Dick Hyland of the Catholic Youth Organization in Cleveland, Ohio, instituted a program requiring all CYO football coaches to pass a stiff coaching certification course before being allowed to coach. Such preparation should be mandatory for every youth sport program in America, regardless of the obstacles and problems involved. In no situation other than youth sport competition do we so willingly and blindly push our children into the hands of people so totally unqualified to lead them.

One sensitive to this is Washington, D.C., high school basketball coach Morgan Wooten who tells prospective coaches at clinics, "Gentlemen, you are the real teachers. You have these children when they are at their emotional peaks and their emotional lows. That's when they are the most pliable. It doesn't take any intelligence to send a kid home with his head hanging between his knees. Any idiot can think up a sarcastic remark to hurt a child's feelings. But to send him home with his head up every night, proud of himself, well, that might show a little coaching."[11]

Elsewhere in D.C., at St. Stephen's school, the fifth and sixth graders are coached in football techniques, but when it comes time for an intramural tackle game the kids organize themselves and invent their own plays.

"We keep score when we play," said athletic director Al (Sleepy) Thompson. "When I see forty-four smiles and forty-four tears coming back from our intramural championships, that's bad. That makes me sick. So I sit 'em down against the gym wall, and we have a little talk. They don't leave until I've got eighty-eight smiles."[12]

Most empathetic to the problems of youth sport coaching and the need for eighty-eight smiles are the professional coaches at the junior high, senior high, and college levels. In many instances they are offering their services to assist agency-sponsored groups. Where the educational system and the recreation departments and civic groups can work cooperatively, everyone is better off. But too often there are padlocks on the educational facilities and a counter "no thanks, we'll do it ourselves" belligerency among the agency-sponsored groups. And the kids are the losers.

In exasperation, football coach Joe Paterno of Penn State said, "It's time we started letting kids grow up naturally. Let them find their own interests and their own levels. Let them be kids instead of forcing them to play at being adults."

The crux of the issue is knowing what it is to let kids grow up naturally. Does this mean play? Or competition? Or both? If so, in what sort of balance?

In a well-known experiment, social psychologist Dr. Musafer Sherif took a group of eleven-year-old boys to an isolated camp at Robber's Cave, Oklahoma, and split them into two groups to compete every day at baseball, football, and tug-of-war. He followed the philosophy that winning is the only thing. He discovered that although adults might be able to operate under that kind of system, children couldn't. Friendly competition became hostility—first with minor jostling, then shoving and cursing, then outright fights among former friends.

To restore harmony, Sherif introduced cooperative competition by having the pipe bringing water to camp turned off and announcing a water crisis. Both groups volunteered to search for the turned-off valve, and they had water in a few hours. After several other joint endeavors, the hostility was replaced by friendship.

Sherif's conclusion was that competition is not inherently antagonistic to human behavior, but pressure to win can override natural tendencies.

Dr. Tutko comments on play and/or competition for children:

"Children use play as one way of growing up, of 'trying out' life on their own level, at their own pace, among their peers. Play is necessary for their development and should have a serious place in society. Instead, adults have taken over children's play, as if to say that unstructured, unorganized sandlot games are no longer possible or important in today's society, especially in the suburbs and small cities. If we continue to plunge children too quickly into a grown-up world and cheat them out of the opportunity to prepare for life in a low-key, low-pressure fashion, we can expect a generation of adults to emerge who are totally alienated from competitive sports.

"I feel that competition is a learned phenomenon, that people are not born with a motivation to win or to be competitive. We inherit a potential for a degree of activity, and we all have the instinct to survive. But the will to win comes through training and the influences of one's family and environment.

WHERE IT MAKES A DIFFERENCE

"It is interesting to note that children often have a different perspective of what sports are about. When they play tennis, for example, and adults aren't around to ask 'Who's winning?' the idea is to keep the ball going back and forth, even if it bounces two or three times or goes off the court. That's the thrill; not to slam the ball down the opponent's throat. Unfortunately, the adults soon come along and start insisting that the youngsters 'play by the rules'; that is, play to win.

"Learning to compete obviously has merit, since one finds himself competing most of his life, either with others or within himself. But adults have a common misconception: that children will not compete unless they are around to take over and show them how. But children are competing all the time—in school, at home, among their friends, on the playground. Given free time, they love to get into some kind of activity; they do it naturally.[13]

Dr. Martens says of play and competition: "Youth sports are not inherently evil nor are they inherently good—they are what we make them. A moderate degree of competitive stress created by an environment where winning is prized and losing is not scorned, is more likely to be helpful than harmful in the moral development of the child."[14]

There are points I would strongly advocate concerning youth competition: no contact sports before age fourteen (ninth grade), and in noncontact sports, no more than the keeping of league standings—no playoffs, no all-star teams, no post-season banquets, no off-season training, and no media coverage of youth sport games before ninth grade except for the printing of scores. No one should become a coach unless he or she has been qualified through a rigid certification program, stressing communication, parental relationships, and player/

228

coach psychology. I'd establish as much cooperation as possible between the educational system and agency-sponsored groups, with taxpayer-provided educational facilities and trained coaches in charge of the program.

The bottom line, however, is the individual decision by each parent and youthful player/competitor as to how we deal with this fuzzy, cuddly monster. The one question each must ask himself is "what price glory?" That's the title of an old movie. Jimmy Cagney and Dan Dailey, I believe. But the question is always contemporary when it refers to youth sports.

What price glory? Watch the Russian and East German children performing internationally and become aware of their life-styles and you ask it. Especially when the voices are raised for the United States to ape this pattern to "keep up." Spend an hour at any kid sport contest and you will eventually ask it.

There is a critical point one must always remember: the youth leagues are the spawning grounds for the competitive philosophies, character traits, and attitudes that undergird and interlace every higher competitive level. We have spent an inordinate amount of time discussing hero worship and the downward flow of influence from one athletic level to another. It is time we reversed our analysis and began to deal with the formative athletic stage and inspect how our mania for the earliest possible formation of organized youth competition establishes physical, mental, and emotional patterns in individuals and, thus, has a direct bearing on subsequent athletic competition, recreation, and leisure play.

So Jesus' words in the Sermon on the Mount in Matthew 7: 24-27 are applicable to kid sports. Are we building the stadium of high school, college, pro, recreation, and leisure sports on rock or on sand?

WHERE IT MAKES A DIFFERENCE

If we are Christian athletes, coaches, parents, and spectators, we have a mandate to scrutinize youth sports and all its ramifications. The Scripture calls us a "peculiar people," meaning a people set aside, a people with different values, a people called to elevate societal standards of living and believing. This should affect our attitudes toward the whole of athletics and competition, including youth sports.

I'm not one for proof texting Scripture and do not see selected Scriptures as being cure-alls for everything from tidal waves to hemorrhoids. But Jesus says some interesting things that you can place like a magnifying glass on the organization charts of youth sports.

Read Luke 11:46. Ever been guilty of putting a load on a child's back too heavy for him to carry?

Read Luke 12:13-21. The parable of the rich fool certainly speaks to youth sports. He was also plagued by the bigger, better, brighter syndrome, and God called him a fool. That was tough talk. The next pro-style uniform you buy or game film you shoot or banquet you work on, ask yourself if it's necessary and valid or simply another form of overindulgence.

Read Luke 17:1. Jesus chastises those who "make sin happen." Some of what we do to children in the name of competition and sport is sinful. Do Christian parents and coaches help make sin happen?

And finally it seems there is a sharp contrast between much of what is seen in youth sports and Jesus' concept of greatness. Much of what is construed greatness in youth sports involves the exploitation of youth and their manipulation to satisfy the whims of adults. We, in turn, teach our children to be manipulators and exploiters in the name of competition.

Jesus defines true teaching and caring and leadership in totally different terms. He talks about servanthood, about the least being the greatest, about the essential and lasting qualities of the Kingdom.

The mother of the sons of Zebedee (Matt. 20:20-28) would have fit into most youth league programs. She was concerned about her children. (We all are.) She wanted the best for them. (We all do.) And she was willing to do whatever it took to get them to the top, to make them happy, to create her little successes.

Jesus asked her if she really knew what she was doing. And then Jesus explained to the disciples that a life of peace and fulfillment is a matter of serving and not just taking in all we can inhale.

As Christians, how can we best *serve* our children? How can we best meet their emotional and physical needs when they are five to fourteen? How can we make them truly great? As far as "little this and that" is concerned, we may find that it means a little less of "this" and a lot less of "that."

COLLEGE ATHLETICS

Though one cannot safely generalize about any level of organized athletics today in America, the college athlete is, in a very real sense, like the man without a country.

To differing degrees, depending on whether he attends a small, church-related school or one of the largest football factories, he is somewhere beyond the fun and games (supposedly!) of high school, but not yet to the big business of pro sports.

So he (and, increasingly each year, she) circles this NCAA or NAIA Sinai, awaiting a decree from the summit indicating just what college sports are all about.

Most college athletes spend their four to six years (if they do even graduate) in shoulder-shrugging confusion. A few filter into the pros. Most retreat to the nostalgia of scrapbooks or to the sandlots to keep the body firm and the dreams alive, at least a little, or to the backyard where fathered likenesses are pointed toward the same Sinai.

I spent a rewarding afternoon with nine college athletes in a cabin at a beautiful retreat center in North Carolina.[1] We discussed their experiences, feelings, and attitudes concerning faith and competition. They represented large and small schools, sports from swimming to football, states spread as far as Oklahoma and Massachusetts.

They had one similarity: all had made commitments to Jesus Christ. After our time, I was encouraged that back-

232

yard tutelage might be marked by more gentleness and sensitivity in the future.

The athletes were: Lem Tucker, football, William and Mary; Doug Michalke, swimming, Navy; Frank Rennie, football, Navy; Pete Billingsley, basketball, Carson-Newman; Mike Fagen, football, Yale; Jim Watts, football, Tennessee; Rich Lambke, soccer, Oral Roberts; Jasper McFarland, track, Vincennes; and Steve Curnutte, football, Vanderbilt.

I asked them to define competition.

Lem: I make a sharp dichotomy between the world's and the Bible's definition. I see the world defining competition as one man beating another. The Bible defines it as one man striving within himself to reach a goal.

Mike: Some view competition as inherently bad, but even though it is at times abused, I don't think we'd be where we are in science or athletics or any place unless people were trying to outdo each other.

Jim: When I'm giving 100 percent of myself and another is doing the same and we meet, that's competition.

Rick: It's not just physical, it's brains and attitude against brains and attitude.

Frank: Competition is the gut feeling you get when you know you're going against someone else.

Steve: Yeah, it's a gut thing. When I know Tennessee is the next game I get more and more emotionally involved—all the butterflies begin churning—I'm scared to death. I'm ready to explode.

Jasper: The gut feeling is an everyday struggle for me. There's that part of you that says you can beat a guy who has a faster time and a part that says you can't. Man, that is a battle!

Author: What kind of competitor are you?

Lem: It's 60 percent mind orientation and 40 percent emotions for me.

WHERE IT MAKES A DIFFERENCE

Doug: I'm a bad loser. I keep Philippians 4:13 in mind.

Frank: I'm a highly intense, highly concentrating competitor. I try always to give 100 percent. If I don't, I feel I've cheated.

Mike: I enjoy the psychology of competition. I don't find it hard, for example, if another guy needs to win to let up a little—I don't throw it—but I let up if he needs to look better. If a guy is a jerk and needs to lose, I'll do my best to help him lose. In team sports it's different. You work for the team; it's not a personal thing.

Jim: I try to do the best for the Lord with the talents he's given me. If that's second place, then I try to find the answers second place has.

Rick: In soccer I only compete against myself. I don't like football; I don't like being pitted against another man.

Jasper: I try to win, but if I come in second I really feel all right. If I come in last, I never feel all right!

Steve: I'm with Frank: intense and emotional. I'm not big; I'm not talented, so to play major college football I've got to be superpsyched. I cry before a game and after a game, win or lose. It's hard to keep things in a Christian perspective. Real hard.

Author: Some of you have philosophical conflicts concerning competition.

Lem: Yes, I do when I become dissatisfied with the gifts God has given me. I should be satisfied when I'm reaching the potential ability God has given me. When my main motivation is to look better than the other guy, I really struggle.

Pete: You can lose perspective; lose sight of your goals and forget about God. My assistant coach is a fine Christian, a fine guy. But it bothers me when I see people who will do anything to win.

Mike: I'm not like Frank or Steve. I really don't get fired up that much. I have a job to do and try to do it. You know, a lot of players take the field and get in a circle and just go crazy beating on each other and screaming. I'm usually the guy on the outside of the circle by himself. I don't get that excited after a win or dejected after a defeat.

Jim: The coaching sometimes bothers me—non-Christian coaches saying and doing things at crosscurrents with your faith.

Steve: Yeah, sometimes I get to the point where I don't want to compete anymore. I'm sick of it. I want to get off with my little sister and play some silly game and let her whip the tar out of me. I enjoy watching her having fun beating me. It releases something in me to lose and not care.

Frank: I get uptight and dejected when I fall short personally or the team loses. It's a matter of going back to the Lord and thanking him for the circumstances—whatever—that I'm in. That's hard.

Author: I would rather play someone better, lose and gain expertise and experience because of it, than play someone poorer and win. How do winning and losing fit into your competitiveness?

Lem: One needs a foundation for competition. For me this is Jesus. He gives my competitiveness an eternal dimension so that no matter what comes my way, it's always a victory. Like the story of the widow's mite (Mark 12:41-44). She didn't appear to do much, but Jesus got excited about it. She gave all she had—more than the big guys—and this was all Jesus asked.

Jasper: Losing can be a great feeling, too. It makes you more of a man when you can lose and accept the fact that you lost and gain from it. The "taking part" is important. It's easy to sit in the stands and criticize. We ought to all cheer anyone who has the guts to get out and compete.

Pete: You have to consistently evaluate yourself. You see

your name in the spotlight; that old, selfish desire creeps back in. You better ask if you're playing for God or for yourself.

Jim: Right, if we do the best we can with the power God gives us, then we have no right to look back and question, win or lose.

Lem: I'd like to challenge Frank on an aspect of his "100 percentness." I may be misinterpreting, Frank, but it seems society breeds into us this idea of finishing first and beating the other guy as the apex. We have to measure our true ability in competition and, if third place is our very best, we should be content with it.

Frank: Well, OK, I understand what you're saying, but for me it's important that I know I've given my very best. If I don't strive 100 percent 100 percent of the time, then I'm cheating myself and cheating God. It's too easy to say, "Well, he's better," or "Well, their record is better and we can't beat them," and be content with less than our best.

Author: Why do you guys compete? Why do you play games?

Steve: It's something you grow up with. Competition surrounds you. You can't escape competition in this country.

Doug: My grandfather was high on the parable in Matthew 25:14-30, which urges us to use our talents for the Lord. If you bury your talents, you'll never grow.

Pete: Yeah, I know I can compete because God has given me that ability. And in competing as a Christian I can help someone else.

Frank: The Bible says our bodies are God's temples. To glorify your body is to glorify God.

Jim: My reasons for competing are different now that I'm a Christian. I compete for fellowship and the opportunities to witness aside from just enjoying the game.

Author: Why did you compete before?

Jim: Well, as Steve said, it's just a thing everybody does.

You play games, and then it gets organized, and you're into it.

Frank: Before I was a Christian, sport was more or less a big ego trip.

Mike: I think we all have an inner need to compete, to be the best in something. People with physical skills use athletics for recognition and achievement.

Author: Our nation often judges by the scoreboard. Do you feel to be a success in life you have to be a competitive person?

Rick: It's natural selection. You compete against nature to survive and you compete against others just to exist. Maybe all this generates the competitiveness in nonessential areas, such as athletics, and in judging a person as to one's standard of success.

Author: We live in a society of the "rat race" and the climb to the top and beating the other guy. Perhaps athletics fits right into this. Are you satisfied with the competitive emphasis and the stress on winning over losing as portrayed by our society?

Frank: Well, that's something (Naval Academy cheating scandal) very close to me. It was a situation where getting to the top and being a success took precedence over basic concepts of morality and honesty. When competition crowds your mind so you can't think of anything else, then it can be destructive.

Steve: Our society doesn't have many places for the loser.

Mike: At Yale the big pressure is trying to get into graduate school. Sixty percent of my freshman class was pre-med. In my chemistry lab the cheating was unbelievable. Grades are everything—the only standard for getting ahead. There are four million volumes in our library and on Friday night—Friday night!—it's so crowded you can't find a place to sit. People have no time for anything but books and getting that grade. I have friends who have compassion and understanding to be fine doctors who cannot endure this brutal competition. I'm generalizing, of course, but there is a bigger element of truth in it than many would admit. To get to the top as a doctor or lawyer or other professional you have to cheat and scrounge and sell your soul. And many who make it are sorry specimens.

Steve: That hits me, Mike. All my life I wanted to be a doctor. But my grades aren't good enough. I don't have a chance for medical school.

Author: How do you fit your competitiveness into your Christian faith?

Pete: They go hand in hand. I believe the Lord is going to use my competitiveness to reach people I compete with and against.

Rick: Competition is good because it helps you grow. And Christianity is a growing process. The Greek word for salvation says it is not just a one-time thing; it's a constant change from the initial rebirth. We grow as Christians and as competitors.

Mike: It should be cooperation more than competition, but mankind is not going to cooperate until everybody has some common bond. That bond is Jesus. I think Jesus would be happier with cooperation to achieve goals than with competition.

Author: Here's a radical thought. I think Lem and I are together on this. I believe love ought to be the primary motivation in all my competition. My main concern in competition should be making me and my opponent better as a result of our interaction. The contest should be a celebration, a party. There should be joy in this shared fellowship. Sometimes we take ourselves and the playing of games too seriously. The real victory in competition is when I have a love relationship with my opponent and we both are better people after our experience together. Winning or losing? That really becomes irrelevant. What do you think?

Steve: I've always taken competition too seriously—up until now. Funny, but Jim and I look forward to the Tennessee-Vanderbilt game. We plan to meet on the field before the game and just walk around a little and pray together. I've never felt so good waiting for something to happen.

Doug: I took competition too seriously. Now I see that games—anything we do, really—is a passing thing. I'm going to try in the future not to hate my opponent but to love him and hopefully gain new friends because of competition.

Frank: If we place competition above love, I don't believe we're acting as God wants us to. If you do that, you shouldn't be a competitor.

Mike: I heard a Grand Prix driver say that when he sees a wreck he grits his teeth and blasts on through it without thinking about it because one of his friends might be in it. Then you read about the Indy driver who stopped his car to help a friend, and the runner who quit the race to go to the aid of a fallen opponent. That's beautiful! I do believe the solution is to compete in the love of Christ, but I don't have much hope that this can be conveyed to the world.

Author: We alluded to this earlier but let's be specific. What is your main personal struggle with competition?

Mike: My problem, whether taking the SAT or covering a guy on a football field, is when I beat him, interpreting this in my mind that I am better than he is. This is wrong. I should be thinking that I'm better than I was yesterday—that I did better than ever before—instead of equating this with how I compare to another guy.

Author: Like putting down another guy?

Mike: Right—a guy who might need a win or at least assurance more than I do.

WHERE IT MAKES A DIFFERENCE

Pete: This ego tripping is tough. When I do beat somebody on the floor, my mind will flash, "Hey, man, you really whipped that dude!" I find my old self creeping back in. It makes me stop and think—I guess that's God talking to me—if putting a guy down really helps him out? No way.

Frank: My intensity bothers me. I lose perspective. I break down and start cussing. Then I feel as if I've let down my Christian brothers.

Steve: If I don't watch it, I easily get bigheaded. My emotions flare; I feel as if I want to fight someone.

Author: You lose self-control?

Steve: To an extent. It's self controlling me, not God controlling me.

Jasper: The problem is keeping cool. When I lose a race, I want to be alone. Someone comes over to me and I may turn away and then immediately regret it. I need to learn to control myself earlier rather than always having to say I'm sorry.

Rick: I really have trouble loving someone who is my opponent. I don't want to get that involved with him. My teammate? I can love him. But if an opponent kicks me in the shin, I not only get sore in my body, I get sore in my heart. But the Bible says love your enemies. I guess I'll just have to learn to turn the other shin.   ◦

(Chorus of boos, hisses, and catcalls!)

Author: Let's wrap up with this: give me your Christian philosophy of competition.

Jim: A total sharing of one's self with the talents that God has given. Jesus did this. He gave everything, walked on and never looked back. No regrets.

Frank: Guess you know by now—tried and true Academy stuff—I'm a 100 percenter. But that is my competitive feeling. However, the 100 percent is for God's glory and not my own.

Rick: Christians are not at one time a secular person and at another time a spiritual person. When we compete, therefore, we're always doing it spiritually. So whatever our overall competitive life-style is—this is our Christian philosophy of competition and our witness.

Mike: To latch on to what Rick says, competition is just one small facet of our Christian philosophy. I sometimes wonder if God doesn't look down and smile a little to see how much importance we attach to athletics. We ought to use athletics for the development of our bodies and for brotherhood with each other and not all the other junk.

Author: Then you think the Christian in his philosophy of competition looks at the spiritual won-loss column and not the physical?

Steve: The spiritual is the life thing; the other is temporary, but it sure can seem the most important at the moment.

Jim: I view Christ as the ideal spectator; he's never going to boo me or turn away from me. I compete with that in mind.

Rick: Mike said it's important we take care of our bodies, so we compete. But I wonder how often we really think of that? We're doing our competing for our egos most of the time.

Mike: Well, that's what I meant when I said we seem to have this need inside to compete *against* somebody rather than compete *with* somebody.

Lem: For my Christian philosophy I point to three Scripture references. The one I referred to is in Mark 12—the widow's mite—giving our all and then being satisfied. The second is Matthew 22 where Jesus gives us the two greatest commandments—to love God and one another. This should undergird all our competing. That's why I stress competing *with* and not competing *against*. We need to encourage the guy we're competing with and rejoice when he does well. That's the kind of competitor Jesus was. And the final passage is James 4:1, talking about the humanness of each guy at war down inside himself. The basic dissatisfaction comes when we don't let God be God and we point the finger at something in us and want it to be bigger than it is.

Doug: My philosophy can be summed up in Romans 12:1—giving ourselves as a living sacrifice and becoming totally acceptable to God in that way. If everyone could compete with a spirit of love and fellowship, I believe we'd all come out on top.

THE PROS
REMEMBER

Quarterback Gary Cuozzo had a star-crossed career, drifting, unsettled. He was beyond a journeyman but never the enshrined hero the myriad of sport publications display on their covers. I was fortunate to see him on his most productive day.

It was December in Bloomington, Minnesota, and I huddled high in the wind and snow-tormented east stands of Metropolitan Stadium, undoubtedly the icebox of God's creation. Cuozzo, filling in for Baltimore's injured Johnny Unitas, was far from frostbitten. He threw five touchdown passes against the frustrated Vikings. Post patterns, square outs, deep sidelines—he hit them all.

Ten years later, Gary, the orthodontist, and I talked about that and other days. "I was the kind who loved to practice," he smiled. "Pro sports can hurt you; you can be sixty-five at age thirty. But not the quarterback with a good line. He has it easier. That's why even practice was fun.

"For awhile after retiring I had to cut myself off from all competitive sports. I substituted jogging for games.

"Several years ago I returned to Baltimore for an old-timers' reunion," he continued, the eyes of this studious man taking on a faraway cast. "I cannot describe the feeling when I walked on that field and felt the sixty-five thousand people surrounding me, heard their noise, anticipated the whistle for the kickoff. I started to quiver . . .

WHERE IT MAKES A DIFFERENCE

I had goose bumps . . . I wanted to cry. You must have competed at that level to know what it's like. It was an eerie, other-worldly experience."

Want to know what it means to be competitive? What bearing faith can have on one's competitiveness? Ask the man who has been in the arena and then finds himself on the outside—watching, but no longer a part.

Sportswriter Ed Linn wrote, "Sooner or later society beats down the man of muscle and steel." Society may wield its hammer, but time is the crueler enemy. Time that ebbs slowly and subtly like the incoming tide, caressing and diminishing the rocky reef of one's reflexes, quickness, speed, and strength. Then the retired athlete must revert to another life. Pele, the world's *numero uno* of soccer, said in an interview before his retirement, "Soon I will be finished with one life. What is next? It must be something, because if I do not play, if I do not do something, I will die."[1]

A significant number of pro athletes have found that it has been the presence of Jesus Christ that has allowed them to transfer their competitiveness to other sectors when the gate to the pro arena slams shut behind them.

Alan "The Horse" Ameche, Heisman Trophy winner from the University of Wisconsin, scored the winning touchdown for Baltimore in the fabled 1958 sudden death championship game against the New York Giants. Then injuries cut short his career after only five years.

"I was bitter," he said. "I was twenty-seven and washed up. I couldn't stand to go to a game. Life was a void; there was no fulfillment. Then I got into a meaningful business. More importantly, my Christian faith, which had been babylike, took on new meaning.

"Know what I remember most? There were few witnessing Christians in the league in the late 1950s. We had two on our team—Raymond Berry and Don Shinnick.

We'd sit in the back of the team bus and poke fun at them. They were out speaking and being with kids. You couldn't have crowbarred any of us to go with them.

"But they are my best memories. I've told this to Raymond and want to tell Don. They helped my faith get started . . . and I didn't even know it."

Ron Burton, running back with the Boston Patriots in the American Football League before injuries forced his retirement after six seasons, said, "I won the battle through my faith. You feel you're in shape and can try again. My faith told me that was wishful thinking. Then I'd dream about playing. I could actually feel getting hit and lowering a shoulder into someone in return. Then your faith wakes you up and you go on. You say, 'It's over . . . thank you, Lord.' And you go on."

Mike Roberts, baseball coach at the University of North Carolina, was a Christian coming out of college, who found his faith the ingredient that helped him transfer his competitiveness from playing to coaching.

"The Lord made me realize baseball was not the biggest thing in my life," Mike recalled. "Pro ball had been my dream, but circumstances were turning it into a nightmare. We lived in a house trailer in Waterloo, Iowa. It was 110 degrees, no air conditioning, my wife was pregnant, and I was riding buses to away games eighteen days each month.

"God also spoke to me about some other things. I wanted to get into a profession in which I was giving. As a player, I was simply a taker. And there were few Christian players. I found, other than the game itself, I had little in common with the guys around me. So I became an 'ex' after just two seasons."

James Michener writes in *A Michener Miscellany* of the retirement of the Mexican bullfighter Calesero, "A fantastic crowd turned out to see the brave old man fight his last bull. He was sensational. When the fight was over, he marched to the center of the ring. His family came out of the stands, a beautiful wife and seven children. The band played 'La Golondrina.' Someone released four hundred white pigeons. Old-timers who had fought with him came to the center of the ring, and with a pair of silver scissors, one of them cut the pigtail.

"Calesero wept. His wife wept. His seven children wept. The President of Mexico wept. The pigeons kept flying and the band kept playing and I wept. It was some afternoon, believe me. Sport can sometimes be like that."[2]

Jesus said, "I came that they may have life, and have it abundantly" (John 10:10). Ask the Christian pro athlete who has seen the pigeons fly and heard the band play: sport and faith can sometimes be like that.

COACHING

It was a humid, somber afternoon. I stood at third base on the diamond at Michigan State University, mulling over a personally disastrous season, wanting the practice to end, wishing commencement would come and all the heartache of failed opportunities would be behind me.

We were out of the Big Ten race, going through the motions with only a couple of nonleague games left. Behind the mound, calling balls and strikes for the intrasquad game, stood coach John Kobs, a legend who would coach thirty-five years at MSU. It was said he would be buried behind the pitcher's mound, his tombstone reading, "Three and two . . . let's see if we have a hitter or a pitcher."

On the field he had lost it years ago; off the field he was like a father to me. While my attitude toward him was a mix of respect for him as a man and resentment at his baseball senility, he'd nonetheless had a strong influence on me.

A foul fly off third shook me from my reverie. I drifted after it, carelessly forgetting to glance and feel my way to the fence. Watching . . . drifting . . . running. Watching it almost into my glove . . . when I slammed into the stomach-high, steel mesh fence. It knocked the wind out of me, and I ended up draped over its zagged top.

The fence cut into my stomach. But I was cut deeper by laughter from the field. I pulled myself free and saw that Coach Kobs had found my predicament humorous. He was bent over laughing at the sight of me making a rookie play on a routine pop foul. Some of the players giggled nervously; others scuffed at the ground. A couple of the seniors hurried over to see if I was all right and stared with me at the coach.

"I'm glad I could bring a little joy into your otherwise dismal season," I sarcastically growled at him. I was a senior on the way out, coming off a bad season. I was no longer important to him. From that day on, he was no longer important to me. A sad, unfortunate way for our four-year relationship to end.

Coach. There is something special, prominent, important about the title. He or she is a teacher, a buddy, a baby-sitter, a counselor, a parent-figure, a man or woman in the crucial role of being able to provide the shelter of love and care for millions of young people.

I believe the coach is as influential a person as there is in our culture.

The coach may be the most vital link in the process of understanding our competitiveness. Influence can lead to hearing, understanding, respect. If, however, the coach is not properly qualified to lead and teach, the opportunity for young people to become whole, balanced competitors is severely restricted.

Walk through the halls in any school in America. Though the good old days of "jockdom" may be gone, many students talk about teachers in lower case while Coach is still upper case. *Coach* can trigger a near reverence. I would have run through a wall for *Coach;* I would have walked around it slowly, if at all, for a teacher or even my parents.

I remember precise moments when Coach paid me a compliment. Ed Bailey was the raw-boned, square-jawed Charlton Heston look-alike who coached our ninth-grade football team. "We'll pass a lot from now on," he said after our first game. And then, smiling at me, "Now that we finally have a passer."

I wanted to dance.

In a high school scrimmage, I ran a quarterback option and cut back against the flow for a sizeable gain before being tackled. As I got up, my theretofore aloof coach, Al Lewis, patted me on the helmet and said, "That's the finest piece of running I've seen this season."

I wanted to sing.

I returned to Michigan State the fall of my senior year. Meeting a teammate coming from the coaches' offices, he said, "I just saw 'Pencils' (Frank Pellerin, assistant coach). He said the pros are really going to be watching you this season."

I wanted to dance and sing.

But compliments always run out. The problem is when respect runs out. And the deepest problem is when decent people in coaching too often run out. It happens because of two critical deficiencies in sport today. The first is "the coaching mentality." It's the reason many coaches are unable to help young people cope with all the elements of their competitiveness and bring sport to the proper perspective.

I know many excellent coaches. Excellent coaches because they see people as people, not X's on a blackboard or pawns to produce wins. A percentage are Christians. This is not always a prerequisite. I know Christian coaches who should be working with machines, not people.

I contemplated becoming a coach and do enjoy teaching and coaching. But the university-level educational process is not the place to learn how to be sensitive to human need. Teammates were physical education majors. In their four years of school there was one class, just one, in their major field for which they actually had to study—kinesiology. The instructor could not be bought. You passed or you were ineligible. That simple. I had friends who thought about the class for years. Years! Putting it off as long as they could, being tutored, actually buying a book, stealing old exams, hoping the instructor would go to another school or die before they got to him.

I took one physical education class, a six-credit course. We spent several weeks dealing cards, first with the right hand, then with the left. We wrote a paper on what we learned. I was never sure how this would allow me to relate to athletes. Unless we set up a casino in the locker room.

I have discussed this educational wasteland at length with John Robert Bell, former football player at Georgia Tech, head coach at East Tennessee State, and FCA staff member. He, too, is saddened by what he sees.

"Too many become coaches," he said, "because, frankly, they are not bright enough to do something else or because they were too lazy to do anything else or because, as athletes, they had no time for a major that required a lot of study. Physical education was the easiest way through school.

"The shocking disparity in our society is that a plumber's helper can make ten to fifteen dollars an hour for working with pipes while our teachers and coaches, who work with human life, aren't apprenticed properly or paid enough to live on. It is a terrible indictment on a society that allows a pro basketball player to make $200,000 a season and then allows sensitive men and women to leave teaching and coaching because they simply cannot afford to stay in it."

Another man who comes to the edge of his seat when talking about the preparation of coaches is sports psychologist Dr. William Beausay. "It's a disgrace," he says, "to have hundreds of men and women leading young people who have no idea how to go about it.

"Our schools teach the coach techniques of a sport but nothing about the people who play the sport. Most coaches can draw X's and O's but have had no training, no preparation, no 'coaching,' if you will, on how to relate as one human being to another. It is changing in some schools but still too slowly.

"So the good coaches make it because they inherently care . . . it comes naturally. And the bad ones? They destroy kids. And you see it everywhere."

"The coaching mentality" produces coaches at one extreme who, despite the low salaries and all the problems, really care, and those at the other extreme who are at it for all the wrong reasons.

Unfortunately, when the public thinks of "the coaching mentality," it too often thinks of the wrong extreme because that's what makes the headlines. And this retards the potential of raising the coaching standards.

Dr. Lyle Owen, professor of economics at the University of Tulsa, wrote in the American Association of University Professors Bulletin, about a monthly meeting of his chapter at which the guest of honor was the head football coach. "The professor of football made it a central point in his oration that no football player had ever become a Communist, therefore the sport is a prime preventive. I had not realized before, when wondering how we should grapple with Marxism-Leninism-Maoism, that football is the answer. The information alone was worth the price of my annual dues."[1]

Steele Harmon, former coach at Centre College (Kentucky), recalls his high school football coach Ben Flora: "We lost our first game my junior year. Ben wandered out behind the stands where refuse was being burned in a bonfire. We watched him through the locker room window. We thought he might tear the stands apart. He just stood there, looking in the fire. Then he took off his sport coat . . . and threw it in the fire! He tore off his tie . . . into the fire. His shirt was next . . . into the fire. We were afraid to watch anymore."

The good old days? No, the good new days. An Associated Press story in 1977 told of the football coach at Eau Gallie High School in Florida who boosted team morale by biting off the heads of live frogs!

There is another side. It is said the real test of a man is to possess power without abusing it. Coaches have that chance. It is said to handle yourself, use your head; to handle others, use your heart. Coaches have that chance.

There are coaches who have been able to keep up with the times and adapt to the needs of young people. Sam Bell, track coach at the University of Indiana, wrote, "My athletes can get involved in anything they want. I don't want them to think about track twenty-four hours a day. That isn't healthy. I want them to leave Indiana as great people first and then perhaps as great track men. Track is only a vehicle to let young men see what life is about; and life is not putting them in a box and smothering them in a narrow, restrictive collegiate atmosphere. If this creates a problem for a man who is coaching, he should reexamine what he is doing in coaching."[2]

The sadness is when the young and gifted leave because of the atmosphere enveloping coaching. This was the case with John Roush, a fine halfback at Ohio University, a standout student, singer, respected rising star in the coaching profession, a Christian. Now working on his doctorate in educational leadership, he commented, "I don't know if I'm cut out to be a coach. I love this chance to minister but, you know, I could go 0-10 and see some personal growth in players and some life-changing things happen and be very satisfied . . . and I'd be fired. Zero and 10 does not make it. While playing, I thought that on Saturday afternoon clocks stopped all over the universe, and the game was as important to millions of Chinese as it was to me. Everyone cared, didn't they? No. I don't care that much about winning anymore. Guess I've lost it."

Given a chance, which of the following philosophies would you choose?

Dave Nelson, athletic director, University of Delaware—"The wide world of football coaching is not round. It has two sides—win or lose, good or bad, sweet or sour, thumbs up or thumbs down. . . . (The coach) actually sees everything through different eyes depending on the bottom line, i.e., win or lose. When he wins, there is a light in his eye."[3]

Joseph A. Margolis, athletic director, Brooklyn College—"The values and virtues attributed to organized competitive athletics have been widely publicized in an effort to gain respect for school sports programs. Unfortunately, the pressure and demands on many coaches have caused them to subvert these values and betray the virtues attributed to sports in order to achieve the bottom line—winning.

"Coaches must remember that coaching is teaching. As a coach, some of the warmest moments have been derived from accomplishments by my athletes not directly related to athletic performance.

"It's like being a father or mother to a large family and taking pride in the children's accomplishments because as a coach you feel you have played a small role in forming their character. If you are only interested in winning, you can never build relationships that will bear this fruit. . . . Perhaps we need new methods and techniques for evaluating a coach's overall performance. . . . The people who really know best how the coach is doing are not the spectators or the media but the athletes on the team."[4]

WHERE IT MAKES A DIFFERENCE

Ask fifty people at random which philosophy they espouse for their children and the overwhelming majority would publicly opt for Margolis. Put those same fifty in a private voting booth with the future of their children on the line, knowing that winners advance and losers are, well, losers, and Nelson might win in a landslide.

This indicates the second great problem for the coaching profession, "the observer mentality."

The Christian coach today may be caught in as ferocious a tug-of-war as any individual in any profession in America. He loves competitive sports. He sees the teaching aid that sport can be. He wants to build relationships and, ultimately, mature people. Yet, always the scoreboard leers knowingly and wickedly at him. Many fine Christian coaches have been fired. Not because they were not exceptional teachers. And not because they lost. One can lose if he wins enough. And the coach has no control over those forces who measure his "enough."

Why do they continue? Because if you've ever coached, if you've ever experienced closeness with players and seen change and growth in their lives, you revel in the highs associated with coaching.

I have coached several youth teams. Halfway through our sixth-grade basketball season on a team that had become close in a hurry, Robert Hoekstra informed me his family was moving to Chicago. This was his last week. I put my arm around his shoulder, and we talked. "I don't want to leave you, coach," he cried. He had known me only a few weeks, but I was his coach. A coach who had shown interest in him. Believe me, the responsibility associated with coaching is awesome.

Greg Laughlin played center on that team. We worked for hours on his rebounding. He could not break the habit of taking the offensive rebound to the floor instead of going right back up with it. In a late season game he leaped, grabbed the rebound, and laid it against the board in the same motion, then was fouled before coming back to the floor. When the whistle blew, he turned to me with a culminating look of joy, amazement, and understanding neither of us will ever forget.

The parents of those boys told me they appreciated the way I played all the kids half the game and stressed fun and learning even though we lost more than we won. But I know had five of them had the chance to trade me for the abusive coach of the championship team, who played five and sat seven all season, they would have bid me farewell. Most parents are just not strong enough individually—and there is little way for them to band together unless they start their own league—to buck the tide of win, win, win.

"How great to realize that every moment and event of life is sacred. God did not give us rich gifts of talent to be hoarded, but rather shared. Whereas the parent, minister, and teacher often have to first get the attention of youth, the coach has it at the outset. And the current coaching profession can be an even more effective witness because of the increased arena of the world of athletics."[5] So stated Don McClanen, the man who believed so strongly in the ministering and witness potential of the Christian athlete and coach that he devoted his life to the founding of the Fellowship of Christian Athletes.

Each word brings an affirmative amen from me. Faces flood my mind; faces of men and women who coach and share Jesus and impart a profound influence on young lives.

Ed Stevens coached basketball at Augustana College in Sioux Falls, South Dakota. Losses far outweighed wins; the pressure was smothering; problems at home were mounting; he had an ulcer; he would probably have had worse.

WHERE IT MAKES A DIFFERENCE

Through a series of events he made a commitment to Jesus. He tells the result beautifully:

"Being a Christian is something. I mean *really* something. Consider our basketball season. This was to be our year. But we've been bad, sad, awful! For the first time in my life, however, I can take it. I still hate to lose, but I can live with defeat because as a Christian I am free; free to win and just as free to fail. The custodian who sweeps out the gym is just as important to me as our biggest money booster downtown, and I've found I can coach for God, my players, and myself in that order.

"Christianity sure wasn't a cure-all for my basketball woes. But I did start loving—my wife, my players, other people. There are some verses in John's Gospel I paraphrase this way, 'If the Son sets you free, man, that's as free as you can get!' I know the truth and I'm free—free to be myself. I don't have to be a fake anymore.

"Right now I'm the biggest failure I've ever been as a coach. But I'm the biggest success I've ever been as a person. For years I was religious. Now I am a Christian. There's quite a difference."[6]

"When I walk through the halls each fall," says Ben Parks, high school coach in San Francisco, "and the kids shout, 'Hey, coach, it's nice to have you back,' I know I have the chance to help some lives. I thank Jesus for that."

And thank God for Christian athletes who care about their coach. "I spent my time drinking with some of the players," said Otterbein College (Ohio) track and football coach Porter Miller. "Then some of the other players said they were praying for me. I watched their lives on the field, in the classroom, around campus. That convinced me. One night alone in my bedroom I gave my life to Jesus.

"We just went 12-0, and two kids accepted Christ.

That's the important thing. I sometimes revert, but my desire as a competitor and coach of competitors is to put the Lord first in every practice and every game."

Frank Truitt coaches soccer and golf at Kent State University. He has been through the wars. A real one and the artificial sport wars. He was basketball coach at Kent State during the tumultuous late 1960s and early 1970s. Frank was dismissed after the 1973-74 season. His successor lasted five months. There have been attempts to bring Frank back. He resists; he is content.

"We in sports take ourselves too seriously most of the time," he said as we sat on the grass at Denison University in Ohio, talking about competition, the protest movement, Kent State, the shootings. "I've had the highs and lows of sport. We lost the 1971-72 Mid-American title by two points to Toledo. Had we won I believe I could have stayed on for life.

"In 1958 my Ohio high school team played Jerry Lucas and his team that had won seventy-six in a row. We won. The next night we played in the state championship game before fourteen thousand people and statewide television for the first time. We lost. Two nights and the extremes of ecstasy and agony.

"You know what it meant? Not much. I was just happy to be there, win or lose. At nineteen I was a combat engineer in the Battle of the Bulge. It took us four days and nights to get one guy wire across the Saar River, the shelling and small arms fire were so intense. I didn't know if I'd see the next day, let alone coach a championship team.

"I saw Christians around me, especially one friend who became a minister. While the tough guys of boot camp were cowering in cellars, the Christians were helping others. I wanted to be like them.

"After the war, sport could never be that important

WHERE IT MAKES A DIFFERENCE

again. Competition could be important but never a priority. Every day of life was to be savored, and sport was only one part of every day."

If only "the coaching mentality" and "the observing mentality" could understand and incorporate this saneness. Or does it always take a war to make life sacred enough for us to get our priorities and perspectives straight?

THE SPECTATOR

Out of curiosity to view this American art form firsthand, a friend attended a professional wrestling match, sitting next to a devoted fan. This human volcano erupted at regular intervals, leaping to his feet to scream obscenities, the spittle coursing down his chin and glistening along his beet-red neck where the veins bulged, as if to burst.

Eventually my friend politely tugged at the man's sleeve. "Excuse me," he ventured, smiling a slight, incredulous smile. "Don't you know this is all fake?"

"Sure I know," he replied. "What's that got to do with it?" And the devotee was back on his feet, shaking a fist at the ringed offender and, apparently, having a pleasant evening.

The spectator.

His frenzy knows few limitations. He (or she) can experience both the height of ecstasy and the ultimate depth of agony in a matter of seconds. He exists in a mesmerized lunacy. He braves rain, snow, bitter cold, and scalding heat to back his team. He screams, hollers, exhorts, prays, pleads, giggles, weeps, and ferments in the turbulent juices of his own emotions. He is a realist and a rationalizer, a dreamer and a doubter. He is the Jekyll become Hyde; the Milquetoast become Spartacus.

He is the spectator. And, to some degree, he resides in most of us.

Certainly in me. I was a watcher before I was a player

and will probably be watching when the capacity to compete and perform has escaped me. I have been obnoxious to opposing teams and fans in victory and traumatized to a state of near shock by defeats that I feared to be the end of me, if not the end of civilization as we know it.

One situation is acutely embarrassing, but it indicates what a drug spectating can be—perhaps the modern day opiate of the people. Our first child was anxious to be born. My wife's labor increased in frequency and intensity; obviously time to go to the hospital.

I warmed up the car but had not turned off the TV. Detroit and Montreal were playing hockey. Joyce was at the door, beckoning. I turned for one last look. It was late in the third period. The score was tied and Detroit had a power play.

"Just one more rush, honey," I said. She gaped at me, unbelieving. I don't believe it either . . . now.

I'm far from alone in wanting "one more rush." Over 35 million fans attend both major league baseball and college football every season. The three major networks now carry over one thousand hours of sports a year— over 11 percent of all available time—and audiences for sports telecasts average almost 13 million.

Want a sure TV success? Take a couple of movie stars and give them a tennis racket or a bicycle or an obstacle course and pit them, man against man or man against woman, and the public rushes to see even this "trash sport" in the name of competition. "The public's love affair with sports continues to be ravenous," said Carl T. Lindemann, sports supervisor for NBC.[1]

And it's not just pro sports or televised sports. Now that apathy has once again replaced activism on the college campus, football Saturday has returned. Whereas students were staying away in droves in the 1960s and even protesting the expenditure of funds on sports, the athlete is again a campus hero. Students sleep in line for days to secure precious football and basketball tickets.

Said one student of the sixty-foot bonfire that lights the sky at College Station, Texas, before the Texas A & M-Texas football game, "If you don't get goose bumps from that, you gotta be dead!" Bonfires are again lighting the once-dark college sports night, and students from coast to coast are wearing the latest in goose bumps.

Stories of fanatical fans have become legends. Each pro, college, high school, even Little League team has its representative tale. Perhaps no one, however, has matched the verbal last will and testament of Charlie Winkler.

Charlie lives in Grand Island, Nebraska, and drives the 200-mile round trip for every University of Nebraska football scrimmage and game. He fully expects to have a heart attack some day.

"And when I do and they take me down to the respirator, I want them to roll me over so I can see the field," instructs Charlie. "Maybe that way I can see one last touchdown."

Charlie has further plans for his demise. "I want a helicopter to hover over the stadium, spreading my ashes. Then people can look up and say, 'Hey, cover your cokes and hot dogs. Here comes old Charlie floatin' down. Ain't he a prize?' "[2]

As fanatical as we are, however, North Americans are still rookies in our spectating addiction. James Michener describes a midsummer afternoon in Madrid, Spain:

"Madrid was throbbing with activity. Streets were crowded. Men were ogling pretty girls. And traffic was impossible.

"Then suddenly this city of more than two million fell silent. Cars pulled to the side of the road. Pedestrians left the streets and a tension developed so real that you could feel it. Madrid became a ghost town.

"For the next ninety minutes the city remained silent, listening to radio and television reports of a soccer game being played in Birmingham, England, between Spain and West Germany.

" 'Why the anxiety?'

" 'Don't you realize what's happening? If we lose, we're out of the World Cup!'

"At half-time the score was 1-1 and Madrid began to pray. . . . Then in the forty-eighth minute of the game, West Germany booted home a goal. . . . Spanish men around me began to weep. One knelt in the street and began to pray. Others stood in shadows, crossing themselves. One man stood on tiptoe for the remaining six minutes, as if by doing so he would help Spain score an equalizer.

"In vain. The whistle blew and Spain was eliminated from the World Cup. In Madrid men cursed, kicked at dogs, snarled at their wives and proclaimed, 'The nation is finished.'

"What I saw that day in Madrid was tame when compared to what happened in Italy and Brazil when their two great teams . . . were ignominiously defeated in early rounds. . . . In Brazil, where the collapse of their champions was a shock of incredible magnitude, fans tried to commit suicide or dropped dead from excitement."[3]

Commit suicide? Over a game? Why?

Experts have analyzed the spectating phenomenon. And their conclusions cover a gamut of psychological, philosophical, and sociological influences.

Mike D'Innocenzo, a Hofstra University professor, in his course "Sports and the American Character," said, "People find comfort in the 'good old days' of sport. Sports is a way of avoiding future shock."[4]

Said Jerry Pyle, former athlete at the University of

Minnesota, "We seem to retreat into sport in order to deny the complexity and ambiguity that marks the political, social, and religious issues of our time. . . . We have found respite and security in the irrelevant drama of sport."[5]

Jack Scott said, "We have become a nation of peeping jocks. If most of your day-to-day work is meaningless, you look for other thrills. You root for . . . the home team."[6]

One of the most comprehensive studies of spectating has been done by Los Angeles psychiatrist Dr. Arnold R. Beisser in his book *The Madness of Sport:*

"The fan is an athlete once removed, an athlete in spirit if not in fact. . . . He is a competitor without the necessity of facing the dangers of competition. He is aggressive without threat of injury either to his body or his pride. Although his competition is vicarious, he can enjoy the pleasure of victory, the sorrow of defeat, the tension of the climactic moment. He knows what it is like to be on the battlefield without going to combat. Moreover, he can, if he wishes, express his emotions verbally and even physically without fear of censure.

"The team supports the players; the crowd the team. . . . The team influences the crowd, and the crowd influences the team, in symbiotic fashion. They belong to each other and rely on one another for their vitality. . . .

"For modern man, social custom and the necessity of living close together preclude very much expression of primitive emotions. Regression, the return to simpler and more elemental stages of adjustment, is acceptable within the matrix of sports watching. Grown men carry banners or wear hats denoting their favorites in the same way that youngsters emulate their idols. Like alumni returning to a class reunion, they act in the stadium in ways different from the way they are free to act in the work world but similar to their behavior in nostalgic, bygone days."[7]

It seems complex. Yet some people opt for the simplicity of sport watching as advocated by California's loose-change Governor Jerry Brown, who commented in *Sports Illustrated* on the Los Angeles bid for the 1984 Olympic Games: "We don't want to have the Olympics for the sake of anything but the Olympics themselves. They're just games, frivolous things. They're not really necessary. But don't forget, some of the least necessary things in life are the most important . . . they make life worth living. There's enough dreariness and seriousness around without making the Olympics into something they're not. They are to enjoy. Period."

When our competitive zeal is channeled through the release valve of sport spectating, there are two potential dangers we must beware.

The first is *the creation of false community*. There is no doubt that sport spectating provides community. Beisser wrote, "The fan enjoys a peculiarly luxurious position between the camaraderie and the anonymity of the crowd. He can share intense feeling with strangers who understand. . . . It is strange, indeed, that it should take a game to allow human beings to feel related to each other."[8]

One student describes going to see the Boston Red Sox play at the height of the youth upheaval and campus protests in the 1960s: "In the pennant year of 1967, I used to say that the Red Sox *stood for* all that's good in the world—happiness, enthusiasm, courage. Then I began to say they *were* all that's good in the world. Because of them I could talk to anybody at all and share something and be together and understand. They were very important in that way."[9]

The spectator finds himself part of a body with like

emotions and goals: sunbathing in the bleachers in Wrigley Field, proving hardy by braving 15-below temperatures in Green Bay, booing a rival, cheering a hero, reflecting in concert upon the ancestry of an umpire. And so it goes. But this community evaporates. It is a fraud—fickle, fragile, futile. It's a home that is as tentative and insecure as the fog that "appears for a little time and then vanishes" (James 4: 14).

The heart longs for lasting relationships. The spectating community may not kiss and tell, but it does kiss and laugh, a deeper insult to the spirit. It is a fiction masked with reality. It is a haughty and cruel lover who rejects her sailors from the stadium and then sings her lusty siren's song amidst the empty popcorn boxes and barren seats until they are drawn to her again.

Finding community, relatedness, is a prominent New Testament theme. What an opportunity for the Christian sports participant—performer or fan—to point the way to the community that alone offers immediate and eternal fulfillment.

Christian community is not for everyone. Those who stand in the ticket line wanting pleasure have always lacked heart for Christianity's tougher dictates: "Because of this, many of Jesus' followers turned back and would not go with him any more" (John 6: 66, GNB).

But for those who choose Christian community there are benefits no stadium crowd can match: "We know that we have left death and come over into life; we know it because we love our brothers. . . . Let us love one another, because love comes from God. . . . If this is how God loved us, then we should love one another. . . . If we love one another, God lives in union with us and his love is made perfect in us" (John 3: 14; 4: 7, 11-12, GNB).

The second potential danger in sport spectating and the competitiveness it evokes is *the tendency toward loss of*

WHERE IT MAKES A DIFFERENCE

self-control in its milder forms and violence in its extreme.

"A few years ago, on an otherwise quiet November afternoon, 6,000 citizens of Columbus, Ohio, poured into the streets for what was to be perhaps the longest and most violent demonstration that city had ever seen. . . . Traffic on the main street was stopped. Cars were walked on, painted on, overturned. Columbus reporters cheerfully reported property damage and pronounced the whole affair delightful. Police joyfully escorted the rioters about. According to *New Republic,* Governor Rhodes, who had previously called out the National Guard at the slightest provocation (by political protestors) felt it had been 'a great day for Ohio.' It was a grand old riot. Clean-cut American sports fans were celebrating football victory over Michigan."[10]

Such behavior has occurred through the sport's ages. There is a "boys will be boys" mentality that tolerates disruption in the name of "sport celebration" not otherwise tolerated. While recent disturbances and on-the-field partying turned to downright meanness have soured the previously unconcerned press and populace, spectating violence is still prominent.

Some say that sport assures a healthy emotional outlet for spectators. Is it true? One can find both corroborating and contradictory testimony.

According to Dr. Christie Kiefer, anthropologist at the University of California in San Francisco, football games may serve the same purpose as various primitive rituals by releasing tensions and solidifying the bonds that hold society together. Dr. Keifer explained in *Parade* magazine that the game permits the fan "to re-channel his aggressions in a socially acceptable way." The doctor said sport watching allows people to "release pent-up feelings of aggression, hostility, or frustration in a kind of free-for-all ceremony."

Not so, indicate the findings of associate professor of psychology at Temple University Dr. Jeffrey Goldstein. Over one hundred fifty fans at an Army-Navy football game were asked to take the Buss-Durkey Hostility Inventory. The results revealed a sizable increase in hostility responses from the fans polled after the game as compared to before the contest. Therefore, he concluded, the fans had become *more* hostile for having been at the game, not less hostile.

My personal experience is that this idea of sport "assuring" a healthy emotional outlet for player or spectator is, in large degree, a myth that needs debunking. I had long sensed the contradictions in the "healthy emotional outlet" theory, but it was not until one specific afternoon that I confronted my own emotions.

It was an eighth-grade football game. My daughter was a cheerleader, and I was "mother" for a Saturday, bringing a carload of cheerleaders and carrying the hot chocolate.

The opponent pulled ahead, but in the second half our team came back. Then there was a fight. Players hitting after the whistle. Coaches charged officials and screamed at each other. Parents screamed at players, coaches—and each other.

I shouted a couple of barbed sarcasms, just to irritate one spectator who was making an idiot of himself. I was doing the same. And I knew it. Yet I did it. Had there been a fight I believe I would have taken a swing at someone, just because it seemed the logical extension of what was surging inside me. And, believe me, I am the nonswinging kind!

When it suddenly hit me how laughable I'd become, I walked away to ponder the experience. I imagined bodies lying in the streets of Belfast and a veterans' hospital and a heroin center. I thought of agonies some people endure and wondered how I could become inflamed over something so totally and profoundly insignificant.

And I also realized how difficult it is to empathize with a photographed body in Belfast compared to what happens internally to player and fan in the athletic context. It is personal. It is now. Seldom does anything bring us to the raw edge of our emotion as does sport. That is the primary reason sport and its performers can play such a vital role in getting man's attention for Jesus Christ.

I returned to the game just to watch people. When it ended the scoreboard read 22-14, but nobody had won. The losers were only further frustrated. The winners gloated the laughter of vengeance, not the laughter of shared happiness. A heavy depression hung over a field surely graded and limed to evoke other feelings.

Contact sports infect us the most. There is real communication through action. A tear-stained face melts us. A child's smile warms us. And men's violent assaults on each other can inflame like passions within us.

Lord, how we need you to make our spectating competition the emotionally healthy release it can be. How hard it is to maintain self-control, to keep events in perspective, to keep the contest from becoming a war without your grace. Even with your grace.

Proposed: a "Sport's Manifesto"—the first seventeen verses in chapter three of the apostle Paul's letter to the Colossians. Read it all, but the essence is—"You have been raised to life with Christ. Set your hearts, then, on the things that are in heaven. Put to death the earthly desires at work in you—anger, passion, and hateful feelings. Instead, put on compassion, kindness, humility, gentleness and patience. Be helpful to one another and forgive one another. Everything you do or say, then, should be done in the name of the Lord Jesus, as you give thanks through him to God the Father."

The competition of sport playing or watching can be that healthy emotional outlet; that uplifting, happy experience. Or it can become a vendetta.

It is not what the game does to us but what we do to the game.

It is not what the game brings to us but what we bring to the game.

Bring Jesus. Or maybe we'd better stay away.

THE OPPONENT

The first "away game" I ever played was in ninth-grade football. We traveled thirty miles to Bedford Consolidated Rural School. We were town school kids, the nice kids. Not big, not mean, not talented, but nice kids.

It was drilled into me that there was nothing nice about the Bedford boys. I had a summer to think about them. "You better be ready," coaches and former junior high athletes warned me. "They're mean. They'll hurt you. You better get mean and want to hurt some people, too."

I did not want to hurt anyone. I wanted to play football.

Every athlete, whatever the sport, knows the trauma of "opponent watching." Waiting for their arrival, watching them run on the field, hearing their screams (to shake you and to ward off their trembling), sizing them up, feeling their strength burrow like moles beneath the field or court or diamond and reach up to paralyze the legs and gnaw at one's courage.

For the young competitor there may be no more important aspect of athletics than the perspective on his opponent as taught and modeled by parent, coach, and peers. It can assure healthy growth or destroy one's sensitivity to people and sport for a lifetime. By and large in America, this need is given little thought. In effect, the adult model is too often the worst enemy the young competitor has.

The Bedford day arrived. The Bedford players wore raggedy uniforms and played on a raggedy field in front

270

of raggedy fans with raggedy cheerleaders. The players' biceps bulged; from lifting plows, I assumed. They had big heads hid in bigger helmets resting on thick necks atop drumlike bodies of concrete.

"Aw, they're so dumb they can't even remember plays," a terrorized teammate scoffed to hide his fear.

They didn't have to remember plays. They only had two, sweep left and sweep right. Sweep right was right over my defensive cornerback position. Two massive blockers and a burly fullback. The picture is still painfully vivid: the raggedy uniforms; the flailing arms and legs; the grunt of bodies coiling to hurt; the warding off; the torn, raggedy sod; the blood and the pain.

They tore us to shreds. It was agonizing. For the first time I wanted to hurt someone in return.

"Two are better off than one, because together they can work more effectively. If one of them falls down, the other can help him up. But if someone is alone and falls, it's just too bad, because there is no one to help him" (Eccles. 4: 9-10).

It has been suggested that this verse could define the opponent's role in athletic competition just as it obviously defines teamwork. (After all, without an opponent, the game could not be played!) But first one must run a gauntlet of stress and emotions. As in every reaction and counterreaction situation, there is the swing of the pendulum between the extremes before the balance point is reached.

From an undefined, neutral position concerning my opponent, I swung first, passionately, toward hatred. With my fear, uncertainty as to my ability, pressure to make the team, and all the other factors—internal and external—a competitor faces, I was easy prey for the "killer coach."

One of my high school coaches instructed me to hate

("intensely dislike" were his words) my opponent. I was to get him before he got me; humiliate him before he embarrassed me. Coach labeled it "competition." We worked at hating each other in practice, friend against friend, to prepare for the real enemy. At times I was able to psyche myself into such a rabid condition. But it was so joyless. When practice ended, the air was fresher up the block.

George Sauer, Jr., former New York Jets wide receiver, wrote in *Ramparts* magazine, "Opponents in sport are not enemies. They are not beasts venting a blood lust into acceptable channels. . . .

"If anything, athletic opponents are brothers in a universal sense. They compete in contests to express something about men in the face of challenge. Opponents mutually enrich their challenges by presenting an intelligent unpredictability that is absent in sports without opponents.

"Opponents reflect ultimately a cooperation in the form of competition. Even the words 'compete' and 'contest' imply a togetherness rather than separateness. Compete literally means to 'seek together,' and contest, to 'bear witness together.'

"Opponents finally are seeking something together and together they are bearing witness to what man can become in the face of challenge. In this way, they serve each other with a means of testing their limits and testing their spirit, while at the same time providing a drama for a dynamic excellence of man.

"As mutual servants, opponents are bound together in a certain equality that announces them as brothers."

A brother? No, I never pictured my opponent that way. It would have been better. It would have made unnecessary so many years of stomach-wrenching fear and combative "psyching up."

Again, someone misled me.

There were certain instincts involved in defining one's foe: survival of the fittest, get them before they get you, crush, intimidate, destroy. Nothing as wholesome and uplifting as brotherhood and cooperation.

Sport competition was war . . . and war is hell.

Most athletes find themselves in a quandary—they cannot get beyond the hatred stage, or at least a masquerade of it. The rationalization sometimes becomes "I can leave it on the field." This holds true for Christian competitors.

"Learning to be a competitor is learning to survive in the world," says chapel leader and Seattle Seahawks offensive tackle Norm Evans. "It's still a matter of survival of the fittest."

"My opponent is the enemy," says Bob Davies, former pro basketball great. "He's the one in the way of my achieving my goals. It always has been that way. But I never made a mortal enemy in pro ball. I had the capacity to leave it on the court."

"I once believed in annihilation of the foe," said John Robert Bell, former highly respected college football coach at East Tennessee State University and former Fellowship of Christian Athletes staff member. "If I were playing you, I didn't feel you had a right to be on the same field with me."

So, where hate seems to rule, flower children often step in. When we swing to the other extreme, we end up with a combination competition/play that is nebulous, even mushy.

"A friend of mine was a superjock at Yale," wrote Kurt Vonnegut, "but in his senior year he quit the varsity ice hockey team. He organized a hockey team where you had to have a beard to play. He challenged Rhode Island School of Design to a game, and the two teams skated to the middle of the rink carrying their jerseys. They made a big pile of them, then chose up sides. That was beautiful. These were friendly, cheerful people and they were doing amusing things. Their goal was to delight themselves, not to defeat each other."[1]

Today there's a healthy variety of newly conceived "fun" events. They involve no projected competition, no specific opponent role. They expand the tradition of Frisbee and jogging. What one must do is carefully delineate between leisure fun and competition. From Frisbee came competitive Frisbee golf. From fun running and jogging has come competitive marathoning with record numbers of participants.

"Some people are amusing," said Trinity College (Illinois) track and cross-country coach Paul Frykholm. "They feel the only way to eliminate the problems of competition is to eliminate competition."

But wait, still others say there are ways around competing and having to have a winner and loser. Why not play for a tie or, in other words, eliminate the scoreboard from athletics?

Horace Spencer Fiske wrote in his poem "The Cry of the High Hurdlers":

We mount the air, a hidden stair
    And shoot their easy height.
And now we feel the final pull—
    A triple struggle hot:
We catch the cries, we feel the eyes,
    We "hit her up" a jot.
We spurt as one, we rise abreast,
    Like horses o'er a hedge;
We hear the cry: "A tie, a tie!"
    We'll drink to each a pledge.[2]

I have been in those situations. And found great delight in co-authoring a win and sharing the afterglow in that blissful but seldom reached never-never land of sport where there are no winners or losers.

In the 1978 NAIA indoor track and field championship, two pole vaulters from Abilene Christian University were left alone in the competition at a NAIA indoor record 17'2'' height. Both failed to clear in three attempts. Given one more try, according to the rule book, they failed again.

The bar was lowered to 16'8''. Now bone weary from day-long competition, both missed again. Rather than going on, they utilized the rule that says teammates can choose to be co-champions. Billy Olson and Frank Estes hugged each other, saluted the cheering crowd, and were co-medalists.

A tie is not always like kissing your sister, but it is an incongruity, an aberration in any activity in which it's normal for one side to have more points than the other. And life is too precious a gift to play it to a tie.

Well, if there can be no tie, others say, then eliminate the humanity from the struggle. Internalize your competitiveness. Compete against yourself or against a standard.

John Mack Carter and Lois Wyse write in *How to Be Outrageously Successful with Women,* "If you really have competitive spirit, it is not the men and women with whom you work that you compete with. Your real competitor is you. Instead of wasting energy wondering what he or she will do, or what someone else's reaction will be, you continually try to do yourself one better. . . . And, if your chief competitor is yourself, you get along a lot better with everyone else."[3]

This viewpoint has merit. In *Desiderata* we read, "If you compare yourself with others, you may become vain and bitter; for always there will be greater and lesser persons than yourself." But in avoiding the comparison, our internalizing of competition can sometimes go to silly lengths. High jump champion Dwight Stones says he turns his hatred toward the bar ... it has a tendency to fall off when touched. A sixteen-year-old Michigan school girl scheduled to play transsexual Renee Richards in a pro tennis tournament said, "I just watch the net and the ball. I don't know who's on the other side of the net."

This is akin to those racists who deny their racism by calling themselves "color blind." How ludicrous. We cannot rationalize or conditionalize our opponent from existence. He or she is there. We must recognize our opponent and deal with our attitude toward him.

The key—and here is where the love of Jesus that confirms our self-worth comes in—is to be able to look at others and ourselves, discern the various gifts and talents, and to feel secure about who we are and the role and the personhood of the opponent. Most aspects of the athletic world involve human opposition. For the Christian competitor to attempt to separate himself from this world is, in effect, to forfeit his position in it. Jesus never calls us from the world in a cosmic sense or from the smaller worlds we each inhabit; only to live at the highest plateau within those worlds.

The athlete alone may best understand looking on an opponent as more than an adversary. And the Christian competitor should understand it better than others.

Columnist Sydney J. Harris wrote, "Most people look upon the Biblical injunction 'Love your enemies,' either as impossibly Utopian or impossibly sentimental. This is because they fail to understand the meaning of *agape*, or love, as Jesus meant it.

"It is the 'personhood' of the other that unites us in something that is above and greater than both of us; and our respect for this common ground of being must take precedence over our likes and our beliefs. . . .

"It may sound odd, but true athletes 'love' their enemies. That is, they respect them as other persons striving toward an opposite goal. And they oppose them only within rules that both obey. This is the kind of spirit Jesus was urging upon us, not a sticky sentimentality that tries to blink away human conflict or pretend that people can like each other better than they do. He was saying that it doesn't matter if you like someone or not, it doesn't matter if you agree or not—the only thing that matters is treating the other as fairly and cleanly as athletes do."

Others have wrestled with this and found competition insulated by love and concern a way to wholeness. Writes *Christianity Today* publisher Harold Myra:

"When we were kids, I tackled my brother in a back-yard game. Years smaller than he, I grabbed his ankle and rode him thirty yards before I tripped him—Thunk!—into the hard November ground. He looked across at me, surprised. 'Way to go, kid,' he grunted—and the rest of that day, I was a tiger!

"Couldn't competition be like that sometimes, Lord? Admiring the brother who outdoes you . . . but still fighting like crazy to win? . . . I don't have to hate the guy who beats me—I can admire his ability, if God is in me. Opponents are made in your image, too. . . . Yet you live within me, telling me to love, even as I compete. Love people, love you, as you loved us, and died for us. Help me to take that to the ball field, Lord."[4]

Writes Dr. George Sheehan in *The Physician and Sportsmedicine*, "Play, then, is the answer to the puzzle of our existence, the stage for our excesses and exuberances. Violence and dissent are part of its joy. Territory is defended with every ounce of our strength and determination, and moments later we are embracing our opponents and delighting in the game that took place.

WHERE IT MAKES A DIFFERENCE

"Play is where life lives, where the game is the game. At its borders we slip into heresy, become serious, lose our sense of humor, fail to see the incongruities of everything we hold to be important. Right and wrong become problematical. Money, power, position become ends. The game becomes winning. And we lose the good life and the good things that play provides.

"A universe where we are to play and enjoy ourselves and our God is one thing. . . . A universe where it is either 'us' or 'them' will certainly make us seek peace in another world. Life under those circumstances is just as Samuel Beckett described it, 'a terminal illness.' "[5]

And how does the athlete keep his competitiveness from becoming "a terminal illness"? Again, the Christian competitor has the best barometer: our heart will tell us, "This then is how we know that we belong to the truth, and how we set our hearts at rest in his presence whenever our hearts condemn us. For God is greater than our hearts, and he knows everything" (1 John 3:19-20, NIV).

To build our attitude toward our opponent on anything less than a heart probed and massaged by the love of Christ is to be the foolish builder of Matthew 7:26. The foundation erodes and we slip to the levels of self-delusion or hatred.

Increasingly, more and more athletes are coming to the brotherhood concept of George Sauer.

"We need the capacity to enjoy someone else's success," said surgeon and avid tennis player Dr. Buddy Whitesides of Gastonia, North Carolina. "If I love you, if I have respect for you, I'll cheer your success, even if it's over me. At times it may be 'Nice shot, you old _____ .' It taxes our pride and ego. It has to become a habit, a discipline, a commitment until it is a real and genuine part of our competing nature."

Said new Christian Rich Saul, center for the Los Angeles Rams, of his concern about being a Christian and playing against Christian brothers on other teams, "The hardest part will be playing against you guys. Tell you what: I'm going to hit you with all the love I have in me!"

Commented coach John Robert Bell, "We were taking passive, nice boys from proper backgrounds and teaching them as offensive linemen to clear a path for a running back. You can do that in several ways. You can turn them into brutes. Or you can teach it as a skill, as team effort. It is evil to turn to emotion and animal instinct that creates an overly aggressive life-style. Sport can be a fun thing to test one's intelligence and endurance against another. Cooperation with teammate and opponent is a major part of sport."

"Some people say they love to play against their friends," said Miami Dolphin defensive back Tim Foley. "Not me. I played against Mike Phipps, a close friend of mine, when he threw five interceptions. We won, but I was really down. I hurt for him. The biggest change I've had in my athletic career is going from the fear of losing and resultant hatred for my opponent to a real respect for the effort, pain, and achievement of my opponent. Mutual respect among competitors is very important."

No one has captured this better than Bill Bradley in his book *Life on the Run:* "I guard John Havlicek—by far the most difficult job I have in a season. . . . Testing my ability against his superior skills gives me great satisfaction. Both of us know instinctively how far we can challenge each other without destroying our mutual respect. If he makes a cut to the basket without the ball, I might try to stop him with a stiff arm to the hip. He might respond by grabbing my arm for leverage and hurtling past me. . . . We will play hard against each other—each doing some holding and pushing, but never turning the natural aggressiveness of the game into hostility."[6]

Blind, unperceptive competition has turned many aspects of our lives into a shambles. In child rearing, in the scramble up the economic and social ladders of success, in the quest for educational degrees, in our political Watergates, in our nationalism, which reflects the "bigger, faster, better, tougher" ethic, competition has sometimes midwifed a mindless cruelty, a cold intensity, a calloused seriousness, and a joylessness that is a far country from competition as Jesus manifested it.

Consider what could happen to the playing of games if every competitor would incorporate these concepts into his play:

Respect the contest, yourself, and your opponent.

"Blessed are the meek" (Matt. 5:5).

Commit first to doing your best, second to team loyalty, and third to the higher total on the scoreboard.

"Blessed are those who hunger and thirst for righteousness" (Matt. 5:6).

Determine to enjoy competition, doing whatever it takes for you, your team, *and your opponent* to have fun at what you are doing. Otherwise, why do it?

"Blessed are the pure in heart" (Matt. 5:8).

Understand that regardless of athletic shop talk about sacrifice, discipline, commitment, and all the rest, unless it is wrapped in an expressed love for the game and all its participants, it is meaningless jock talk.

"Blessed are the peacemakers" (Matt. 5:9).

What would happen? We would have a sport revolution.

A WORD
FOR MY CHILDREN

Dear Jeff,

It's OK to fail, son.

Not that failure has been much a part of your life. Not at all. Maybe because we have guarded so hard against it. Yes, we. Father and son. I see this struggle with all the implications of failure so apparent in you because I still battle it so hard in me.

It began before you were born, Jeff. Over twenty years ago. The firstborn. The culmination of two people becoming one. Oh, I'd be the all-time "most valuable" father. I said all the right things: "He can be anything he wants and I'll be proud of him. If he likes sports, fine. If he doesn't, that's OK."

Not like sports? The thought was staggering. Prefer the clarinet, working under a car, getting a job, hanging around a street corner? You had to like sports. Just had to.

Or I would have failed? Maybe that was it. If it was, your genes got a piece of it. We're "like father, like son" in too many ways. I passed along some problems, Jeff. Sorry about that.

Like appearance. Remember when you were eighteen and in the hospital and the receptionist said to me, "Your brother is right down the hall." Your brother! I loved it. And did I ride you about that. "If you ever get sick again," I grinned, "I can fill in for you on your dates."

But the beneath-the-skin stuff is where it counts.

WHERE IT MAKES A DIFFERENCE

That's another story; a tougher, more important story.

I had seen so much parental abuse of children in the name of sport that I had determined to do better. Remember little Tommy next door? At age three his dad had him in the backyard in helmet and shoulder pads, teaching him how to tackle and take a handoff. Dad screaming and son sweating and, eventually, crying. It was sickening.

I wasn't that way. No, but to a lesser degree, I got my vicarious kicks in subtler ways. I wanted you to like baseball. So we took batting practice. A lot of batting practice. And you were terrible.

I'd throw the pitch down the pipe and you would duck away. I'd walk to the plate, show you, talk to you. You'd look at me so disappointed, say you'd try harder . . . and wonder when we could go home. I'd throw again. A foul tip buoyed my expectations. But they were infrequent. Most of the time you'd just back away. And I'd shout sarcastic things, eventually, mean things.

Then you were hit in the batting helmet by a pitch during a game. You didn't get visibly upset. Just wondered when we could go home.

We took you to the eye doctor after a school checkup indicated a seeing deficiency. The day you received your glasses you read street signs for the first time. You couldn't read them before, just as you couldn't clearly see my pitches. I felt desperately wicked and tried to explain. "That's OK, dad," was all you said.

If you had only told me months before, "Dad, I'm sorry. I can't see the ball. Baseball is not for me. At this game I'm just a failure." But how could you say that? You'd never seen that attitude modeled. Failure was for others, not a Warner. But I'm getting a little more comfortable failing. And I believe you are, too, son.

In football you played defensive end. "It's up to you,

Warner," your coach would admonish. "You must box in that sweep. If they get around you, it's six points."

I'd watch practice, see you studying your plays, notice the tension build in your eyes as game day approached. "Everything OK, son?" I'd ask. "Want to talk about it?" Knowing your reply would be, "No, it's OK, dad." It's hard to talk. It was for me; will be for your son. Hard to talk about "what if . . ." Hard to talk about failing in a world where failure is not acceptable.

Down inside where you live you kept looking for your thing. That's the way you are, persistent, introspective, independent. The only guy in a graduating class of twelve hundred to wear blue Adidas under his cap and gown. Nice going, buddy. Your mother loved that one.

I know you can name the moment you discovered gymnastics, just as the sawdust trail convert can name the moment he discovered Jesus. For me, gymnastics was a set of parallel bars in the corner of the gym on which guys did chin-ups. For you, in a school system extolling the sport, the first time you chalked up, mounted the apparatus, and took that first awkward swing, you were home.

At first you were overly cautious. One or two events, some simple moves. Then you got the message from good coaches: it's OK to fail, Jeff. And you were on your way. For failure is the only way to growth in any sport.

Through a standout high school career and now collegiate gymnastics, I've seen you grow, become freed-up, and be purged of some of your father's sins.

Remember the day you came home from high school with your hand swollen and bloodied? You finally admitted you couldn't get your stutz on the P-bar and had jumped to the floor and smashed your hand into a cement wall. You were failing and failure was untenable.

That's why your calls from college in your freshman

year were so gratifying. You talked about the compulsory routines and what was tough to learn and your pratfalls and the coaches kidding you and some things "I may not be able to learn for awhile."

You were learning how to fail. And it's OK to fail, son.

But, more than this, I see you maturing in other ways. Remember the time we took that long walk and talked about relating to women? Maybe it helped for me to explain how I had often failed to communicate with your mother, preferring to quietly ride out the storm and hope for a new day and a lapse of memory (which never happens with a woman!) rather than facing up, communicating . . . and perhaps failing in the process. I failed, but in my own acceptable pattern.

You talked about how hard it was to say you're sorry. Sure. Sorry implies failure; that you were wrong. But sorry is also the cement of repentance that binds relationships and restores fellowship.

And I used to get a kick out of throwing you a ball. It might take you five bounces to capture it. Hands like cement. Gregg, six years younger, could handle you in basketball, tennis, you name it. So you'd avoid these games at all costs.

Now you'll try most anything. Sure, you still get upset at times. But you've a new capacity to laugh at yourself, give the game and the opponent their due, and not carry the burden of perfection.

It's OK to fail, son.

Maybe I could have saved us this mutual grief had my faith not been so immature when you were young. I had the words then, but I didn't know how to bring them to life. I had all the answers but I didn't know anything. Now I don't have many answers, but I do know the Answer—the Lord Jesus—in a deeper way.

And that's why we, father and son, can fail. Because

Jesus says it's OK. He lets us know we are acceptable in our failure. We will fail; that's a given fact in our relationship with Christ. But perfection is to be sought, not acquired; and the end of this rainbow is a long way down the road, all the way to glory.

Consider the apostle Paul. The beautiful thing about Paul is he was so successful because he was such a failure. He failed all the time and was God's man in the process. God told Paul that "my power is made perfect in weakness" (2 Cor. 12:9). Therefore, when we fail, when we admit our weakness and invite Christ to fill the void, we have access to his strength. And it is that way into eternity. For if the body is "sown in weakness, it is raised in power."

There is power in athletic failure, Jeff. For we have tried, we have learned, we have enlarged our base of experience. We can be more an athlete for all that failing involves.

And there is power in life failure, Jeff. For it is here that Jesus offers more of himself so that each failure, and all it implies, may become another step toward that perfection that is only found in Christ.

It's OK to fail, son.

Love,
Dad

Dear Wendi,

Where did my little girl go?

The little girl who used to beat the boys on Field Day in elementary school and be so anxious to show me her blue ribbons. Now the ribbons have turned to medals and photos and radio interviews and newspaper clippings and state championships and college scholarships. And while it is not a life and death thing, it is edging that way.

Don't lose the joy, honey.

WHERE IT MAKES A DIFFERENCE

Wendi, you'll always be "my little girl." Even when you're thirty and I have grandchildren to spoil and then hurry back to you when they ride my nerves. Just don't grow old on me before it's time. Stay a little girl for awhile. Don't become gray-haired and too serious at nineteen. There ought to be a lot of joy at nineteen.

Remember the night I came to your Fellowship of Christian Athletes meeting? And the tennis player talked about competing and life and death in the same breath? And the way her dad had trained her? And how she wanted to quit? And how there was no fun, just drudgery? She is an old person as a competitor and such a child in other ways.

Don't lose the joy, honey.

You've become so much in such a short time. A high school cross-country All-American; a state cross-country and track champion; a scholarship college freshman. Happiness . . . and heartbreak, too; some agonizing loss- es. And it's far from over. Your aspirations are so high— record runs, college competition, marathons. I'm proud and yet afraid. I want to cry "no more!' and shelter you from it all, but such shelter only suffocates a soaring spirit.

Soar on. Neil Diamond sings "the higher the top, the longer the drop." It's not the drop I fear for you, just the sudden stop. Just the abruptness of reality at whatever level of competition each of us eventually reaches our reality. I wanted the major leagues once, fell far, and landed hard. But I survived the jolts of competition and learned from them, and so will you, whenever they come, however it happens.

Athletic daughters and dads share special things. We've laughed. Remember the dark, bitter winter morn- ing you were totally bundled—only nose and eyes showing—to run distance, and how you stopped at a gas station and the rest room door wouldn't open because the attendant had given you the men's key, and how you informed him of his error?

We've hurt. Like the day you finished second in the AAU regionals and I caught you when you fell exhausted at the finish and your eyes were glazed and all you could say over and over was "What happened?" And there was nothing I could answer, only ache with you awhile.

We've shouted the joy. When you broke the mile mark by thirty seconds and the radio interviewer congratulated you on "being out there all alone and running such a great race" and you told him that you weren't alone, that Jesus was running with you, and he got flustered and didn't know what to make of all that.

We're been short with each other (the momentary barriers of age and gender and experience and emotion). There are times I've wanted to hug and comfort but had to stay away. The curse of being a father. Sometimes the people closest to us just can't be close.

You could stop right now and I'd be proud. My, what determination. When you were a child, I'd spank you and you'd refuse to cry. You were building that stubborn spirit that now runs miles up and over hills and says "catch me if you want to hurt that much." I've seen you run ten miles in the boiling Kansas sun; seen you put in five miles at 5:30 A.M. in the frigid January darkness and another five that night . . . and wondered why. And have known why at the same time. Because there is something inside you that says run. There is another second to be taken off. There is another challenger to overcome.

Why? Because. And that's enough.

Remember the times we have run? Especially at night. No sound but the reach for air and the rhythm of our shoes on pavement. A syncopation. And we have gone on and on with only that sound, that feeling of being in a slow-motion fantasy removed from our physical presence. It is a spiritual thing. How many other dads and daughters have known that? There was no finish line (although you like to stay that one step ahead!). No conclusion. Just the doing of it is enough.

Perhaps that is too pure. Now there are times to be lowered, races to be won, new plateaus to reach, competition to test and be tested by. The finish is so vital. But the essence of the journey—the getting there—yes, we'll always have that.

Don't lose the joy, honey.

I hope you are learning all the healthy things that play and physical activity and competition (in the best sense) can teach: a commitment to an effort; a satisfaction with the knowledge that one has given her best; a resilience to overcome pain and defeat and try again; endurance, perhaps the most overlooked but important quality one needs in both the Christian and competitive lives; loyalty; appreciation for teammates and opponents; a willingness to learn and to be taught; self-sufficiency in some areas, dependency in others; pleasure gained from seemingly insignificant moments and encounters; and so much more.

And I hope that you—and all the young women coming along in record numbers in athletics—can avoid the nasty side of sports that plagues your male counterparts. Don't let "In Title IX We Trust" be the catch phrase that takes you along the same problem-strewn road that men have constructed and rued. Will recruiting wars begin? Will professional leagues spring up? Will the youth-league monster create as many old women out of twelve year olds as it has old men? Will the current enthusiasm for female sports create the same sludge pile of excesses and abuses faced by males?

Don't lose the joy, honey.

One day you'll know the ambivalence of being a parent. I look forward to the next season with such anticipation. I'm always wishing it would be here, but I also wish it would never come because it is over so quickly and we are older and there is less of it left. Help me be the right kind of dad. Let me be aware of and equally interested in all the facets of your life. Don't let me push, but do let me help. Don't let me pressure, but let me always make you aware that I am interested. Don't let me be around too close at times when dads are simply in the way, but do let me be there. Just be there somewhere nearby. Don't let me patronize you with advice or concern or pat answers or unrealistic experiences ("back when I was a boy"), but do let me share my feelings and what makes me hurt, and you do the same with me.

And just let me love you as best I can. And love me in return as best you can. And love Jesus as you do now, because in that way you really love me best.

And don't lose the joy, honey. For I never will. You have already given me too much. There's no way your dad will ever be without it.

Love,
Dad

Dear Gregg,

It's going to be all right, son.

I wonder how many times I have told you that. Not always verbally. Sometimes with a smile or the clenched fist of encouragement.

All fifteen years, as a starter.

You were number four. Jeff, then Wendi, then a little brother none of you ever saw. He died at birth. We've stood together at his grave. "Baby Boy Warner . . . of such is the Kingdom of Heaven." And we pulled the weeds away from where it read "May 13, 1963."

WHERE IT MAKES A DIFFERENCE

And then you came along. Born early, too early. It seemed God wanted you back in a hurry. One lung was collapsed. And you lay in the nursery, little blue fingers and toes. No sound from that isolette.

The doctor gave you twenty-four hours. If the lung did not expand by then, well . . . but you fooled him. Fooled a lot of people. Only you took ninety-six hours to do it. Always the ham. Just a "wild and cra-a-a-a-a-a-zy guy," as you like to say.

I knew you'd make it. I stood by that hospital window for hours, watching, praying. You know what I told you?

It's going to be all right, son.

And then the lung decided to cooperate. And you let out your first cry. The first of many. Such energy! Still! We nicknamed you "Chaos" until you became sensitive about it. We tried to recall some of our prayers. "Lord, we wanted him well, but this is ridiculous!"

God seemed to smile back and remind us, "It's going to be all right."

It was natural you'd like sports in this family. But you are unique. You still can't comprehend Jeff's discipline. For you to concentrate on something for thirty minutes is a minor miracle. Your sister's fierce determination leaves you almost amused. You wouldn't run across the street if you could hitch a ride . . . or con someone into going for you.

But you've a special ingredient. Life is fun. Each day is a joy. What boundless enthusiasm. Coaches call it being a little "loosey-goosey." You've always had enough loosey and goosey for ten guys. How many other six year olds can fall off a second-story fire escape, laugh, and run off playing?

Talented athletes can be loosey-goosey. And you've that talent. It all came so easily. Perhaps too easy. How many other twelve year olds break 45 for nine holes on a stern country club golf course? Baseball, tennis, racquet-ball, golf—your body seems completed by the addition of a bat, racquet, or club

And I saw another quality emerging that I knew would one day intersect your joy to deepen and enrich its essence. Sensitivity. You're a caring person. It hurts you when your buddies pick on people because they are a different color or have some physical handicap. I like to think God gave you a caring heart during those ninety-six hours.

Watching you play with the little neighborhood kids is a rewarding sight. Especially with Jimmy, the boy in Special Olympics three houses away. He thinks you are God, Gregg. And John, the black youngster, feels at home in your bedroom. And Marty, who has such a hard time speaking, calls so many nights, and you are patient with him for long, long minutes.

Stay like this and it's going to be all right, son.

Then I saw this sensitivity intercept your play. I remember the day you became a competitor. The day play became important; the day it mattered. It was nothing so obvious that anyone else noticed. But I knew.

It was a June day at the baseball complex. You'd been a little worried about your hitting. The competition was catching up. The pitchers were bigger, stronger, threw harder. You weren't getting around on the pitch. It was no longer a simple matter to casually stroll to the plate and pull the ball to left field.

You were in the on-deck circle, practicing your stride and swing. Usually you'd kneel, check out the stands, talk with a teammate, the umpire, the catcher, anyone who would talk back. Not now. You were all concentration. And something was wrong. You seemed uncomfortable. You steadied, took your stride, swung . . . and then turned to silently mouth to me, "Look all right?"

WHERE IT MAKES A DIFFERENCE

And I saw it. In your eyes. The fear of a frightened animal that senses danger. Your world of fun and games had been invaded by your initial impression of their difficulty and importance. You have not been the same since. You are learning about sacrifice, commitment, winning and losing, and all the elements that competitive sports introduce and can help foster in the life-styles of young people.

It's going to be all right, son.

It's going to be all right because you won't let sport beat you down. You are still loose enough to try a behind-the-back dribble, which makes your coach bury his head in his hands so you won't see him grinning. You can still throw down your mask in mock horror at baseball practice when someone complains about a bad throw, spread your arms, and shout, to the delight of your teammates and coach, "Well, Excuuuuuuuuuuuuuse me!" You can give up football because you would rather do other things. You can give up striving for excellence because you simply do not want to spend the time and effort it would take to approach that excellence. And that's all right if one is content with that decision.

That's why it's going to be all right, son.

Finally, I believe it's going to be all right because you have another rare gift. The gift of sensing joy and appropriating it amidst life's struggles.

Remember the bad ice storm several years ago? Your teacher asked you to help your blind friend, Todd, home. Todd is a rare sightless youngster, attending the neighborhood school. But that day was too much for even Todd to negotiate his way home.

You started out, two little guys in a storm.

The day was eerie and beautiful with its muted gray-white coloring, burdened trees and shrubs, and sadistic wind. Occasionally a transformer would blow, illuminating the scene in a blue orange glow.

You trudged along, steadying Todd, helping him over broken branches, and describing what everything looked like. Then he gripped your hand and you stopped. "Wait a second," he whispered. "I hear the birds singing."

A flock of disoriented starlings had found haven in a tree and were venting their wrath at the storm. But to a blind boy, it was the sound of singing.

Both sports and faith are like that, Gregg. If you enter the competition of sport you must be willing to walk a difficult course through pain and struggle and have the branches of heartache come falling down around you. But if you have pledged to yourself to be a bit loosey-goosey and not take yourself or games too seriously, it's going to be all right.

You can pause and hear the birds singing.

It's the same with faith, son. Even today there are wise men (like Todd) who hear a song in the screech of starlings, just as other wise men once heard the love call of the Savior in a baby's crying from a manger.

To know Jesus is to know love. And Jesus says his perfect love "casts out fear" (1 John 4:18). You never need look so frightened again when your hope is sunk in the bedrock of Christ's love.

And your hope is. That's the reason I know it's going to be all right, son.

Love,
Dad

26
COME COMPETE WITH ME

And so it is finished. The book that, for me, had to be, were there no books before it and none to come. Four years in the research, two years in the writing, a lifetime in the living. I am alternately cheered and embarrassed by it. I only pray it informs, enlightens, stirs, helps.

There are yet two matters on my mind.

THE FIRST MATTER

The first has to do with "what now?" If the competitive attitudes, mindsets, and theologies of athletes, coaches, parents, and spectators are to be swept by a fresh breath from God, the organizations functioning in the sport/faith ministry must bear a considerable portion of the leadership.

FELLOWSHIP OF CHRISTIAN ATHLETES—This is the granddaddy of the sport/faith groups. After eleven years as an FCA staff member, I am convinced this is the one body in a position to have a major beneficial impact on the competitive attitudes and actions of significant numbers of athletes and coaches.

FCA was a forerunner and a prophet in its evangelistic outreach and its fellowship emphasis. It has, and has had, great opportunity to be a forerunner and prophet in the decisive areas of relating faith to competition and dealing forcefully with the issues and problems that plague sports today, from the youth leagues to the pros. Thus far it has opted to be conspicuously silent or adapt a "let Jesus do it" approach rather than undertake the risks involved.

The reasons are obvious. The Fellowship advertises itself as broad and inclusive. Actually, in leadership perspective, financial backing, and program emphasis, it is conservative and one-dimensionally salvation oriented. Raising funds, building a national headquarters, resurrecting plunging staff morale, and trying to find some semblance of spiritual leadership are problems at the top. Dealing with sport-related ethical and moral dilemmas and the deep concerns of being competitive and being Christian are taboo as FCA chases its bureaucratic tail and tries to overcome severe financial limitations.

But life goes on at all levels of the Fellowship. It is an organization whose problems at the peak of the pyramid may, in effect, be the strongest hope for a new priority at the base—a priority emphasizing the application of faith to competitiveness. For the Fellowship's strength has historically been that it is a loose federation of thousands of little islands of athletes and coaches, many of whom meet under the FCA banner with no organizational tie. These hundreds of groups are free to wrestle with the questions of competition and bravely move to a deeper level of faith, commitment, and action than the national leadership seems ready or capable of going.

It is an opportunity . . . if it is not left to others.

PRO ATHLETES OUTREACH—This is the sport boot camp where Christian soldiers are prepared for war. It was initiated in 1974 by a handful of pro athletes—Greg Brezina of the Atlanta Falcons, Mike McCoy of the Oakland Raiders, and Norm Evans of the Seattle Seahawks—tired of being jostled between the various sport/faith bodies and wishing to implant a perspective of their own. The purpose is "aggressive evangelism"—basic training for the pro Christian athlete in the Scriptures and their application in witnessing.

In this sport battleground, the business of training and

sharing is grim, hard work. There is a fierce competitiveness for recruits. As yet, however, the movement has shown a reluctance to even talk about issues in sports and the competitive drive, which too easily surfaces as greed, pride, ego, and other pertinent problems of the play-for-pay vocation. All this has been left to others.

ATHLETES IN ACTION—This is an arm of Campus Crusade for Christ with the same purpose and fervency. This is the most team- and competition-oriented of the groups. And no other sport/faith ministry is as win-conscious.

The direct ministry is to introduce athletes to Christ. The second part of the outreach is to disciple these athletes and give them a broad platform for worldwide sharing with other athletes and the sport spectator.

The ministry's primary emphasis takes the form of traveling teams in a variety of sports—basketball, gymnastics, weightlifting, soccer, volleyball, wrestling, track, and field. Excellent teams. Winning teams. Teams that fill arenas and attract TV coverage. Teams that are playing with the big kids . . . and by the big kids' rules. This is Madison Avenue chic in jock strap. No other group is as media- and-PR conscious.

AIA has much to do *with* competition. It has not had a lot to say *about* competition, allowing anything other than momentary introspection to lapse into the hands of others lest the game fail to go on as scheduled. President Dave Hannah was quoted as saying, "Infidels don't listen to losers."[1] He claims it was an overstatement but does say, "We sure didn't get much of a hearing when we were losing." So winning becomes imperative in the "success gospel" approach. And anything that hinders winning is an obstruction. And expendable. Dealing with one's competitiveness can be an obstruction to winning. So it is left to others.

SPORTS AMBASSADORS—This is the sports arm of Overseas Crusades. Through the years these hardy bands of college athletes have had a unique and exciting ministry. This is back-jungle basketball, soccer, and baseball. The concerns are battling dysentery, winning, and sharing the gospel in other countries. One can deal with his or her competitiveness when the tour is over. So it is left to others.

THE SPORTS CHAPELS—Never have so many given so much to so few. The Sunday Morning Touchdown Club, sometimes resembling a group shot from National Lampoon, indicates again that God has a sense of humor and that Jesus can use us both because of and despite ourselves.

This is the mushrooming aspect of the sport/faith movement whose genesis was a blessing but whose direction and emphasis must elicit concern about its dubious phases. Every pro football and baseball team has a weekly chapel. The pro golf and tennis tours have chapel. Hockey is honing in. "Let us pray" now echoes alongside "play ball!" The problem is, it is sometimes translated "let us prey."

The spotlight shines brightest here. And the sport gurus are out in number. Chapel is populated with the unique and zany characters of sport and faith—the Billy Zeolis, Tom Skinners, Ira Eshlemans, and others from ex-cons to seminary presidents have lined up at the locker room door. Not everyone can be the President's pastor but most anyone who works at it hard enough these days can be a pro athlete's buddy.

The most publicized and commercialized aspect of sport/faith, the chapels can become self-serving exercises in evangelizing the overevangelized. It is in the maturing trend toward Bible studies and one-on-one encounters that the wrestling with one's competitiveness and the deeper issues of being athletic and being Christian can take place. This is the heart and the hope. Beyond that, the chapels themselves and the ensuing locker room exploitation by athletes and the media of "I'm on God's team, I promise" are too often an embarrassment and a hypocritical mirage in the pro sport Sahara.

THE INSTITUTE FOR ATHLETIC PERFECTION—This is the "other" to whom it is left. Forget the presumptuous title. Salute the effort and cheer the results. The sole purpose of IAP is to help the participant become like Christ in his or her competing, a lofty expectation but certainly headed in the right direction. President Wes Neal left Athletes in Action, where his views were considered too cerebral and visionary and not integral to the AIA win concept. So he founded IAP and set up a training center in Arizona (P.O. Box 2021, Prescott, AZ 86301).

Now the desert near Prescott is alive with the sounds of competition. To this remote outpost come small groups of Christian competitors to receive training in how to actuate their faith/competitiveness in ways that are honoring to Christ and uplifting to the spirit of sport play and sport competition.

I have taken the IAP course. While it is flawed by oversimplification, I nonetheless endorse its serious approach to helping one understand and cope with the competitive drive as one strives to create, in IAP terms, a "Christian athlete's commitment": "In every athletic situation, whether practice or actual competition, I will dedicate myself to give a total release of all that I am— mentally, emotionally, and physically—to become just like Jesus. I will determine to conduct myself in a way that will please the Lord rather than gain any recognition from men."[2]

There is much to do in learning what it means to be

competitive and how the competitive drive exists in concert with the yearning to believe in a power beyond ourselves. And once we square up to our competitiveness and how it molds into our faith experience, to learn how this is adapted to our love for sport and all the issues, pressures, and forces which can operate to disrupt the joy and harmony that pure play and competition can bring.

The sport/faith ministries have labored faithfully and successfully in sharing the saving Jesus with the athletic community. Now they must consider the urgency and necessity of sharing the whole Jesus and not avoiding Christianity's implications in the competitive sport life. It is a sizeable challenge. But these groups are in the best position to take on the challenge. To ignore the opportunity, to negate the need, to miss the calling would land these groups on the current sports spectrum somewhere between disappointing and tragic.

THE SECOND MATTER

Several years and thousands of words ago this pilgrimage began with my personal odyssey through athletic play and competition. Who am I now? More competitive? Less competitive? More playful? More intense? What does the simple playing of a child's game mean to a man to whom the play of his childhood is becoming a blurred memory?

When Michael Novak depicts himself in his marvelous book *The Joy of Sports,* he also sketches my portrait— "How could I be forty years old and still care what happens to the Dodgers? . . . Is it time for sports to be discarded? Is it time to put away the things of childhood? Quietly, I knew the answer. . . . My love for sports was deeper than any theory I had. The reality is better than its intellectual defense. . . . But why? Why do I love sports? How can I explain it to myself, let alone to others, especially to those who are skeptical unbelievers? Sports is, somehow, a religion. You either see or don't see what the excitement is."[3]

Sports competition is such an integral part of me there could be no escaping it if I wanted to. I'll be running, throwing, and catching until all there is left to do is watch. And I'll be watching until all there is left to do is remember. And I'll be remembering until all there is left to do is pass into a life where, I have to believe, there will be more and better running, throwing, and catching than this life was meant to offer.

Sport is somehow intertwined in the roots of me. I have lived in Kansas City for over a dozen years. But I am no more a Kansas City Royals or Chiefs fan than the day I arrived. However, mention the Detroit Tigers or Lions, and my pulse quickens. Let the Tigers mount a modest winning streak. I await the score on the evening TV sports. I devour the box score next morning. With every Detroit win, life seems just a little better.

Why does it matter? I am not sure. But it does. Very much. The Detroit teams were "my teams" when a boy-child was awakening to the enchantment of sport. My competitive life was nurtured, in part, by my fascination with those teams. I came as child and man to be a competitor, my appetite whetted by the magnificence of sport, my heroes modeled for me, or so it seemed in my innocence.

So, to play. And to compete. As a Christian. Not to alibi away its importance, or to be ashamed of being a "jock" or a watcher and admirer of "jocks," or to exclude it from my life as a nonessential. It is essential to my completeness. I acknowledge the place of sport and competition as necessary fiber in my physical, mental, and spiritual muscle.

When asked if I enjoy writing, I sometimes echo the

response of fellow author Philip Yancey, "I like to have written." There were agonizing sessions with this book when the typewriter mocked me and prose poured as rapidly as cement through an eyedropper. I would day-dream of some riotous celebration when the last of these seemingly insurmountable writing "walls" had been scaled. Some of the fantasies were not affordable. Some not practical. A few not commendable.

And so I settled, one might imagine, on a silly thing. I competed. It was a why/because experience. And it further confirmed for me my deep love for sport and competition.

I had gone to a high school cross-country meet at the park where I had watched my daughter, Wendi, run for three years on her way to becoming the state champion. So many times I'd watched her perish and be reborn in the course of a two-mile run.

I floated through a sea of strangers. Now and then one would turn and offer, "Hello, how is Wendi?" But this was no longer her field of testing. Her place had been taken by other anxious girls, and mine had been taken by those who suffer and delight as onlookers of the testing.

One thing does not change: the sensation of what is to transpire, the competition, the intensity, the doing of a hard thing. Not just to run two miles, but to run it well. And to beat the clock. Beat the clock better than others. Maybe better than all the others.

I watched the girls. And the coaches. And the parents. And wished I could encompass the scene in the lens of a camera and freeze it with stop action and then walk through the statues and study what was on each mind at this moment nearing competition. To feel their expec-tancy and nervousness. To know the special relationships this form of communion was creating between parent and child, child and coach, child and teammate, child and

opponent. To make them promise me they would trea-
sure each moment and not take it for granted, for it is a
beautiful experience. I already felt like an outsider. A
loneliness clung to me.

I went back the next day, at twilight. I loosened up
behind the starting line. To jog two miles was easy; I run
two to four miles five times a week. But to run it well—to
bless the course and let it bless me—was quite another
thing.

The silence was delicious. My thoughts seemed to be
screaming so forcefully I glanced around, as if they
would reveal my intentions. The flag made a whipping
sound as it rode the breeze, and miles away the undercurrent of rush-hour traffic gave a presence to the grassy
hills. Dark, delicately patterned cirrocumulus clouds
rode high overhead, blotting the sun and muting the
colors on the dying leaves of October. I remembered
Wendi at these moments. It was so different for her. She
was occupied by a vortex of emotions. I wondered if she
ever felt so alone and so pure?

I imagined the crack of the starter's gun and broke
away, down a wide expanse to where it narrows into a
beaten path several yards wide and then points up a
gentle incline toward the pine trees at the perimeter of
the course. I ran easily, trying to establish a rhythm in my
breathing. Who would do a thing like this to celebrate a
book? I wondered if anyone would understand. If I had
to explain it to them, it really did not matter.

The course took a hairpin turn and returned me toward the start. Wendi would have the lead here. I would
watch her coming at me, eyes down on the path, legs
powerful in their proud and sure prancing, arms pump-
ing, the breathing controlled like a race horse under rein.
"You're looking good. Run, girl, run!" I would call, and
she would not look at me.

The course swung to the right, slightly downhill, and then sharply right into a long downhill. I lengthened my stride; I was flying. Too fast, I thought. Each thud sent shivers into my hips. A runner could fall. Or ram a leg up into his stomach. At the bottom of the chute I sprinted out and angled left toward a softball backstop that marked the western edge of the course.

Around the backstop and then right again up a short, steep hill. My breathing sounded more desperate than it actually was; my legs protested the activity but did not demand a halt. Across the flat terrain at the center of the course and past the one-mile mark. Toward the road, then another sharp right.

By this point Wendi and one or two other girls were always well into the lead. Her face would start to show the strain here. The eyes slightly glazed; the neck cords tightening. I remembered times her breath came in little gasps, like the muffled sounds of young lovers. My breath was coming in noisier inhalations as my lungs put out a Mayday for more oxygen. I dropped my hands and shook out my arms, trying to loosen my shoulders and neck. The temptation was to slow the pace. But instead, I passed a cornering tree, turned into a downhill straight-away and sped up, smiling at my ability to do so when my lungs warned against it and my abdomen was beginning to rip at the edges.

Into the steep downhill again. Somewhat cautiously this time. Wanting to save something for the long uphill ahead. Around the backstop. This was the point, with about a half mile to go and out of view of the spectators at the start/finish area, where races were won and lost. The feelings came back from those times I'd waited arduous, suspenseful seconds that seemed like hours as the competitors ran west to north out of sight. Finally, I would spot figures in the distant pines and try to distinguish running styles and uniform colors and length of hair until the forms broke into the stretch and became real people again.

Now I knew what Wendi had felt. The uphill was deceitful. It did not appear treacherous but ate at your strength over the long, long moments it took to conquer it, lasting for nearly a quarter mile.

I was hurting, aching all over, as they say, except for the parts that were numb. I had seldom attempted to run two cross-country miles this fast and with such nostalgia and emotion playing inside me. Worse yet, I was not alone. A high school cross-country team I had not noticed was running quarters up the hill. Boys and girls. They started ahead of me. I was relieved. I didn't know if I could pretend I was doing better than I was if I got too close.

Three of the runners—two boys and a girl—began to trail the team. I would catch them. I needed the incentive to escalate me up that hill. Besides, they were there and could be caught. I picked up my stride against the frantic admonitions of my legs and my mind.

Got one!

Got two! And feeling stronger.

Got three! Just as we neared the team. Had he slowed before I reached him? Don't believe so. I'm counting it.

Their coach spotted me. A man who looked like Ichabod Crane and thought of himself as Napoleon. I had listened to him berate runners for three years. He is the kind who ruins twenty kids in the process of making five exceptional. I did not like him.

"Hey, get out of the way. Give the runner room. Way to run, coach! Looking good!"

Looking good! Maybe he's not so bad after all. I ran past and did not look at him.

The pines admitted me. The edge of the course. The

edge of the world. I could lie down, or stop and walk away and no one would ever know. There was a county road department building across the fence. Surrounded by large piles of sand. And I had thought all the sand in the world was in my legs.

Out of the trees and into the stretch. The last 440. As far as I could see there was no movement, no one, just a long, worn path in the prairie grass pulling me along. The course ended atop a little indentation in the earth. That, surely, was the end of the world. I would run there and fall off and tumble deliriously, letting all the pain melt away.

Downhill to the edge. My stride was lengthening, although I could feel little from the waist down. I could hear the impact of my feet like a whisper from some distant past. The spit lay on my chin and it didn't seem important to brush it off. The flag was pointed my way, but it was a lie. The wind was so obviously at my back. Everything was at my back.

What had Wendi felt running here, the finish line, the applauding, cheering crowd in the distance? Holding the lead. Looking like some straining figure in a slow-motion dance. Three years of watching her and now finding out what it might have been like.

I was smiling and there were tears in my eyes. I was exhausted from the pace and the nostalgia, and yet feeling so totally in place. There was a part of me that wanted to fall into the earth and bury myself, tears and smiles, in her coolness and release all the joy and feeling sport had spent forty-two years building in me.

There were two hundred yards to go.

There was another part of me that wanted to keep running. Run the course again. Run all night. Run and never stop. Run for Wendi. Run for the child-me and the grown-me and the known-me and the secret-me.

WHERE IT MAKES A DIFFERENCE

There were one hundred yards to go.

I dropped my hands a last time and shook my arms, then slipped gears into the final sprint. There had been another race here. Two seniors who had competed against each other for several years. It was the National AAU Junior Olympic regionals. Easily the best, assured of qualifying, they had gone into the lead and run side by side, laughing and talking the entire way. In the last few yards they had put out their hands and run across the finish line in a dead heat with hands held high and broad grins on their faces.

A little ripple of joy caressed my spirit when I thought of that. It was one of the Lord's pleasant interludes. His special hugs of grace. I was reminded again why I competed and why I would always compete as an athlete. I was laughing out loud now, the only noise to be heard across that course as the tears and the sweat rolled down my face.

There were ten yards to go.

And I put out my hand.

Come compete with me.

SPORT/FAITH MOVEMENT ADDRESSES

FELLOWSHIP OF CHRISTIAN ATHLETES, 8701 Leeds Road, Kansas City, MO 64129
PRO ATHLETES OUTREACH, Box 15736, Phoeniz, AZ 85060
ATHLETES IN ACTION, Campus Crusade for Christ, 1451 E. Irvine Blvd., Suite 12, Tustin, CA 92680
SPORTS AMBASSADORS, Overseas Crusades, Box 66, Santa Clara, CA 95050
SPORT CHAPELS, Baseball Chapel, Inc., 4775 Cove Circle, No. 501, St. Petersburg, FL 33708

APPENDIX:
PERSPECTIVES ON
COMPETITION

KYLE ROTE, JR. . . .
THE PLAYER

The man behind me was obviously British and obviously quite lathered.

"Put Kyle in," he demanded. "You must get Kyle in there."

I questioned the imperative of substituting the injured Rote at this juncture.

"We must change our attack," he sighed, showing tolerance for a soccer neophyte as if explaining birds and bees without pictures. "We play an air game with Kyle because he is so strong; he dominates the goal area and can score with headers. Now we're playing a ground game and, as anyone can see, going no place.

"It shall be interesting," he persisted, stuffily, "to see how long we continue being stupid."

The Dallas Tornado, mired in a losing streak, was trailing lowly Colorado, 2-1, and in danger of missing the playoffs. The team's finest player, Kyle Rote, Jr. (traded to the Houston Hurricanes after the 1978 season), had torn up an ankle and had missed the last eight games, and there were only six more games to play in the season.

A scattering of fans freckled the bleachers, meaning thousands of Dallasites had successfully ignored T-Shirt Night. Some of the faithful surveyed the joggers on the adjacent track; others thought they recognized faces in the full moon and inhaled the aroma of bread from Mrs. Baird's downwind emporium.

The program, with three ads featuring Kyle, assured

us this was big league soccer. The ticket was six dollars, the parking was two dollars, and the Cokes were seventy-five cents—all in Lamar Hunt, big-league fashion. The bodies on the field had the dark-haired, sharp-featured look of immigrants and the squat, stocky, powerful bodies of soccer immigrants. The voices in the stands were of distant derivations. One took them for serious soccer afficionados, which explained their presence.

There was no mistaking the blond on the Tornado bench. Kyle Rote, Jr. Six feet, 180 pounds. Born Christmas Day, 1950. Born that day as a sign he was to be the savior of soccer in the United States, some would say— "The Great White Hope" as he became known in 1973 when he was NASL Rookie of the Year and the league's first American scoring champion.

Kyle Rote, Jr.—America's All-American all-American. Certainly every mother's son. Apple pie and Chevrolet garbed in Episcopalian robe. The superstar of Superstars. A three-time champion. Son of Kyle Rote, Sr., one of Texas's all-time sports greats.

Then "Hope" was beckoned. The crowd did not notice. But then, no one cheered Casey until he got to home plate.

"Hope" ran up and down the sidelines. Ran like the classic athlete. Arms rhythmically washing his chest. Little pitty-pat steps elopers use crossing the front lawn or religious fanatics employ tippy-toeing through hot coals. But it is the legs you notice. Heavy in the thighs. The base from which the pendulum of his athletic balance and agility swings. Two bombs packaged between knee cap and hip joint waiting to be detonated.

With 17:15 remaining, Kyle was announced as a candidate for competition. Hope springs eternal. The Tornado would be all right now.

He had come barefoot to the door that morning in blue shorts and white T-shirt. As always, the smile, revealing a formidable exposure of front teeth. He is twenty-eight but may always look twenty. He flopped back on the time-worn couch. He had awakened with a temperature to accompany the disturbed ankle and, since there was a game that night, he drank juice all day long, except when his wife, Mary Lynne, was dropping a thermometer into his mouth. The phone rang. Six rings and it gave up.

"I'm intrigued by your study of competition," he said. "We Christians seem to open the easy parts to Jesus. Some athletes and coaches are like the straight guy who slips into the closet for a shot of booze. We go to the closet to compete; it's our escape. It's too difficult to give that to Jesus.

"When I think of athletic competition it evokes three phrases. First, equality of opportunity. There is a set of common, accepted rules. Everyone begins equally. Second, self-determination. We can pretty much determine our own fate. Third, framework of growth. Sport competition can be a yardstick to measure yourself, a grounds on which to test your attitudes and beliefs."

Kyle entered the testing beneath the banner of a famous name. His father, Kyle Rote, Sr., of SMU and New York Giants football fame, was not present at his birth, the Hula Bowl in Hawaii taking precedent. The Rotes moved to New York the next football season. Kyle, Jr., lived in a hotel and played games on the streets of the Bronx near Yankee Stadium before the family moved to the plush suburbs of Westchester several years later.

Everyone in his neighborhood dreamed of being Mickey Mantle or Willie Mays. Sport was fun. This fun aspect was innate with him, Kyle feels, but his competitive models were serious, and he learned, perhaps too well, the serious side of competition.

APPENDIXES

"I expect, in a sense, that sport is a miniature of life," Kyle reflected, "but not as much so as some think. Sport competition is basically fair; life isn't. The public eye on sport is a primary modifier of behavior. Athletes complete their actions to meet the expectations of the coach, the officials, the opponent, their teammates, and the crowd. In life there is less pressure to do this. You're not being watched and graded."

Life is not always fair. Kyle's parents divorced when he was twelve. His mother moved back to Dallas, a paralegal secretary by day and SMU student by night. Kyle, the oldest, assumed the father role for brothers Gary and Chris and sister Elizabeth.

He was a storied athlete at Highland Park High School. He entered Oklahoma State on a football scholarship and was a much-sought baseball prospect. A year at OSU was enough. Kyle found the athletic dorm and football factory atmosphere restrictive and isolated from reality.

He had picked up soccer as a high-school summer conditioner. Several friends advocated the University of the South in Sewanee, Tennessee. Kyle transferred. It was love at first kick. He became a soccer standout, delved deeply into books and campus life, and met Mary Lynne, a strong, emotive, fundamental Christian from Georgia who balanced his pragmatic, high church approach. They were married the day after graduation in 1972.

Returning to Dallas, he spent a year in law school, then entered Perkins School of Theology at SMU. But soccer and Superstars soon consumed his time. He turned down several NFL and WFL offers to join the Tornado. He earned $1,400 his first season. Mary Lynne worked so Kyle could be a professional athlete.

He has a genuine affection for soccer as a children's game and a family recreation. The figures gush from soccer's roving Chamber of Commerce: "I grew up the typical American sports isolationist. . . . Soccer is the world's game, played in more countries (142 to 134) than there are countries in the United Nations. . . . It is the world's cultural common denominator. . . . If the command of the Gospels is to take the message of Jesus to the whole world, there is no better vehicle than soccer."

The vehicle that took Kyle to the whole world was Superstars. He entered four times, winning three times and finishing third the other year. He will not enter again. He has accomplished all there is to accomplish and, as he says, "ad infinitum becomes ad nauseum." And the promoters are happy. The first several times it was nice to see the underdog conquer. But niceness wears on the ratings. Kyle was too good, too bland. The TV network and sponsors wanted a personality hero.

I was reminded of a conversation with a movie producer who had interviewed Kyle in hopes of making a movie on him. "I dunno," the man shook his head. "You know what he and his wife do for excitement? They ride their bicycles around the block. I'm afraid the film will be, well, dull."

He made the film. Depending on how you define "dull" and "exciting," it could be either.

"I was fortunate to get in Superstars," Kyle recalled. "They needed a soccer property. I was coming off my good 1973 season, had the Rote name, which gave me visibility in New York, and was the blue-eyed, blond-haired stereotype they wanted.

"But I approached this competition differently than the others. I took it seriously. I was representing soccer, I liked the challenge of the multiplicity of sports, and I wanted to represent myself, my family, and the Lord well."

As only a competitor the likes of Rote would do, Kyle

picked his seven required sports from the possible ten and then checked out fifty-six books from a Dallas library to bone up. He sought coaches to train him in each of the sports. He trained by the hour, the week, the month. One of his strongest competitive strengths is admitting to deficiency and seeking help from those more skilled. His first year in pro soccer he sought players whose skills paralleled his weaknesses and had them drill him until he was proficient.

The first day of Superstar competition the superb Austrian downhill skier Karl Schranz said, "I know all zese guys except zis Juneeor. Who ees zis Rrrowt Juneeor?"[1] But it was all uphill for Schranz and the others. Perfectly tuned, Rote ran away with the title and gave $5,000 of his winnings to Special Olympics. The next several years the other entrants also began preparing as the money and the prestige soared. But Kyle was always the man to beat.

"I wanted to get out of Superstars before I got addicted to the fame and the money," Kyle said. "Its real importance was how it helped my relationship with God and with people. I enjoyed the Christian fellowship with such men as John Havlicek and Stan Smith. But I am primarily selfish as a competitor. I want sports competition that will uplift me spiritually. If it doesn't, and I felt Superstars was beginning not to, it's time for other things.

"Sport competition is not the ultimate thrill for me. I was interviewed after Superstars and the reporter said I was the least excited champion he had ever seen. That was true. My competing is based on preparation, not psyching or adrenalin.

"Had I finished forty-eighth out of forty-eight in the Superstars and yet performed to what I felt was my potential, I would have been satisfied. Not many people understand this, but I had made my peace with the competition before it began. Winning is a standard in competition; we need to win at times. But it is only one standard among many, including the rate of improvement and attaining our current potential.

"I really love sports for what they are—fun and a way to establish relationships. Winning the NASL championship, for example, would not be a big thrill for me. But I'll tell you what is: God entering into the circumstances of my life. I'm injured. OK, no sense getting uptight about that. It's a hazard of the athletic vocation. But during my rehabilitation I have been running to strengthen my ankle. And our equipment manager, John Myers, has been running with me. We have become friends. And we have talked a lot about Jesus. John has a lot of questions.

"I believe Romans 8: 28. I believe there is a reason why John is running with me. I could enter the game tonight and score a goal and we could win. But what does that mean compared to the eternal importance of talking with a friend about the Lord?"

Mary Lynne called time-out for lunch—sandwiches and soft drinks while William Kyle III scampered about the floor. He has the Rote legs. But the speed of a one year old is not measured in forty-yard time. He can make it from the kitchen to the basement steps in "the time it takes to pour a Coke," said Mary Lynne. His speed appears adequate.

Kyle had his temperature taken again and more juice was poured down him. Mary Lynne excused herself to run errands, and Kyle and I picked up again while chasing Will across the hardwood floor. What sort of faith experience would father be sharing with son?

"I went through three stages," he said. "My boyhood faith was fire insurance. God was then a God of nature and of justice. Good will eventually gets its due and, in the eternal answer to evil, evil will eventually turn on itself.

"In high school I started going to Young Life. At a summer camp in Colorado when I was sixteen, I saw the love of Christians. But because of my nature I couldn't take the blind leap of faith. I told God, quite practically, that he could show me he was real, and I would inspect it and determine then whether or not to believe and follow.

"Since then I would describe my faith as a constancy of growth. I have seen my personality, my outlook, my attitudes change. I attribute that to the reality of God. I even tried to quit playing dictator with my brothers and sister. God became a God of love as well as justice.

"The third phase has come after our marriage. Mary Lynne has been a strong influence on me. I have been opened to the Holy Spirit, the constant, powerful companion. The second stage brought me a more personal God, and the third stage has revealed the God in me."

Kyle is a celebrity Christian and faces all the pressures of a public Christian. In constant demand to speak and share, he has found ways of coping. He seldom gives a testimony; instead he will speak about social issues or world needs.

"I may mention Federal spending and how much we spend for recreation in comparison with how much we spend on philanthropy," he said. "Or I may wonder out loud how we can know the heartbeat to the thousandth of a second of a guy on the moon and not know the hunger of people in Alabama."

Yet he finds the typical listener would rather discuss such deep issues as "what is O. J. Simpson really like?" He understands, but it disturbs him. It has forced him to wonder when one reaches that balance of witness on one hand and self-improvement and personal spiritual development on the other. He is learning to say no and to feed himself in his faith experience—through a weekly Cursillo fellowship with eight other men, through a pro athletes Bible study, through his church, Saint Albans of Canterbury on the SMU campus, through his times of reading and quiet prayer—even with the phone ringing and Will exploring.

The base for the superstar's serious spiritual nature is a mother's legacy. One can see in his eyes the separation—like water and oil—of present peace and pain from the past when the subject is broached.

"Mother is in a San Antonio nursing home," he explained. "In 1973, she developed an aneurysm when a blood vessel broke in her brain. She is paralyzed on one side and must use a wheelchair. She had remarried just before her stroke.

"When she became physically disabled, he took off," he said. There was anger in the slow, even pace of his words.

"She has every right to be bitter. Losing two husbands. Her first husband remarried and is making a good living in the city she enjoyed. She is only in her fifties but in a wheelchair. Yet she is closer to God than ever before. She is a counselor and speech therapist in the home and has a strong Christian influence. She feels God will honor her faith. He has."

Will was demanding a little action. I suggested a tour of the house. Before the Rotes bought it, it was a home for unwed mothers. We meandered along, through sliding doors, up winding stairways.

In one room hangs a picture of great-great-grandfather Rote, the first mayor of San Antonio. The Rote name parallels the growth of Texas. Yet there was a fresh gouge in grandpa's forehead, as if he had been ambushed only that morning.

Scattered through the rooms were memorabilia of his father—blankets from SMU, pictures of senior and junior. Dad's face is stern in comparison to son's, and when there is a smile, the eyes narrow . . . the intense look of the competitor. Had he been in Superstars, according to junior, he would have won.

"My father never played catch with me," Kyle stated. "He never saw me play in high school until my final football game. At meals before the divorce he would ask about my studies, my music lessons, and, occasionally, as if it were an afterthought, about sports. I got no recognition in the home for being an athlete. Dad did not want to force the pressure of his name on me. He'd seen parents ruining their children in the name of sport. He went to the opposite extreme.

"I knew what the Rote name meant. I did not want to appear on page 1 of the *New York Times* for lighting a firecracker in school. I narrowed my behavior and put my emotions in check.

"I see dad's reasons now and I understand, partially. I didn't understand at all as a boy. Dad and I are fairly close now, but we weren't when I was a teenager. He was in New York; I was in Dallas. We just didn't run across each other much.

"I missed the normal father/son relationship. I'll have to determine how to handle Will's introduction to competition. I hope we can at least play catch."

He cradled Will and we walked onto one of the balconies.

"The problem with being Kyle Rote, Jr.," he said, "is that you miss the highs and lows of life. I don't lose my temper; I never yell. Lynne gets frustrated; she wants to fight and I just stay calm.

"But I miss a lot from competition that way. I don't seek failure, but I'm not destroyed by it; winning does not mean that much; and I seldom push beyond the limit of what solid preparation can take me to. I'd rather use my body to commune with God, corny as that sounds. The highs of sport are the fellowship and the giving to each other, the coordination of separate wills and abilities that brings team progress."

I studied him. Here stood, to many, the epitome of the all-around athlete. Yet the contradictions. Where is the killer instinct such a champion is supposed to have, according to American folklore? And if emotion is not the critical factor, where is the cold, polished, menacing, impersonal callousness of the hired gunslinger who can dispatch a challenger without an emotional twinge? Somewhere between lies Kyle Rote, Jr. Maybe at the point where competitiveness and grace intersect.

"Pride and ego have never overwhelmed me," he said, "because I do not equate athletic success with personal worth. This is the great danger of competition for kids. They begin to think if they do not succeed in sports, they are failures as people. My opponent, whether the best player or the worst, still has the same eternal worth. It is as important for me to witness to the ball boy as to the owner. We are only special because God says we are special.

"My primary competition is always with myself. If I play the twelve year old down the street, I'll handicap myself by, say, only dribbling lefthanded. If he wins, I'm tickled to death. I can applaud any opponent's good play and not lose my intensity. Competition is a means to get to know yourself and your opponent and develop a relationship. You can learn to face failure and not deny it, to face success and not worship it.

"Perhaps I miss out because I don't have killer instinct. I will play intensely against someone who can accept defeat and come back with grace and intensity at me the next time. If I play someone who cannot handle losing, I will let up and perhaps not play him in the future. I guess I look for the same maturity in my opponent that I like to believe is in my competitive makeup."

In the maze of rooms and clutter, there was something missing. But what? It occurred to me: trophies. There were no trophies. "Oh, there are," said Kyle, "someplace. In boxes, I guess. Dad had lots of trophies. All trophies do is remind you of what used to be and can no longer be."

And Kyle lives in the now and plans for the future. As another element of his practicality, he and Lynne have saved enough money that they could take two years off after pro soccer for law school or seminary or whatever Kyle feels is next.

Kyle has already achieved a stardom few people get near in a lifetime. And he has a lifetime ahead. Walking around the house, he pointed out "Will's tree," barely taller than a yardstick, that will "grow along with our son."

"One of the challenges I want to take on," said Kyle, "is to run a marathon. And I'd like to shoot par golf. (He has run thirteen miles and his best golf score is high seventies.) Just to see if I can accomplish it. The good thing about competition is that it gives me feedback on myself. Not on performance but on attitude.

"My other goal is to actualize 1 Timothy 4: 7-10. I want to transfer my commitment as an athlete to my spiritual outreach."

Kyle lives by the clock. It was 4 P.M. Time for a light training meal and a nap, more juice, and one more thermometer.

And he was living by the clock again five hours later. With 17: 15 to play, the moon spectating from the balcony, Mrs. Baird's fragrance moistening the air.

The crowd applauded when Kyle went into the game. Kyle is suited to soccer. It fits his competitive temperament almost perfectly. While casual sports fans appreciate the touchdown pass, the home run, the overhead smash, the goal scored, the 300-yard drive, true devotees appreciate the flow of a game, its inner majesty, its intricate patterns and teamwork, its subtle variances and ploys and deceptions.

Soccer is a game of cat and mouse, of wait to strike. The beauty is the little contests within the grand design: the confrontation of attacker by defender, the deft footwork, the intermittent bursts of speed, the penetrating and the preventing.

Kyle prowled restlessly in front of the goal area, waiting for a pass, looking for the opportunity to head a shot, trying to make an opening. His defender shadowed his every step as Kyle pivoted, spun, darted in, and then retreated. It was Kyle's life-style in miniature—to plan, to work, to discipline moves for eighty-five of the ninety-minute soccer time limit and then score in the last five minutes for a very satisfying 1-0 win.

But the competition and its meaning are not in the scoring and the winning of the five minutes but in the preparation and the relationship to your opponent and your teammates and the crowd and the night of the eighty-five minutes.

However, there would be no Tornado victory despite the quickening, desperate attacks of the Dallas team. Kyle did not have opportunity for a good shot and in the last forty-four seconds, Colorado put together a rush against the trapped-up Tornado defense and slammed the clinching goal past the sprawling Dallas goalie Ken Cooper.

When the final gun sounded, several opponents rushed to Kyle to shake his hand and welcome him back. He chatted amiably with the Colorado players and then walked off the field with his arm around Cooper. In the brief write-up in the Dallas paper the next morning, the Tornado coach blasted his team's play. There was no mention of Rote, only the inference that it was all over for the Tornado this season.

But the season is never over for Kyle. He was set to run with Johnny Myers and continue their conversation about Jesus. And Will had to be watched and loved. And there was another project in the house to initiate. And the Bible study for the week looked interesting. Then there was the postseason trip to plan for. And several speaking engagements. And calling mother in San Antonio. And a basketball game with a twelve year old.

There are many ways to be a competitive superstar. Some ways seem to be better than others.

DR. WILLIAM BEAUSAY...
THE SPORTS
PSYCHOLOGIST

We sophisticates from southern Michigan have historically assessed Toledo as "The City of B's"—a bleached blond with a bottle of beer in a bowling alley—feeling this most appropriately describes the northern Ohio populace. Then, thanks to John Denver's demoralization in song, Toledo officially moved into the standup comic competition with Peoria and Newark as the ever-disputed armpit of the nation.

However, having grown up only thirty-five neighborly miles northwest, I'd been quite comfortable in this industrial city in the middle of the fertile Michigan-Ohio truck and grain-farming belt. Until now. Until driving from the Toledo airport to Perrysburg, the bedroom suburb on the Maumee River, to visit sport psychologist Dr. William Beausay.

I felt somewhat intimidated. I am leery of the "gists." Archaeologists dig in the earth, which seems harmless and almost playful, but sociologists, physiologists, neurologists, psychologists, and other "gists" dig inside people, which makes me queasy. I am not exactly sure what they dig for or why. I only know for certain that a psychologist's degree and forty cents will get you a cup of coffee. Our educational mills are grinding out more "gists" than lawyers, and whoever digs deepest survives. It is unsettling.

I'd met Dr. Beausay on the pages of *Sports Illustrated*. The chilling headline read, "Winning One for the Ripper."[1] There he was—balding, mustached, eyes glowering, fronting a computer and holding what appeared to be an electronic torture instrument over a plastic replica of the human brain. My brain? Would this Rasputin-looking explorer of the mind want to determine what, if anything, made me tick?

I read the article. The second mistake. The good doctor had once punched a Toronto Argonaut center in the mouth to raise his hostility quotient.

In another situation with a New Orleans Saints kicking specialist who scored low on hostility, he discovered the passive punter went berserk when pinched. Just before the punter entered the game an assistant coach would give him a sharp, painful pinch on the bicep. I wondered what this modern Dr. Frankenstein would do to me.

But his credentials are so impressive it was worth the chance. What a triple-threat! How many people can analyze you, perform your wedding, and pull your teeth in the same day?

Bill has his B.A. in psychology, his M.A. in counseling, his doctorate in administration, and is an ordained minister in the Church of Christ. He has graduated from Messiah College, Ohio State University, Bowling Green State University, and Dallas Theological Seminary. At Ohio State, in his spare time, he also became a Certified Dental Technologist. (Another "gist"!) He has a private psychology and counseling practice, teaches at Bowling Green, is personal consultant to business and institutions, and can take to the pulpit when called on.

He is president of the Academy for the Psychology of Sports International. He has been described as a "snoop who prowls the sports scene with his meddlesome 180-part quizzes, computer printout codes, and charts and graphs . . . drilling, quizzing, and searching souls."[2]

He has conducted psychological tests on (1) pro football's Eagles, Bears, Redskins, Browns, Saints, and Bengals; (2) Detroit Pistons and NBA referees; (3) college football and basketball teams; (4) Indianapolis 500 drivers; (5) the United States Olympic Rifle Team in preparation for the 1980 Games; and (6) the American Motorcycle Association.

I had quoted Dr. Beausay in a magazine article on sport and psychology. It was the kind of thing one hears from the spotlighted sports psychologists, Thomas Tutko and Bruce Ogilvie: race drivers are hostile, dominating, uncontrolled, insensitive, nervous, withdrawn, self-absorbed, and depressed; linebackers and defensive linemen are just like race drivers—only more so; quarterbacks made the best companions because they are extreme perfectionists, cool, light-hearted, compassionate, and self-disciplined; and the best bet is the long distance runner who is passive, tolerant, compliant, and more self-disciplined than the quarterback.[3]

A letter followed from the doctor: "What the article did not say is that I am a born-again believer and follower of Christ. What's more, I've found in my studies with the top professionals of every major sport that the spiritual dimension contains a powerful potential force for super performance."

It was Dr. Beausay's relationship in the early 1960s with now evangelist-then Detroit Lions/Cleveland Browns defensive end Bill Glass that had initiated his sport psychology interest. To get Glass "up" for his quarterback marauding, Beausay had introduced him to autosuggestion—a repetitive process involving command words Beausay termed "super psyching." Glass was successful and began regularly popping this psychological pep pill.

"It was incredible," Beausay told *Sports Illustrated*. "Bill Glass, a completely warm, outgoing and friendly guy . . .

played like a carefully programmed machine. It really got me interested in the psychology of sports, especially when I discovered that little testing had been done on athletes."[4]

It was dark and rainy that Sunday in October when I drove across the Maumee River and entered Perrysburg. There was nothing apocalyptic about the house, a wandering frame ranch in a shaded middle-class neighborhood. The doorbell had a peaceful sound, not the ominous bass clap I'd anticipated. There was no rumble of footsteps, just a rustling, and no one bellowed "fe, fi, fo, fum."

The woman—Milane or Millie—one of those sweet ladies who comes across as everyone's mother, dispelled my anxieties. A wisp of a person with melting eyes, she met Bill at Messiah College, keeps the house in Early American with candles trimmed and the fireplace on alert whenever temperatures plummet, and works in a hospital with crippled children.

Bill Beausay is a large man—six feet two inches, 215 pounds—with unruly patches of speckled gray hair jockeying for position around his head; but he resembles an accommodating overstuffed couch more than the Jack-chasing, bean stalk-descending giant of my imagination. We retired to one of many quiet little nooks, and he talked about his trade and his sport avocation.

"The Indianapolis 500 in 1968 was my first major test ground," he said. "Astronaut Neil Armstrong gave me some tips on personality tests used by NASA. I combined parts of this with the Taylor-Johnson Temperament Analysis Profile into a 180-question test.

"Tutko and Ogilvie, in my estimation, aligned themselves too closely with coaches and owners. My purpose was simply to help the individual athlete improve performance through knowledge of his own psychology.

What goes into making a superathlete is an overlooked and highly valuable subject for study.

"We are in the Dark Ages of athletic excellence. Giving 100 percent is one of the great myths of competition. The human organism is adept at self-delusion. We never give our best; we don't come close to our potential.

"The ethics of our profession do not allow psychologists to advertise. I believe, however, that every pro team will one day have a staff sport psychologist. We offer testing and bio-feedback. We can perform hypno-analysis. It's amazing what people can perform under hypnosis.

"I worked with a jet pilot who had flown fighters in Vietnam. He was certain he performed better under pressure. I said if he did, it was a learned procedure, and I showed him through instrumentation that we all deteriorate in stress. It is perfectly normal for people not to compete well under pressure.

"You've heard of having 'cold feet' on a date. In sports competition we get cold feet and hands. Under stress, the blood centers in our visceral organs, our body temperature drops, and our appendages get cold, stiff, and immobile. The psychologist can teach athletes how to relax under competitive pressure, how to keep the skin temperature up, and keep the blood circulating to the extremities.

"One day you'll see the 100-yard dash run in 7.5 seconds, and we could help take ten seconds off the mile record right now. It will happen."

I asked him about the competitive instinct. And learned to watch my semantics.

"Ah!" he frowned. "That word *instinct* is a bad word to the psychologist. We'd better define our terms.

"I believe there is a survival apparatus that is inherent and genetic. Hold a baby by its feet and it will struggle to right itself. The baby knows this position is abnormal; his world has been disoriented.

"We will become aggressive for spiritual survival, physical survival, and psychological survival, in that order. There is a human drive for self-preservation. One fights not to be canceled out or destroyed. But in sports, business, or whatever, competition is a cultural development and has nothing to do with self-preservation "

He defines competition from the core of his personal beliefs.

"The Bible says to grow in grace and knowledge of the truth and to admonish each other when we're with the brothers and sisters," he said. "The apostle Paul's writing in 1 Corinthians 9:24-27 is the classic statement on competition. He fought hard; he did not fool around.

"When we're in competition we both have the chance to come away better men. Now, this causes some Christians a problem. I've heard ministers say trying to beat someone is not Christian. They are confusing competition with hostility. I believe not trying to beat someone, when that is the framework and understanding of the situation, is un-Christian. If I lose and my opponent and I can talk it over and I can grow from it, I am better. If he wins and feels he is better and I am a 'loser,' then he is replacing healthy competitiveness with hostility."

In a sense, the issue of hostility prompted a textbook response. However, for Dr. Beausay, it is also a matter of vivid and painful personal experience.

His grandfather, a lawyer, died when Bill's father was only two. Bill's dad was a high school dropout, of necessity, finding work in the post office. The family grew up at 28 Main Street in Upper Sandusky, Ohio—Bill, his sister, and a year younger brother who died when Bill was seven years old.

Bill was always large for his grade and age. And he was

poor. School was no fun and certain days were traumatic. On opening day the teacher would ask for addresses. Everyone knew 28 Main was downtown. Kids would call out neat addresses, like 1424 River Road, and Bill would give anything to live there. On "shoe day" an agency donated shoes for children who needed them. Bill already wore a man's shoe. His name would be called in class, and he would go get his shoes. Everyone knew he lived at 28 Main Street and needed shoes—to go with the clothes his mother made for him.

He did not go to parties; was not invited to class activities. But he was fast for his size. And sports was his salvation. A race to him was not just a race; it was life. When he was a sophomore, the football team was ranked eighth in the state. He played three years on teams with 10-0, 9-1, and 8-2 records. His senior year he was an All-State halfback. Every time he carried the ball he was saying he was as good as anyone else. He got his strokes from competitive sport. The "shoe boy" was worth something.

"Sports got me college," he said. "Without sports competition, we wouldn't be talking now."

He had some papers and equipment at his office he wanted me to see. We climbed in his car and headed back across the Maumee. A football game was on the radio— Browns and Bears. He caught the score and then turned it off. I questioned his lack of interest.

"There are three categories of sport," he said. "Leisure and recreation, which is not competitive; competitive sport, which has the capacity to make us better people; and pro sports or the business level. In analyzing the pros, I have too often felt business sport to be turning out worse people.

"The only clear conflict between competition and my faith involves either kid's play or the pros. Certain man-

329

ifestations of competition at the pro level are immoral. One pro team I worked with had pills by the water fountain, bottled and labeled, regardless of what Pete Rozelle may report. That's immoral.

"And I'm appalled at the treatment of injuries. There is 'morbid pain,' like arthritis—pain that has no function other than to make us miserable. We can alleviate that through hypnosis. But most pain is a signal that bodily wrongs need righting. When teams approve injections to deaden pain—inviting serious complications—that's immoral and dangerous."

His office was a letdown. Is this where a man of degrees, a master of the mind, functions? A square, concrete building painted brown. He busied himself while I browsed the endless bookshelves. There was a major section devoted to children.

"Ah!" he began again. "Kid sports is a book in itself. I don't believe competitive sport has any place in the development of a child before age thirteen. All children need a series of happy, victorious experiences. The normal defeats will come in the routine give-and-take of their own play. But they must learn to succeed before they can accept defeat. After thirteen, they then must be defeated to instigate further growth."

A half skull lay on his desk. Inside was the plastic brain, like a jigsaw puzzle with different colored pieces. I fingered it, trying to imagine this in my head. His head, maybe. I pictured my brain smaller, perhaps only one colored piece.

He loaded my briefcase with data, statistics, graphs, charts—everything you've always wanted to know about the mind and forgot to ask. I asked him about competition in terms of winning and losing.

"There's nothing worse than an athlete who has never lost," he said. "Being defeated is healthy. Winning and losing is the opportunity to teach or be taught. The danger is when one attaches superiority or inferiority to the result of competition.

"This is especially true for Christians. We all need certain basics—love, security, and to compete against each other's excellence. We have the responsibility to help each other be the best child of God we can be. So when you and I compete athletically, I have a Christian responsibility to you to compete against you and try to beat you and inspire you to be the best person you can be. You owe it to another to not only do your best but to beat him.

"Competition is resistance. My jet pilot friend learned to perform better when he faced the resistance of stress and pressure. Winning and losing in the competitive milieu is a matter of growth. The essence of competition should be growth, not results. And one cannot grow without resistance.

"We need to be beaten. We view life too self-centeredly. In a Christian setting, my brother's responsibility is to help me excel. This means growth, which means competition, which means losing and growing from it.

"Jesus was a magnificent competitor. And he always taught while competing. What appeared to be defeats were matters of growth on his way to ultimate victory. I get excited reading the Bible. I feel like a cheerleader for Jesus, because he was always competing.

"Jesus competed against himself. The Greek word *agon* means stadium or place of meeting. *Agon* became *agonia,* which means to strive, to struggle. When Jesus sweat drops of blood in Gethsemane, the word used was *agonia.* He was agonizing, struggling, actually competing against himself. I believe Jesus wants us to go through that."

Would Bill ever let up to let someone else win? I interrupted.

"No, not if the stated purpose of our play is competition. I taught my son Jeff to play chess when he was five. I told him he'd never win a game, and after each game I'd show him what he had done wrong. He knew what to expect. He kept losing and learning, and one day he beat me. It was not a sign he was better than I. It was a sign of growth. He then went over the game and showed me the mistakes I had made!"

Well, then, you believe everyone should compete?

"Yes. If we don't, we miss the chance to come nearer our potential. Even when pushed most people don't come close to their potential, but competition gives us the opportunity to get closer."

But what if a person does not want to compete or simply tires of it?

"I went to the dentist last week. He asked how many times I brush my teeth each day. I said once. He said three times should be a minimum for healthy teeth. I want healthy teeth but not *that* healthy. So I still brush once. If I sneeze someday and my teeth fly out, it's a choice I have made. The parallel applies to competition.

"Competition is not some enzyme. Competitiveness is only a means to an end. In my theology of competition that end is to become a worthy, acceptable child of God. To become a better person and more like Jesus. Now, most people are not competitive. This is why TV sports is such a phenomenon. Maybe 2 percent of us are competitive; the other 98 percent are passive. Most people want a paycheck and to let others do the thinking and creating. Athletes, in general, are your most competitive individuals.

"People may choose leisure or recreational play. When a friend and I play racquetball, we agree on the rules ahead of time. We'll say today is for fun or today may be for the Super Bowl of the universe. We know how to play and what to expect. Recreational sports are OK—the Scripture approves of 'fun sports'—but they are selfish. They help no one but you and they help you only get some exercise or to relax; they do not help you improve your skills or potential.

"We will compete to survive. Beyond that, one can exist in this world and opt not to compete culturally, socially, or athletically. But this does not, must not, apply spiritually to the Christian. This is Satan's system. We are in conflict and must compete spiritually to survive spiritually, to grow, to initiate change. Look at the Beatitudes. They are all about being defeated and coming back.

"You know how Jesus might have been stopped? If Caiaphas and others had ignored him. But the leaders created a dogfight. And the Christian ought to love a dogfight."

Dinner was pleasantly mellow in the rush-hour atmosphere. The fireplace and candles did their thing, and the food looked delicious in the fluttering light. The phone rang constantly; kids came and went; cars drove in and backed out. But Bill and Millie were content on the eve of another full week.

"Kids," Bill smiled. "They know so much—and have so much to learn. I had four football scholarship offers out of high school—Minnesota, Ohio State, UCLA, and Northwestern. But my girl friend was going to Bowling Green. So I tagged along. What a mistake, but what does a kid know? I tried out for football as a walk-on. My equipment was thin and tacky. Boy, it hurt when I got hit.

"I laid out a year to work. Then I transferred to Ohio State in Woody Hayes's first year. I got the tacky equipment again and knew I didn't have a chance. I damaged my knee in a scrimmage and had to quit. They took my book card. That hurt the most. They could have let me keep my book card.

"By that time I'd had a taste of college and liked it. I worked every day of every year I went to put myself through. Sports got me to college, and I learned the degrees were worth fighting for even when the sports ran out."

I was interested in his breadth of interest, especially his ordination.

"I grew up in a Christian home, as they say, but it was not a part of my life," he said. "It was all part of being poor and feeling inferior. We went to a storefront church, one more reason the kids could call me a kook. I hated it. It was terribly embarrassing. I never talked about religion.

"But after years of dealing with the mind and what makes us function, it was obvious that the Christian faith has merit. I ask people in my church, 'Do you really believe that you are a fabulous person because of what God has done for you?' And this is not the self-hypnosis of positive thinking. It's that Jesus Christ died to make us something special.

"God has destined us to be super people. Anything I can do, God and I can do better. And competition is a part of this process. We can't come close to being God's super people without it."

And how can a passive Christian become competitive?

"The motivation should be to become the best child of God we can become. If that doesn't motivate someone, I'm not sure anything will.

"When we are motivated, we compete. Competition is not just a small part of being God's special people. It is necessary . . . necessary."

PATSY NEAL . . .
THE WOMAN

I know that many men
  live their lives
      in twilight zones—
Walking through the darkened portions
    of being without once
        touching
          upon the stream of caring and daring,
Tiptoeing where
  only running would be sufficient,
    Whispering where
      only shouts would carry the void,
        Flinching where
          only supreme daring would win
            the right to live.

The note was terse: "Come to the courts; there's someone I want you to meet."

The expansive two-court pavilion at the YMCA camp in North Carolina was deserted except for two figures. The echoing *thump-thump* of a basketball was a prelude to the tableau of these figures gesturing and laughing while lazily arching shots at the wooden backboard.

The six-foot-nine, slightly stooped frame—like some contorting windmill when he hooked right or left—was easily distinguishable as FCA colleague LeRoy King. The second was about six feet, lithe, sprightly, smooth and sure in its movements. And different from anything I had seen on that court—it was a woman.

"Meet Patsy Neal," LeRoy said. "She teaches down the road at Brevard College. And she's a basketball player."

Her eyes were a light, shimmery blue; her hair conveniently cropped. Her handshake was firm yet not emasculating; her manner unpretentious yet not barren. She was traveling somewhere, I figured, between country and cosmopolitan.

Her diction was Appalachia—a shot was "unspired"; she wanted to try "anotha"—and when there was space to fill in the conversation, she would dribble away to a world of stutter-step, fake, and shoot that she was more comfortable in.

"How about a game of HORSE?" LeRoy suggested.

I was to follow Patsy. Simple enough. Sure! I was in each game a matter of minutes. She did not bounce the ball, she caressed it to the concrete. She lofted hooks right and left, jump shots, set shots, reverse layups. Seldom did her radar shots touch the rim. I just waited for the swish and trotted to the spot from which she had shot. And with every swish there was an apology—"I'm sure lucky today." "My gracious, I never make that shot." "Gosh, why couldn't I do that when it counted?" "You're just a little rusty, that's all." I kept expecting her to eventually polish me off with a two-hand reverse slam dunk.

LeRoy wore an impish look when I remembered I had an appointment. I told Patsy it had been fun, and she wished I had time for "anotha." I was relieved to see there was no one else around the pavilion. Now if LeRoy would only keep his mouth shut.

That was 1967. Ten years later I watched a hundred women coaches and players file into the gym at Rockhurst College in Kansas City, Missouri, for a Kodak National Women's Basketball Coaches Clinic. The subject was "Individual Offensive Moves."

Patsy Neal was introduced. A 40-point per game high school scorer. A three-time All-American at Wayland College and in AAU ball. Captain of the U.S. team in the 1964 World Basketball Tournament in Peru. A member of the 1959 Pan American team. On U.S. teams that played in Europe and Russia and hosted the touring Russian team. Here was the Babe Didrickson Zaharias of women's basketball. Not only one of the greatest women players of all time, but a forerunner, a pioneer, in women's sports.

She had aged gracefully in the decade. There were lines creasing the weathered, freckled face of this athlete/coach/teacher/writer. The eyes had a luster, but not the same girlish sparkle. Instead they shone with the steady defiance of experience and perceptibility one acquires who has fought so hard for so long to be her own person.

She had been the only woman invited to attend the Multidisciplinary Symposium on Sport and the Means of Elevating International Understanding sponsored by the State Department. She had written poetry, books, essays, and articles on coaching techniques, the psychology of sport, and the Christian faith and sport. She had appeared on ABC's "Wide World of Sports." All at the expense of play. "Oh, Gary," she said, puffing, while warming up. "I'm embarrassed. I'm so out of shape. I'm gonna do bettah, I promise."

The girls sat around the edge of the court. Most were attentive but several giggled inanely, popped their gum, and listened indifferently. But what did these kids know? Who was Patsy Neal to them? Then Patsy called a gum popper to the court.

"The most fun in basketball is faking," Patsy began. "Basketball is a one-on-one game. That's the competition, the thrill."

Patsy posted the girl and told her to stop her from scoring. The girl, known as a good area player, smiled confidently, crouched, anticipated the challenge as Patsy backed in on her.

It was over in a second, like the mongoose moving on the cobra. Patsy faked left and, with an exaggerated movement, brought her right arm and the ball up as if to hook right. As the girl shifted her weight and reached in anticipation, Patsy pivoted to face her, swung the ball inches from the nose of the startled youngster into her left hand, dribbled forward, and deposited the ball gently against the backboard on the other side of the basket before the girl could recover.

The gum popper looked at her feet. The gym was quiet; then several coaches gasped and another squealed delightedly and began to write in her notebook.

"Now let's get into offensive moves," Patsy said. "If you all will put up with me being so out of shape, I'll try to make it cleaah."

The rest of the day was hers.

Because of various factors, one of which is the mixed blessing of Title IX, women's competitive sports have exploded in participation and gained a large measure of public acceptance in the 1970s. One woman said, "I never thought I could do anything but look pretty. I want more than that for my daughter."

Not that intractable attitudes don't still persist, even in the Christian community. As recently as 1972 when Olga Connolly was selected to carry the U.S. flag in the Munich Olympics opening march, a member of the weight lifting team, Russ Knipp, a leader in the Athletes in Action program, testily exclaimed, "The flagbearer ought to be a man, a strong man, a warrior. A woman's place is in the home."[1]

Patsy Neal is still watching society catch up with her.

She has endured it all—the slurs, the alienation, the raised eyebrows, the forced acceptance instead of willing friendship—and now she writes about it in a book she coauthored with noted psychologist Dr. Thomas Tutko.

"There are three major myths of women's competition. (1) The female is physically unable to engage in strenuous activity. (2) The female is psychologically unable to cope with the stress of competition. (3) The female is unable to remain 'feminine' while she participates in sports.

"Accordingly, most women today have paid a high price for their involvement in play activities and sports. One of these prices has been unpopularity with men. Some of the other prices have been a lack of social approval and acceptance, a sense of guilt about 'being different,' an inability to develop full athletic potential because of limited training for girls and women, and culturally induced psychological factors that influence girls and women to be losers rather than winners.

"It is my hope that the female athlete will strive for excellence while maintaining a proper perspective of the values of competition—which does not mean that 'victory is everything'—but that humane behavior, pride in accomplishment, enjoyment of play, and an understanding of the self are sufficient rewards for taking part in competition."[2]

We sat in her hotel prior to the clinic. She was nervous; she is always nervous before lecturing, just as when she played. She remembered North Carolina. A long time ago when things were, in a way, less troublesome.

"I'm excited and afraid about what is happening for women in sports," she said. "Sports for girls have historically been a spontaneous, fun endeavor. It is a chance for girls to develop physically and have a healthy release for feelings and nervous energy.

APPENDIXES

"The beauty of sport competition is that it can give you a better self-concept. The way we view ourselves as persons has a lot to do with our physical bodies. So many girls never know what they can do physically. If you believe you are weak and can't take discomfort and pain, that's what you'll be.

"In the past, girls have been taught to be competitive only in 'acceptable ways'—being pretty, getting a husband, keeping house better than someone else. Sport competition was for men. For women it had to be a learned thing.

"I fear what we are learning. Title IX was necessary, but where will it lead us? I see sports becoming for women what it has become for men—a win-oriented job. Women coaches are rude to officials, are sarcastic with their players, scream from the sidelines. What have we done to ourselves?

"There is nothing like sport and competition to allow us to relate to people at the gut level. You are more yourself in a competitive situation then at any other time. If you and your opponent care about each other and respect each other, you are both the better for it.

"In girls' sports years ago it was not unusual for a girl to tell the referee the ball had gone out of bounds off her. I did not hesitate to tell an opponent if she would just set up offensively a foot wider she would not be called for being in the lane. That was accepted, even expected. Now, when winning is so important, a coach might bench you if you did that.

"I wouldn't consider that I had lived had I not been able to play and compete at a physical level. I try to explain in my clinics what sport has been . . . can be . . . but girls don't understand. They just want to learn insights, tips, secrets to win. And when there is so much outside pressure to win, it is hard for them to see the purity of sport and competition. If you win you are somebody; if you lose you are nobody.

"We can't throw out competition. As long as our values and priorities are worthy, competition is good. Competition allows us to reach out, to be all we can be.

"Leisure time and recreational sports can be good if they're what people really want. But if you are going that route to avoid competition—which I see some female athletes doing—you're only fooling yourself and failing to aid sport. We need to work to make competition all it can be, not run from its problems."

Patsy was a child who never ran *from* anything, only ran *to* play. She was raised on a farm near Elberton, Georgia, a town of 6,500 in northeast Georgia, an area relatively liberated in the ways of sports for girls. Patsy competed with her older brother and his buddies while her twin sister, Peggy, was the "lady" of the family.

"Peggy and I were so different," Patsy said. "She lives in Houston and has a family. She had great potential as an artist. But she never developed it. There are times of loneliness when I envy her married life. And there are times when she sees me—single, traveling, writing—and envies me."

Patsy has no bad memories from childhood. All of life then, as she has written in her book *So Run Your Race,* was joy:

> I was born
> > an athlete . . .
> I was young then,
> > and life to me
> > > was just another game . . .
> I did not care to know
> > how or why,
> > > for I was a child,

> and children just *are*
> without knowing.

It was a period of bliss.[3]

There was even girls' basketball in elementary school. By the time she reached high school, she was a star. In those days she played the three-player offense, three-player defense game. In college two players could rove the court. It was not until AAU and international ball that she played the five-player, full-court, regulation game. Regardless, Patsy always played offense and was always a high scorer.

She faced no serious competition and had no thoughts about college ball or scholarships. Wayland, a Baptist college in Plainview, Texas, was the perennial powerhouse of women's basketball. The team was in the midst of a 131-game winning streak.

She discovered competition at Wayland:

> But the rules changed . . .
> Sometimes
>   I even worked
>   at my play . . .
> The supreme pureness of movement slowly gave way
>   to other things—
>   practiced and rehearsed things.[4]

Patsy found herself among All-American players. She rode the bench as a freshman and had to work diligently to start as a sophomore. There were the "I just can't do this again" times every competitor faces. But she did, again and again. And for one reason.

"I had nothing to prove," she said. "I just loved to play. Had to play. Without the physical, I was not a complete person."

At Wayland, the women were accepted as more than an aberration. On the road—and the team had to travel nationwide for games—attitudes were primitive. The players were not only socially but sexually suspect. If not lesbian, at best asexual. Surely you would not want your daughter to be a basketball player when she could be anything else a "real woman" is supposed to be.

And Miss Neal was almost like a real woman. She was graduated cum laude in psychology, was the first woman president of the student body, was in a beauty contest, and was even Homecoming Queen.

"Dealing with my feelings about being feminine was, at times, a problem," she admits. "I just knew I had to play and compete. I could accept the criticism and adjust to it, or give up sports. I saw a lot of girls buckle under. But I had to play. More than they did, I guess."

It would get worse before it got better. Beyond college there were few amateur teams. One was in Salt Lake City where Patsy worked in a recreation department tennis program (she has been ranked among the top ten amateur players in singles and doubles both in Utah and North Carolina), taught junior high school, got her master's degree in physical education and then taught at the University of Utah, and played basketball for six years.

Utah was the pits for women's sports. The team members paid their own expenses and piled into cars and drove for hours while eating from brown paper bags. They returned from games hundreds of miles from home through early morning storms and flat tires, sprawled asleep across each other while one drove and another stayed awake to keep the driver awake. All for the game. All for a couple of hours of suspended magic when a woman could feel physical and alive and whole.

So keyed up by it all,

> as voices of faceless sounds push me
>> into the rapids swirling around
>>> my soul . . .
> Cheered on,
>> jeered on,
>>> booed by . . .
>> and yet pulled even deeper
>>> into the raging action that
>>>> forces me into the river of thought.[5]

The years of struggle and proving wear thin, even on a woman of steel and velvet.

"I've always tried to be me," said Patsy, "and, just so I don't hurt anyone else, do the things I feel are right for me. I am a feeling-oriented person. If I have a conflict between feelings and reason, I'll usually follow my feelings. I believe we are connected to something primitive there, the source of all of life."

She was so involved teaching, coaching, playing in Utah that she felt a need to change her life. Her existence had been so devoted to the physical she felt it time to emphasize the spiritual and the intellectual. She abruptly resigned her position and went home to her parents. She wrote thirty colleges; twenty-nine responded. Brevard College (North Carolina) did not. Intrigued, she called Brevard. Because of renovations to the dorms, school was late in opening. And Brevard had a position. For ten happy years she coached the men's tennis team and was associate professor there. And she developed the other facets of her personality.

"I first wrote poetry in elementary school," said the author who has received four Freedom Foundation awards for essays and has had her poetry published in literary magazines and the National Anthology of College Poetry. "You know, 'Little birdie in the tree; looking down at you and me.' I love to read and to write. And there just wasn't time. I felt I was not being true to myself.

"And my spiritual life had deteriorated. I was caught up in other things. My childhood included church and bedtime prayers. I can remember making deals with a God I've always seemed to believe in. You do this for me and I'll do this for you. I could picture in my mind God and me shaking hands. God kept his end of those deals. And I always kept mine; that was part of it."

We had talked more about religion, she commented, than she had ever talked with anyone. I found that paradoxical for someone who is so spiritually cored. Yet it is a private center. And, as with her competition, her faith is emotionally geared. For this reason she suspects others might not understand. It is easier to keep it hidden in speech and share it in her writing.

"There have been times when the Lord has been so close and I have been wrapped in such a sensation of grace that I would give up everything to keep the feeling," she said. "This seems silly, I know, but it's real. In 1957 I entered the AAU national free-throw contest. I shot 100 to 200 free throws a day until my tongue was hanging out and my toenails were bleeding inside my shoes. You had to hit at least forty-five of fifty to qualify for the finals, which I did.

"The night before the finals I was so nervous I had trouble falling asleep. When I did, I dreamed about shooting free throws. And every time the ball swished, the net turned into a picture of Christ. Look, I'm not a mystic, but I awoke with such a feeling of peace. I hit forty-eight of fifty to win and was so confident and relaxed I don't know how I missed those two. Those times of blissful grace are infrequent, but I wish I could sustain them. I don't believe the Lord meant us to, though. I believe they are a sneak preview."

APPENDIXES

Several years ago, between the game of HORSE and the Kodak clinic, I drove to Brevard along a beautiful winding road through the Blue Ridge Mountains. The red brick of the college buildings stood in twilight relief against the backdrop of green as I hunted the gymnasium.

Patsy was conducting a basketball clinic. Dozens of girls played in the several gyms. On the main court, two high school teams battled. The novice was in most of them but several displayed an emerging knack for the game. One husky gal was unstoppable on the dribble and shot the eyes out of the basket. Another Patsy Neal? Good, but probably not that good.

The game ended and the two college girls who had been officiating shot baskets. Through a crowd of players came Patsy, the queen bee in her hive. Among basketball-playing girls in the southeast, Patsy is legend.

I remarked that the college players appeared talented.

"Talented, yes," she said, "and very nice girls. But they have the struggles I once had. It may be harder to compete now. Even when I was playing, people always asked me who won or lost; not how I had played. Believe me, I like to win. I don't believe anyone should practice three hours a day and then not care to win. But when it distorts your values, it's wrong.

"People used to question my attitude. At times, I questioned myself. But, overall, I was comfortable with my feelings. That's why I don't coach basketball. I don't fit, especially today. I can't gear my life to other people's expectations about winning. I was not a good coach in that respect and was relieved to get out of coaching."

It was an older and even wiser sportswoman who awaited her Kodak clinic appearance. As always, as honest, as comfortable with who she is as was the little girl who played football in the Georgia fields.

"I would be foolish to say I have not had conflicts with my faith and my competitiveness," she offered. "I believe that admission is the only start to wholeness. The reason we can't change sport and make competition wholesome is because people who confess to be Christian are not living like it.

"We must treat people the same in and out of competition. I've been ashamed for things I've done on the court. And if you can't come to grips with your values and priorities and be sensitive to others, you should not be a competitor, either player or coach.

"And I know it's easier for me to say this. I'm single. I have no family responsibilities. Playing and coaching are no longer big ego needs for me. I don't face the pressures and economic realities others do. But I can't answer for them. I only know what I feel and what I must do.

"In Psalm 139:14 we read, 'I will praise thee; for I am fearfully and wonderfully made.' We are wonderfully made. To know your body is to know yourself. And we can't let false values and a distorted emphasis destroy the beauty of competition."

I no longer jump.
    I
      soar!
I no longer jog.
    I
      run!
I am free to live,
    thank
      God,
        with
          dignity.
Oh, God,
    what a joy
      it all is![6]

GRANT TEAFF . . .
THE COACH

While Teaff has religion and football in their proper perspective, the fact remains that few coaches in Southwest Conference history have left such forceful personal imprints in a school's existence and in its football team.

George Breazeale
Austin America-Statesman

Baylor football coach Grant Teaff enjoys telling the story about the time in 1973 he and assistant coach Bill Yung went off for a day of deer hunting on the property of a Texas rancher after the frustrations of a 2-9 season. (Teaff is a fearsome hunter who, as a boy, went rabbit hunting, chased down a cottontail until the bunny turned and gave him a mournful look, at which Teaff lowered the rifle, went home, and has not hunted since.)

The rancher gave his approval on one condition: Teaff would shoot his mule, an aging, diseased beast whom the rancher loves and cannot bear to shoot himself. Teaff agrees and on the way back to the car decides to have some fun with Yung.

"We can't hunt here, Bill," he laments. "That rancher said we were the worst team ever this past season, I was the worst coach he'd ever seen, your offensive line was pitiful, and Baylor stinks academically.

"Well, I've had it, Bill. I can't take any more. See that old mule over there? Watch this." Teaff pulls his rifle from the back seat, inserts a slug, takes aim, fires, and the mule drops dead. Before Teaff can explain, he hears two shots from the other side of the car.

"I got two of his cows, coach," Yung cries. "Let's get the heck out of here!"

Of course, the story brings down the house. And then Teaff becomes serious about loyalty and other coaching virtues. He is acutely aware of all the potential and problems relative to the coaching profession in America today. He is, as is any major college coach, a man on a tightrope.

Even at Baylor, the mecca of Southern Baptists, winning is seen as essential, necessary. Baylor won three of thirty-one games the three seasons before Teaff arrived in 1972. The two coaches before him, one a past national president of the Fellowship of Christian Athletes, were fired. Not for failing to carry their Bibles to practice. For losing. Simple as that.

When Teaff arrived, several businessmen, pillars of the Christian community in Waco, told Grant he could have all the money or whatever he needed to win. Simple as that. Don't tell the good old boys at First Baptist Church in Waco that "it's how you play the game that counts." They know better. God loves a cheerful winner.

Since 1972, Teaff has put himself on the road and Baylor back on the map. He puts in ninety-hour recruiting weeks. He speaks at more clinics than any other college coach in America. And not just clinics, but churches, youth groups, civic clubs, businesses, institutions, wherever two or more are gathered.

And the message does not vary. His autobiography is titled *I Believe.* His cassette tape is labeled "Motivation: The Key to Success." Motivation, to Teaff, is a force, tangible or intangible, that propels man into action. The key is self-motivation: finding a person's "hot button." He stresses love, not gushy or " 'huggelin' and 'kissin' love," but man-to-man love. He calls for goal-setting, communication, positive thinking, never giving up (quoting Winston Churchill's famed ten-second graduation address—"nevah, nevah, nevah give up"), and that athletics is the last bastion (appropriately, though unintentionally, pronounced "Bastogne") of discipline in America.

The dialect is West Texas panhandle. His voice swells and softens like a Southern Baptist preacher. On becomes "own"—"we got to get own with it." Doggone becomes "doggown": "The doggown kid won't hit a lick at a snake."

He is an outwardly placid man who becomes emotive wherever his pulpit because "I want to leave them with something, want to touch their lives." And so he goes on: "I am only one, but I am one." And on: "There's no one else in the whole human race with your kind of style and your kind of grace." And on: "Man's relationship to God is the most important relationship in life."

But wait. There is more to Grant Teaff. His kind is truly the hope of the coaching profession in America. Because when you separate the wheat of his commitment and caring from the chaff of the cliches and platitudes, you begin to see the effect and impact a Christian coach can have on the competitiveness of those who play and watch the game.

"My daddy had a saying, 'Always let the boss know that you know who he is.' During games I wear a head set and sometimes the coaches in the press box will say, 'What did you say?' I'll answer, 'Oh, I wasn't talking to you.' God is part of the real world. When I coached receivers at Texas Tech, I made them get into a three-point stance like the linemen. I wanted them to get their hands dirty, to get into the real world. Being spiritual is like that."

Baylor is still in football's rah-rah tradition. At the end

of home games the team members go to the student side, take off their helmets, and raise them in a salute. The student body stands and all—every last Bear man and woman—lustily sings the school song.

Maybe it could happen only in Texas. Maybe Grant Teaff could happen only in Texas.

"I was small and slow," said Grant, "but I figured if I could become the toughest kid on the field the coaches would find a place for me to play. I have a high pain threshold. I don't hurt physically very easily. And I always had this hot coal, this burning, down inside me. I would do anything to be the best, to please people, to live up to what I felt were my responsibilities."

His father seldom praised him. It bothered Grant. What do I have to do, he thought? And he would have walked through fire for his college coach Wilfred Moore. In four years Moore seldom spoke to him. After his last game of Grant's career, Moore walked through the locker room, slapped Grant on the hip, and nodded.

"That was worth a million dollars to me," Grant recalls. "But if he had done it earlier, I wonder how much better I could have been."

Perhaps more than any other college coach, Grant is a sucker for the walk-on—that scrawny kid with a world of guts and no heralded talent who will brazenly walk into his office and demand a chance to compete. Grant gives four or five scholarships a year to walk-ons.

"If God has given me a gift, it is to let people see their potential and provide them with incentive to maximize it," Grant said. "When you help develop a solid self-image, you have helped someone for a lifetime."

In the glory year, 1974, when Teaff was named Southwest Conference and National Coach of the Year, the honor that meant the most to him was when a player was quoted in the paper on why Baylor was successful:

"Because Coach Teaff expects it of us, and we want to please him."

Teaff is a lover of young men. There are many stories but perhaps one player and one game stand out. The player was quarterback Neal Jeffrey. The game was with TCU.

Texas Christian led, 35-7, with eleven minutes to play. Jeffrey began a fantastic passing show and with seconds to play, Baylor was inside the TCU ten, trailing only 35-28. Then Jeffrey, becoming confused and thinking it third down, threw the ball out of bounds to stop the clock on fourth down.

In the dressing room, with the team kneeling in prayer, Teaff called for his quarterback and said, "Neal . . . Neal . . . get your head up, son. You played a fantastic game. We all love you, Neal." It was something out of Rockne, Ronald Reagan, and Paramount Pictures, but these things seem to happen to Grant Teaff and the kids who fill his life because he really does love them.

"I say it to coaches in every clinic," he says. "Don't be afraid of that word *love*. Tell it to your wife—and mean it. Tell it to your children—and mean it. Tell it to your assistant coaches—and mean it. Tell it to your players—and mean it. I tell my team every day that I love them. Some days I have to say, 'You guys are driving me crazy, but doggown it, I love you.'"

And with such competitive intensity, he knows he's fortunate his zeal tipped to the plus side.

"There's a fine line between toughness and meanness," Grant said. "But it was not a problem for me. I was never a mean person. God put something inside me. I can be mentally and physically tough and not be flagrantly mean. I was only tough between the lines.

"I believe football's physical contact can be pleasing to God. It's a game and not a war. One can be competitive and not combative. I've had to straighten out a few assistants on this. To some, football is war."

While coaching at Texas, another assistant cussed and kicked one of Grant's players. The next day in staff meeting Grant raised the issue and told the coach never to do it again. The assistant invited Grant outside to settle it right then, but the head coach intervened. Fortunately. The aggressor was a former Navy heavyweight boxing champion.

"He would have killed me," Grant admits. "But I don't believe you have to coach that way."

If Teaff feels a calling today, it is to remove the stigmas attached to the major college coaching profession.

"I'm still sold on coaching," he said. "Athletic figures will be looked to with awe or disgust, but they will be looked to. I seldom talk technique; I talk motivation, communication, respect, love. I am more encouraged today. There are fewer 'animals' in coaching. The younger men are more concerned even if still poorly trained and prepared. I've considered opening a department especially designed to teach coaches in a new way. For now I'll continue going to any clinic that will invite me."

If anyone can help cure the illness in the coaching profession, it may be doctor Teaff who has shown a talent for healing sick football programs. He was the youngest head coach in the nation at age twenty-five when he became coach at his alma mater, McMurry College. He not only turned the football program around but even coached a championship track team, although up to that time he thought a track was what held the football field together!

It was while at McMurry that he experienced one of two personal crises that turned his spiritual life around. Following a Saturday night game in Monroe, Louisiana, twenty-eight of the players and four coaches took off for home in a DC-3. But the left stops on the tail section elevators remained locked and the plane clipped the pine trees at the end of the runway.

Twice the pilot tried to land. Both times the plane miraculously maintained power and bounced back into the air. It was then ascertained that the plane, loaded with fuel, had locked elevators, demolished landing gear, and a shorted electrical system. The pilot headed for a Strategic Air Command base thirty minutes away at Shreveport for a crash landing.

The coaches gave the players emergency instructions, Grant led in a team prayer, and the coaches felt their way through the inky black to the rear of the plane. As they huddled silently, Grant did a lot of thinking.

"I thought about all the usual things," Grant remembers. "About the family, about dying, about God. Mother taught me in Sunday school when I was six years old, and she teaches that same class today. I accepted Christ when I was twelve, but I'd never been religious. Dad was never religious, either. Guess I was like him.

The plane was demolished on impact but did not burn. The crew chief said he'd never seen a plane so hot fail to explode. The team formed a club, The Brotherhood of the Indians' Belly Landing Experts—B.I.B.L.E.

The next night, finally recovering a little from the shock and exhaustion of the experience, Grant sat in church and listened to pastor Earl Sherman say he believed the team was spared for a reason. Grant walked out and hurried two troubled miles to the campus field-house to be alone. Inside, he prayed, believing God did have a plan for his life.

"That night my career took some needed detours," he said. "I began to feel there were other aspects to the competitive life, people aspects. My dad, my coaches, all had expectations of me. And I wanted to please them. I now felt God also had expectations of me. I wanted to please him. This is the root—the expectation and the pleasing—from which my spiritual life has grown."

Another crisis came when middle daughter Tracy was eighteen months old. Returning by car from Plainview, the Teaffs became frantic when Tracy could not sit up in the seat. She kept flopping over. They went to the emergency ward. Doctors anticipated spinal meningitis and requested a spinal tap. The Teaffs spent two hours in a waiting room in prayer. The doctors told them to be prepared. It was not spinal meningitis, but the incident helped Grant get prepared.

"Faith has made the difference in my competitiveness," he said. "It helped me better handle football. Baylor may never win another game, and it wouldn't make a lasting impression on the school or on Texas or on anybody. It would to me, but as much as I love sport and coaching my faith would allow me to walk away because of the peace I have about life.

"Faith helps me deal with winning and losing. I hate to lose. It hurts me physically. That hot center in me that reaches out as I compete reaches back in and burns my insides when I lose. I feel responsible to so many people. But at the same time I'm aching, I'm still at peace further inside me because of my faith. I know it's going to be OK. That separates me from some coaches and competitors who, after a loss, actually believe their world has ended."

Teaff believes honest personal assessment is a key to life. A man has to learn what he can and cannot do. He can share with coaches. He can see problem areas in competition. And he feels he can and must do something about that.

"I feel keenly about the application of faith to coaching and playing," he said. "I have made the commitment to building men of God in the coaching profession.

"If I could do one thing with my life right now, just one thing, it would be to do away with the negative stigma major college sports have. And it's there because it is largely true. Lots of people are busting their tails to have a clean program. But a lot of what you hear about recruiting and other things is true. When a boy sits in your car and cries for forty minutes and wants to come to your school but tells you he has to go someplace else, it makes you want to cry. You know how dirty it can be."

When Grant said it was "difficult" to keep your faith as a total, integral part of your competitiveness, I asked him about a quote from Jim Hilyer, a doctor of psychology, associate professor, and assistant football coach at Auburn, who said: "A college football recruiter cannot be totally Christian in his dealings with young men and be a consistent winner. He'll lose the immature kid, the kid snowed by the immature. So one must choose between some form and degree of compromise in his faith and win or being Christian and losing."

Again the smile at the edge. The difficulty of his position was evident in his manner and his response.

"Remember, I'm sitting on a million dollar business," he said. "You've got to keep the crowds coming and the interest high to get money and you've got to have money to recruit. Many things can happen among the alumni without the coach knowing. Everybody breaks certain NCAA rules that are unrealistic and unenforceable. It is impossible to keep on top of it all. Even the Christian coaches push to the edge. Nothing is simon pure.

"I guess I'm fortunate that I have the same hot button competitively in my spiritual existence that I do in coaching and playing. I want to please God. I want to do what I do the best it can be done. I want to do it right. When I don't, it's like losing. That hot coal burns my insides."

DR. DAVID WEE . . .
THE SPORTS
CONSCIENCE

I had known Dr. David Wee for only a few hours. But I had met and respected him six years earlier when I read and reprinted his exceptional article "Athletics as a Human Experience." His perspective of sports competition was an impetus toward this book.

He had written, "As an athlete and a lover of sport, I am involved in a lover's quarrel these days. I believe that sport can play an important function for man, and it hurts me deeply to observe the unfortunate ways we are using sport in this country.

"When we think about sport, we often forget to ask the most important question that we should ask about all of our human activities: What is its effect upon the quality of the human experience? Or what is its effect upon the human spirit? Professional and university athletics has rarely asked that question and might not be committing the present malpractices if they had.

"Man is not only *homo rationis capax*—man capable of reason—but also *homo ludens*—man playing. Too many of us have forgotten how to play—or have lost the desire to play—and thus have diminished our creatureliness.

"The tone of sport in our culture should be established not by the big leagues but by you and me having fun playing tennis on a summer evening. A few professional and collegiate athletes have begun to rebel against the dehumanization spawned by financial athletics; you and I must support their protest by refusing to accept the abuses of sport and by throwing ourselves into a lifetime of the kind of sport that counts—the playing of games among human beings who do it for fun and fellowship and the kind of personal renewal that we rightly call re-creation."[1]

A "sport conscience" periodically emerges, just as false Messiahs once kept surfacing. There is the measure of truth and wisdom in the belligerency of a Harry Edwards, the jabs and barbs of a Jack Scott, the offended "Did you know?" of the play and tell athletic/writers. But eventually one realizes each doth protest too much. The quest for righteousness begins to erase around the edges to reveal a self-serving avocation.

Dr. Wee, a slight, bearded Scandinavian, would not claim to be a sports conscience. He does not offer counsel unless asked. He lives what he espouses, and the consistency of the life-style lends authenticity to the words.

David Wee does not lack credentials to take his place among the scholarly. He is senior tutor of the Paracollege at Saint Olaf. He has his Ph.D. from Stanford and has studied at University College in London and Mansfield College at Oxford. His dissertation was on "The Forms of Apostasy: The Rejection of Christian Orthodoxy in the British Novel, 1880-1900," and he penned an article for *Modern Philology* titled "The Temptation of Christ and the Motif of Divine Duplicity in the Corpus Christi Cycle Drama."

Had he assured me that my white shirt was red, I would have had to consider it.

David's sport theology is simple: "Seldom do you have an argument when you are running with someone. I love to run anywhere, anytime, with anyone." In 1960 he finished fourth in the NCAA college division national cross-country championship while competing at St. Olaf. His best two-mile time was 9:24. He still runs every day, leaving his office at 11:30 A.M., taking different routes through the countryside, and returning to his work about 1:30 P.M., eating from his lunch sack with his first afternoon appointment.

He competes in road races and, twelve years after graduating from St. Olaf, ran a 9:32 two mile, a mere eight-second loss. He runs unattached in intercollegiate meets. He usually finishes fourth or fifth but has won a few. He wants one day to run the Boston Marathon because "it is the ultimate challenge for the American runner."

"I ran with a friend yesterday," said David. "The sun was bright, it was invigoratingly cold, the silence was so inspiring; we'd chat and chase the white puffs of our breath up the next hill.

"The most important thing is that people have a good time together in the process of play. Destruction comes when the stress is on having to win or having to excel. Having fun is much more important than beating someone or performing at your peak, and I place importance on both of the latter. But neither is worthwhile when accomplished at the expense of another."

David's kind make coaches nervous. He is faculty representative for his school's intercollegiate program. And though St. Olaf, as with many small colleges, has a sane and sensible approach to varsity sport, the views of a sports conscience are never popular with people whose livelihood is somewhat dependent on a relative measure of success, which means winning.

The contradiction is seen in his own brief coaching career at St. Olaf. He began the women's cross-country program several years ago as a volunteer coach. He ran with the girls, racing with the faster ones, jogging beside and encouraging the slower ones. His goals were to have the girls enter into a lifelong, enjoyable running experience and to allow St. Olaf to have a competitive team.

Thirty-three girls came out. He told them they could compete if they desired but could run for fun if that's all they sought. What he wanted was for them to write him when they were sixty and say they were still running.

"We'd eventually have had a good competitive team," he said. "That emerges naturally in the process. The last thing I wanted, however, was to apply competitive pressure and have the girls become exhausted and decide running was no fun."

David then turned the reins over to a full-time woman coach—a coach he likes and appreciates. But their philosophies differ. She told those not interested in competing and practicing every day to find other pursuits. There are now thirteen girls on a strong competitive team.

"That's fine," David shrugs, "but if I had my choice I'd have the whole student body running as a lifetime fun activity. The competitive team is of secondary importance.

"Karen and I read today about a jury dismissing charges against a coach whose player had died following a 'punishment drill,'" said David. "You see the value? What was important? Not punishment. That could have been accomplished by suspension from competition. But that might also lessen the team's chance to win. The physical punishment not only shamed and whipped the boy into obedience under the coach's authoritarianism but kept him available for the game. At such schools young men are there to play football, not to become better human beings. They are used by the institution for its own ends. But educational institutions are supposed to have higher concerns for their students and better uses for their money."

Ask David to expose his philosophy/theology/

perspective of sports competition and he divides sport into three categories—the professional, the educational, and the recreational. He does not reserve a place for "fitness."

"Fitness has its place," he said, "and there should be more. Partly because of the American mood for fitness over the past ten years, people are again learning to play. But do not confuse fitness with recreational fun. I see faculty members at St. Olaf torture themselves to grind out their required twenty laps around the indoor track. Sport provides some pleasure to somebody. If one suffers through a run, he is merely exercising, not sporting, and I wish him a better fate."

What he would expose us to as a matter of his personal values is his love affair with recreational sport.

"What's wrong with sport in our culture," he said, "is our misplaced values. Sport should and can serve to enrich the lives of most of us. But as a nation we content ourselves with watching the great athletes perform— often through television—rather than performing ourselves. We pay homage and money to the brilliant few because their skilled performances thrill us; too few of us discover the greater thrill of having a body that can perform games for a lifetime of fun.

"We have explosions both ways," he said. "More Americans are discovering the joy of leisure play. At the same time there are more games in monstrous artificial protective atmospheres, and the Super Bowl is almost a religious pilgrimage. On one hand we worship at the feet of specially endowed and trained athletes. On the other hand we are finding those of us with no special endowments can still play and have fun. There's no way I can ever score a touchdown against Dallas. But I can dream of playing a good competitive game of tennis—and then do it and get great satisfaction from it.

"Recreational sport has emancipated me to experiences with athletics I never had before," he said. "I'm able to place sport in its proper niche in my life rather than a niche created by false cultural values. It would not make me feel horrible never to run another race. But I do like to run races. And I like to win. I try to win. There are lots of people I would like to beat. I try to beat them. But I don't have to beat them. In college I used to try to psyche-out my opponent; I was furious if I was beaten. Now I like to train with my opponent, run my best against him, and then have a grand party with him when it is over.

"Sporting competition is no longer a grim and serious business; it's a physical and even aesthetic game I play. I covet for others my joy in sport, and many do share it. The best sports are those that can be done virtually anytime, anywhere, in any weather, alone or with others, and for free.

"I was the skinny runt kid who was either chosen last or left out," said David. "But as with many skinny little kids, it was a sensitive coach who really helped me—Art Keller, fifth-grade gym class, Carthage, Illinois. He watched me running, pulled me aside, and told me I ran well. I was in heaven.

"We moved to Duluth and in the seventh grade I was the fastest kid in the sixty-yard dash. That summer at my parents' cabin in northern Minnesota I ran two miles a day down the gravel roads to stay in shape. But I wasn't growing. By eighth grade all the other kids had gotten bigger and faster. I was the slowest. I became a hurdler because no one else wanted to hurdle. The coach worked with the stars. He didn't even know I was around. I was embittered.

"One day in tenth grade I was standing by my locker when a friend told me I was going out for cross-country. I told him no, that I'd had it with sports. He picked me up, literally, and carried me to the coach's office—me kicking and struggling—and said, 'Here's a new candidate for the team.'

"Well, I found out I'd built up a lot of endurance. I was the first member of my class to win a varsity letter. My love affair with running had begun."

Aren't there problems when one set of value priorities is imposed on people with other sets of value priorities?

"Perhaps your children teach you best about imposing competitive value priorities," David said. "Rebecca, who is fifteen, is our oldest. She is not an athlete. She tried to be a runner. It was hard for her to quit because she knew it would disappoint me. Quite honestly, it did. But she did not like running. I was the one who had the problem of values.

"She is a cheerleader who is still bothered by some competitive values and attitudes she sees. On varsity football trips, if the team loses, no one—varsity, JV, or cheerleader—is allowed to say a word on the bus coming home. Isn't that tragic? Win or lose, the kids should be singing and dancing in the aisles.

"When one takes defeat as something shameful, we are measuring against the purely human and fallacious standard of winning and losing. That is worshiping at the wrong shrine.

"Jonathan is eleven. He has leg problems and never will be a good athlete. In sixth grade he wanted to go out for football. Karen and I were petrified; we were sure he'd get killed. But we figured he'd come to his senses and quit first. Instead, he loved it! He scored touchdowns for the Green Bean Pickers, an original name, at least. But I won't care when he quits. As long as he does things that make him happy.

"Our athlete is Allison, who is eight years old. She's as

tough as a fullback. At age six she ran in a mile race. None of the other teenage girls in the race was taking it seriously. Allison was. With their cooperation, she won the race. We still run together at times, but she'll soon get distracted and go off to play in the broad jump pit. And that's a good sign."

How do these values fit into your spiritual life? I asked.

"Humans are religious creatures and religion is the expression of those things we consider most important," said David. "We worship what gives the most satisfaction to our existence."

(I thought of Coach George Allen's comment, "The pursuit of victory is my religion.")

"The fact of Christ's redemptive act allows us to live with our humanness, our faults, and our failure. The Christian has discovered the truth of God's intervention in our world, and this allows him to be joyful and optimistic. He can look at tragedy, evil, and corruption and not totally despair; he can look at death and rejoice.

"The Christian can more easily understand sport and play as natural activity. But activity superceded by other larger, more important things in life. So instead of despairing or becoming discouraged when one loses—either skill levels to age or injury or a game—one takes it as the natural order of things.

"The Christian can see that in the ultimate scheme of things, 'being better' than someone else is not important at all. The important thing is that human beings who are playing games with and against each other are people whose worth is measured by the sum total of their human behavior and, more importantly, by the fact that they are the children of God. We are valued in an ultimate sense regardless of our shortcomings, whether they be in matters of moral behavior—good and evil—or skillful behavior, winning and losing.

Dr. David Wee

"It is natural to compare ourselves. Sometimes the standard of comparison is another person's performance; at other times it is winning or losing. But when this becomes an ultimate—a religion—our attitude toward sport becomes unforgiving and we have little recourse but to degenerate to levels of despair, bitterness, and pessimism.

"Because I am a Christian I can see the way to putting competition into a perspective that does not demean others. The Lord tells us that seizing earthly existence is not the ultimate meaning. How, then, can we reasonably make something as trivial as competition the ultimate?

"In the final measure, our value must come because we are loved, forgiven, and valued by God, and for no other reason."

Dr. David Wee has faced the problem of equating his love for sport with his competitive and faith values. He has made his choices.

And on he runs. Not in an agonized frenzy but with light feet and a lighter heart. He will one day run Boston. They say there is magic in Boston in the camaraderie, in the children along the way, in the pure doing of it. Some runners migrate there to touch the magic once. The David Wees, who serve as the conscience of sport and competition, have long ago found this magic. They touch it every day. They may run Boston but they don't need to.

CHAPTER NOTES

CHAPTER 2
1. Bill Bradley, *Life on the Run* (New York: Bantam Books, Inc., 1976), p. 236.
2. Howard Mickel, "Going Beyond Competition," *The Complete Runner*, by the editors of Runner's World (Mountain View, Calif.: World Publications, 1974), pp. 5, 7, 8.

CHAPTER 5
1. "Open Season on Sports," *The Christian Athlete*, June, 1973, p. 8.
2. "Stone Walls, Stout Hearts," *Sports Illustrated*, March 6, 1978, p. 78.

CHAPTER 6
1. "All Quiet on the Western Front," *New York Times*, Nov. 11, 1976.
2. "The Athletes" film series. Southern Baptist Radio and Television Commission, 1977.
3. "Mountaineer with a Message," *The Christian Athlete*, January, 1968, p. 5.
4. "My Most Meaningful Christian Experience in Athletics," *The Christian Athlete*, December, 1973, p. 10.
5. "A Special Case," *The Christian Athlete*, July-August, 1972, p. 12.
6. "My Most Meaningful Christian Experience in Athletics," *The Christian Athlete*, December, 1973, p. 8.
7. "Choosing Sides," *The Christian Athlete*, March, 1976, p. 31.

CHAPTER 7
1. Institute for the Study of Athletic Motivation, a division of Winslow Research, Inc., Santa Clara, Calif. Quoted in *Coaching Girls and Women: Psychological Perspectives* by Thomas Tutko and Patsy Neal. (Boston: Allyn and Bacon, Inc., 1975), p. 91.
2. Quoted from *The Encyclopedia of Religious Quotations*, edited and compiled by Frank S. Mead (Old Tappan, N.J.: Fleming H. Revell Company, 1976).
3. Mike Durbin, "I'm Mad About the Game, But I'm Not Angry Anymore," *Guideposts*, May, 1973.

CHAPTER 8
1. William Bengston, "A Man in Combat Against a Hill He Respects and Even Likes," *New York Times*, October 23, 1977.
2. L. Pierce Williams, "Learning the Difference Between Play and Sport," *New York Times*, October 23, 1977.
3. Philip Yancey, *Where Is God When It Hurts?* (Grand Rapids: Zondervan Publishing Co., 1977), p. 49.
4. Dietrich Bonhoeffer, *The Cost of Discipleship* (New York: Macmillan, 1963), pp. 102-3.

CHAPTER 9
1. Gerald R. Ford, "In Defense of the Competitive Urge," *Sports Illustrated*, July 8, 1974, p. 17.

COMPETITION

2.   Leonard Shecter, *The Jocks* (New York: Bobbs-Merrill Company, Inc., 1969), p. 4.
3.   "Letters to the Editor," *New York Times*, March 12, 1978.
4.   Thomas Tutko and Patsy Neal, *Coaching Girls and Women: Psychological Perspectives*, p. 162.
5.   "Ready for This? Winning Isn't Everything—Udall," *Kansas City Times*, January 23, 1973.
6.   Lewis B. Smedes, "The Winning Spirit," *The Reformed Journal*, October, 1973, p. 3.
7.   Timothy Gallwey, *The Inner Game of Tennis* (New York: Random House, Inc., 1974), pp. 119-25.
8.   "When the Pack Was Back and the Payoff Was in Dimes," *The Christian Athlete*, January, 1977, p. 19.

CHAPTER 10
1.   Alvin Toffler, *Future Shock* (New York: Random House, Inc., 1970), p. 97.
2.   "Open Season on Sports," *The Christian Athlete*, June, 1973, p. 8.
3.   Bill Bradley, *Life on the Run* (New York: Bantam Books, Inc., 1976), pp. 239-40.
4.   Reuben Welch, *We Really Do Need Each Other* (Nashville: Impact Books, 1975), pp. 31, 32, 37.

CHAPTER 11
1.   Mike Spino, *"Running as a Spiritual Experience,"* Appendix B of *The Athletic Revolution* by Jack Scott (New York: The Free Press, a division of Macmillan Co., 1971), pp. 224-25.
2.   "My Most Meaningful Christian Experience in Athletics," *The Christian Athlete*, December, 1973, p. 11.
3.   "Sport and the Human Spirit," *The Christian Athlete*, May, 1972, p. 31.
4.   "Unforgettable 'Mrs. Wightie,' " *Reader's Digest*, October, 1977, p. 103.
5.   "Cutthroat Competition," *Campus Life*, March, 1974, p. 71.

CHAPTER 12
1.   C. S. Lewis, *Mere Christianity* (New York: Macmillan, 1943), p. 109.
2.   Ibid, pp. 109-10.
3.   Earl Jabay, *The Kingdom of Self* (Plainfield, N.J.: Logos International Publishers, 1974), p. 79.
4.   Dietrich Bonhoeffer, *The Cost of Discipleship* (New York: Macmillan, 1963), pp. 125-26.
5.   Lewis, *Mere Christianity*, p. 112.
6.   Paul Hoch, *Rip Off the Big Game* (Garden City, N.Y.: Doubleday and Co., Inc., 1972), p. 155.
7.   Runner's World editors, *The Complete Runner* (Mountain View, Calif.: World Publications, 1974), p. 334.
8.   Lewis, *Mere Christianity*, pp. 112-13.
9.   Ibid, p. 114.
10.   C. S. Lewis, *Surprised by Joy* (New York: Harcourt, Brace and Co., 1955), p. 144.
11.   "Pat Haden at Oxford," *New York Times*, February 27, 1978.

CHAPTER 13

1. George Sauer interviewed by Jack Scott, *Intellectual Digest,* December, 1971.
2. Paul Petrie, "The Old Pros Lament," *Sports Poems,* ed. R. R. Knudson and P. K. Ebert (New York: Dell Publishing Company, Inc., 1971), p. 170.
3. Pat Jordan, *A False Spring* (New York: Dodd, Mead and Company, 1976), pp. 9-10.
4. Ogden Nash, "The Hunter," *Sports Poems,* ed. R. R. Knudson and P. K. Ebert, p. 116.
5. Roger Kahn, *The Boys of Summer* (New York: Harper and Row, Publishers, Inc., 1973), p. 20.
6. "Talk of the Times," *Kansas City Times,* November 30, 1972.

CHAPTER 14

1. "Let's Bring Back Heroes," *Newsweek,* August 15, 1977, p. 3.
2. "Reflections by the FCA's Founder," *The Christian Athlete,* February, 1969, p. 13.
3. "Olga a Big Problem for the Russians," *Kansas City Times,* March 28, 1978.
4. William F. Buckley, Jr., *Execution Eve and Other Contemporary Ballads* (New York: Berkley Winhover Books, 1976), pp. 218-19.
5. Peter Gent, *North Dallas Forty* (New York: William Morrow and Company, 1973), p. 65.
6. Richard C. Halverson, *Perspective,* reprinted as "The Big Man," *The Christian Athlete,* March, 1971, pp. 16-17.
7. Gary Warner, *Out to Win* (Chicago: Moody Press, 1967), pp. 33-34.
8. Hermann Hesse, *If the War Goes On . . .* (New York: Bantam Books, 1976), pp. 156-57.

CHAPTER 15

1. John Steinbeck, *America and Americans* (New York: Bantam Books, published by arrangement with The Viking Press, Inc., 1966), p. 13.
2. "Cost of Collegiate Athletics, 'Competing,' Disgraceful?" *Kansas City Times,* March 25, 1974.
3. "Sports Pay Soars with Demand," *Kansas City Star,* November 17, 1976.
4. Ibid.
5. "Basketball Restyles McGinnis," *Kansas City Star,* November 17, 1976.
6. "Sports Pay Soars with Demand."
7. "Sporting Comment," *Kansas City Star,* March 13, 1978.
8. "Sports Pay Soars with Demand."
9. "The Sound of Money," *The Christian Athlete,* November, 1974, p. 20.
10. "Open Season on Sports," *The Christian Athlete,* p. 5.
11. "Old Lament: College Sports, Reform!" *Kansas City Times,* March 30, 1974.
12. "College Athletic Recruiting Becomes Basic to Survival," *Kansas City Times,* March 28, 1974.
13. "Superstars Recall Pressure Brought by Recruiters," *Kansas City Times,* March 29, 1974.
14. Ibid.

CHAPTER 16

1. Leon Morris, "The Way It Is Today," *Christianity Today,* March 12, 1976, p. 64.

COMPETITION

2.   Jack Scott, *The Athletic Revolution* (New York: The Free Press, a division of Macmillan, 1971), p. 127.
3.   Robert M. Davis, *Aggressive Basketball* (West Nyack, N.Y.: Parker Publishing Company, Inc., 1969).
4.   "The Moment of No Return," *Inspiration,* Winter, 1976, p. 105.

CHAPTER 17
1.   Nelson Price, "Jesus the Competitor," *The Christian Athlete,* February, 1976, pp. 9-10.
2.   Kay Lindskoog, "Making It Big," *The Reformed Journal,* January, 1976, p. 4.
3.   Ibid.

CHAPTER 18
1.   Erich Sauer, *In the Arena of Faith* (Grand Rapids: Wm. B. Eerdmans Publishing Co., 1955), pp. 14-49.
2.   Ibid., p. 47.

CHAPTER 19
1.   Thomas Tutko and William Bruns, *Winning Is Everything and Other American Myths* (New York: Macmillan Co., 1976), p. 61.
2.   Ibid., pp. 61-62.
3.   Ibid., p. 62.
4.   "Youth League Sports: A Den of Iniquity or a Land of Promise?" *The Christian Athlete,* November, 1976, p. 4.
5.   Tutko and Bruns, *Winning Is Everything,* p. 9.
6.   "The Case for Little League," *The Christian Athlete,* November, 1976, p. 11.
7.   Ibid., p. 11.
8.   Tutko and Bruns, *Winning Is Everything,* p. 59.
9.   "Early Sports Training: Is It Worth the Price?" *The Physician and Sportsmedicine,* April, 1977, pp. 37-52.
10.   "The Lords Win and Win and . . .," *Los Angeles Times,* November 18, 1977.
11.   "Children in Sports," *The Washington Post,* December 19, 1976.
12.   Ibid.
13.   Tutko and Bruns, *Winning Is Everything,* pp. 53, 55, 61.
14.   Ibid.

CHAPTER 20
1.   "College Athletes' Symposium," *The Christian Athlete,* January, 1975, pp. 18-23.

CHAPTER 21
1.   "Pele Knows Importance of Retiring 'When the People Want You In,' " *Detroit Free Press,* July 31, 1977.
2.   James A. Michener, *A Michener Miscellany* (New York: Random House, 1973), p. 254.

CHAPTER 22
1.   Paul Hoch, *Rip Off the Big Game* (Garden City, N.Y.: Doubleday and Co., Inc., 1972), p. 195.
2.   "Athletes Are Human Beings," *The Christian Athlete,* May, 1971, pp. 14-16.

3. "A Coach Finds More Agony than Ecstasy," *New York Times*, January 1, 1978.
4. "Coaches Must First Be Teachers," *New York Times*, January 1, 1978.
5. "Reflections by the FCA's Founder," *The Christian Athlete*, February, 1969, p. 14.
6. "As Free As You Can Get!" *The Christian Athlete*, March, 1978, pp. 2, 5.

CHAPTER 23
1. "Spectator Sports: The All-American Mania," *Collegiate Challenge*, 1975, p. 34.
2. Ibid, p. 34.
3. James Michener, *A Michener Miscellany*, pp. 255-56.
4. "Spectator Sports: The All-American Mania," *Collegiate Challenge*, p. 35.
5. Ibid.
6. Ibid.
7. Arnold Beisser, *The Madness in Sports* (New York: Appleton-Century-Crofts, Division of Meredith Publishing Co., 1967), pp. 139-41.
8. Ibid.
9. James Simon Kunen, *The Strawberry Statement: Notes of a College Revolutionary* (New York: Avon Books, 1968), p. 93.
10. Paul Hoch, *Rip Off the Big Game* (Garden City, N.Y.: Doubleday and Co., Inc., 1972), pp.16-17.

CHAPTER 24
1. Kurt Vonnegut, in *Psychology Today*, October, 1971, p. 60.
2. Horace Spencer Fiske, "The Cry of the High Hurdlers," in *Sports Poems*, ed. R. R. Knudson and P. K. Ebert, pp. 132-33.
3. John Mack Carter and Lois Wyse, *How to Be Outrageously Successful with Women* (New York: William Morrow and Company, 1975), p. 47.
4. Harold Myra, "Sports and War," *Campus Life*, April, 1973, pp. 29-30.
5. George Sheehan, "Come and Play," *The Physician and Sportsmedicine*, November, 1974, p. 33.
6. Bill Bradley, *Life on the Run*, p. 114.

CHAPTER 26
1. "Religion in Sports," *Sports Illustrated*, April 19, 1976, p. 90.
2. Wes Neal, *The Handbook on Athletic Perfection* (Prescott, Ariz.: Institute for Athletic Perfection, 1975), p. 54.
3. Michael Novak, *The Joy of Sport* (New York: Basic Books, Inc., 1976), p. xi.

APPENDIX 1
1. Kyle Rote, Jr., *Beyond the Goal* (Waco, Tex.: Word Books, 1975), p. 8.

APPENDIX 2
1. "Winning One for the Ripper," *Sports Illustrated*, November 26, 1973, p. 46.
2. Ibid., p. 47.

COMPETITION

3. Ibid., pp. 46-47.
4. Ibid., p. 48.

APPENDIX 3
1. "Part I: Women in Sports," *Sports Illustrated,* May 28, 1973, p. 94.
2. *Coaching Girls and Women: Psychological Perspectives,* pp. 3, 17, and Preface.
3. Patsy Neal, *So Run Your Race* (Grand Rapids: Zondervan Publishing House, 1974) pp. 11, 13.
4. Ibid., p. 17.
5. Ibid., p. 27.
6. Ibid., pp. 61, 63.

APPENDIX 5
1. "Athletics As a Human Experience," *The Christian Athlete,* May, 1972, pp. 2-7.